TAKING ACTION

A Handbook for RTI at Work™

Austin **Buffum** ◆ Mike **Mattos** ◆ Janet **Malone**

Solution Tree | Press

a division of
Solution Tree

555 North Morton Street
Bloomington, IN 47404
800.733.6786 (toll free) / 812.336.7700
FAX: 812.336.7790

email: info@SolutionTree.com
SolutionTree.com

Visit **go.SolutionTree.com/RTIatWork** to download the free reproducibles in this book.

Printed in the United States of America

Library of Congress Cataloging-in-Publication Data

Names: Buffum, Austin G., author. | Mattos, Mike (Mike William), author. |

   Malone, Janet, author.

Title: Taking action : a handbook for RTI at work / Austin Buffum, Mike

   Mattos, and Janet Malone.

Description: Bloomington, IN : Solution Tree Press, [2018] | Includes

   bibliographical references and index.

Identifiers: LCCN 2017020034 | ISBN 9781942496175 (perfect bound)

Subjects: LCSH: Response to intervention (Learning disabled children)--United

   States. | Learning disabled children--Education--United States. |

   Individualized instruction--United States.

Classification: LCC LC4705 .B85 2018 | DDC 371.9--dc23 LC record available at https://lccn.loc.gov/2017020034

Solution Tree
Jeffrey C. Jones, CEO
Edmund M. Ackerman, President

Solution Tree Press
President and Publisher: Douglas M. Rife
Editorial Director: Sarah Payne-Mills
Managing Production Editor: Caroline Cascio
Senior Production Editor: Christine Hood
Senior Editor: Amy Rubenstein
Copy Editor: Ashante K. Thomas
Proofreader: Elisabeth Abrams
Text and Cover Designer: Abigail Bowen
Editorial Assistants: Jessi Finn and Kendra Slayton

I dedicate this book to my six grandchildren—A.J., Alyson, Brooke, Jennifer, Julia, and Luke. Success for *all* of you—whatever it takes!

—Austin Buffum

I dedicate this book to my dear friend and mentor, Dr. Robert Eaker. The wisdom and kindness you have shared with the Mattos family are truly priceless.

—Mike Mattos

I dedicate this book to the students and educators who have inspired me throughout my career. First and foremost, my son and daughter, Greg and Katie, consistently remind me to view each and every student as a priceless and unique gift, never as a test score or statistic.

Additionally, I have been honored to work with many skilled, dedicated, and passionate educators. To those special few who helped me stay focused on "true north" and who were the wind beneath my wings, this book is for you.

—Janet Malone

ACKNOWLEDGMENTS

We are so grateful for our association and collaboration with Jeffrey Jones, Douglas Rife, and the exceptional professionals at Solution Tree. We know this collaboration has been so successful because we share a common vision: *To transform education worldwide to ensure learning for all*! The publications team has edited and improved every sentence of all our books, and the events team has made this content available through RTI at Work™ institutes and workshops. We would specifically like to thank Christine Hood for her outstanding editing of this book. Shannon Ritz and the professional development department have extended our work to schools and districts around the world. Most important, Solution Tree's efforts to promote our work have demonstrated the highest level of passion and professionalism. It is not surprising that this focus on quality over quantity has made Solution Tree a global leader in educational publishing, events, and staff development. We look forward to our continued collaboration for years to come.

We call our intervention recommendations RTI *at Work* because they are built on the Professional Learning Community at Work® (PLC at Work) process. We believe that it is impossible to develop an effective system of interventions unless it builds on the guiding principles of the PLC at Work process—with a learning-focused culture, collaborative structures, and a results orientation. The leading authors of this process—Richard DuFour, Rebecca DuFour, and Robert Eaker—have generously shared their knowledge, expertise, and friendship. A special thank you to Becky, who read every word of our draft to ensure that we clearly and accurately capture how the RTI at Work process fits within and is driven by the PLC at Work framework. We hope that our work, in collaboration with Bob and Becky, will lead others to the power of the PLC at Work process and honors the life of our mentor, Rick DuFour.

We are also blessed to work with an exceptional team of RTI at Work associates: Kim Bailey, Tim Brown, Brian K. Butler, Daniel Cohan, Luis F. Cruz, Darin L. Fahrney, Paul Farmer, Paul Goldberg, Aaron Hansen, Brandon Jones, Dennis King, Greg Kushnir, Dave LaRose, François Massé, Maria Nielsen, Geri Parscale, Garrick Peterson, Will Remmert, Laurie Robinson Sammons, Rich Rodriguez, Paula Rogers, Julie A. Schmidt, Sarah Schuhl, W. Richard Smith, Bob Sonju, Timothy S. Stuart, Eric Twadell, and Nicole Dimich Vagle. They are all outstanding educators from around the world. Serving as practitioners, they have gained the depth of knowledge and understanding only achieved through actually doing the work at the highest levels. They graciously share their expertise with us and with educators from St. Louis to Singapore and beyond.

Like virtually all educators, we view our work as a labor of love. We have a singular focus—to help every student have the kind of future we would want for our own children. When your career requires you to give to others, it is essential to have people in your life who fill your heart and soul with their love. We are so blessed to have these people in our lives. We would like to thank Anita Mattos, Laurel Mattos, Lesley Buffum, and all of Janet's growing family. This book is an extension of the inspiration you fill us with every day.

Visit **go.SolutionTree.com/RTIatWork** to download the free reproducibles in this book.

TABLE OF CONTENTS

Reproducible pages are in italics.

CHAPTER 3

CHAPTER 4

PART TWO

CHAPTER 5

PART THREE

CHAPTER 7

ABOUT THE AUTHORS

 **Austin Buffum, EdD,** has forty-seven years of experience in public schools. His many roles include serving as former senior deputy superintendent of California's Capistrano Unified School District. Austin has presented in over nine hundred school districts throughout the United States and around the world. He delivers trainings and presentations on the response to intervention (RTI) at Work model. This tiered approach to response to intervention is centered on Professional Learning Communities (PLC) at Work concepts and strategies to ensure every student receives the time and support necessary to succeed. Austin also delivers workshops and presentations that provide the tools educators need to build and sustain PLCs.

Austin was selected 2006 Curriculum and Instruction Administrator of the Year by the Association of California School Administrators. He attended the Principals' Center at the Harvard Graduate School of Education and was greatly inspired by its founder, Roland Barth, an early advocate of the collaborative culture that defines PLCs today. He later led Capistrano's K–12 instructional program on an increasingly collaborative path toward operating as a PLC. During this process, thirty-seven of the district's schools were designated California Distinguished Schools, and eleven received National Blue Ribbon recognition.

Austin is coauthor with Suzette Lovely of *Generations at School: Building an Age-Friendly Learning Community*. He has also coauthored *Uniting Academic and Behavior Interventions: Solving the Skill or Will Dilemma*; *It's About Time: Planning Interventions and Extensions in Elementary School*; *It's About Time: Planning Interventions and Extensions in Secondary School*; *Simplifying Response to Intervention: Four Essential Guiding Principles*; and *Pyramid Response to Intervention: RTI, Professional Learning Communities, and How to Respond When Kids Don't Learn*.

A graduate of the University of Southern California, Austin earned a bachelor of music degree and received a master of education degree with honors. He holds a doctor of education degree from Nova Southeastern University.

To learn more about Austin's work, follow him @agbuffum on Twitter.

Mike Mattos is an internationally recognized author, presenter, and practitioner who specializes in uniting teachers, administrators, and support staff to transform schools by implementing the response to intervention and PLC processes. Mike co-created the RTI at Work model, which builds on the foundation of the PLC at Work process by using team structures and a focus on learning, collaboration, and results to drive successful outcomes and creating a systematic, multi-tiered system of supports to ensure high levels of learning for all students.

He is former principal of Marjorie Veeh Elementary School and Pioneer Middle School in California. At both schools, Mike helped create powerful PLCs, improving learning for all students. In 2004, Marjorie Veeh, an elementary school with a large population of youth at risk, won the California Distinguished School and National Title I Achieving School awards.

A National Blue Ribbon School, Pioneer is among only thirteen schools in the United States that the GE Foundation selected as a Best-Practice Partner and is one of eight schools that Richard DuFour chose to feature in the video series *The Power of Professional Learning Communities at Work: Bringing the Big Ideas to Life*. Based on standardized test scores, Pioneer ranks among the top 1 percent of California secondary schools and, in 2009 and 2011, was named Orange County's top middle school. For his leadership, Mike was named the Orange County Middle School Administrator of the Year by the Association of California School Administrators.

Mike has coauthored many other books focused on response to intervention (RTI) and professional learning communities (PLCs), including *Learning by Doing: A Handbook for Professional Learning Communities at Work*; *Concise Answers to Frequently Asked Questions About Professional Learning Communities at Work*; *Simplifying Response to Intervention: Four Essential Guiding Principles*; *Pyramid Response to Intervention: RTI, Professional Learning Communities, and How to Respond When Kids Don't Learn*; *Uniting Academic and Behavior Interventions: Solving the Skill or Will Dilemma*; *It's About Time: Planning Interventions and Extensions in Secondary School*; *It's About Time: Planning Interventions and Extensions in Elementary School*; *Best Practices at Tier 1: Daily Differentiation for Effective Instruction, Secondary*; *Best Practices at Tier 1: Daily Differentiation for Effective Instruction, Elementary*; and *The Collaborative Administrator: Working Together as a Professional Learning Community*.

To learn more about Mike's work, visit AllThingsPLC (www.allthingsplc.info) and http://mattos.info/welcome.html, or follow him @mikemattos65 on Twitter.

Janet Malone has thirty-five years of experience in public schools, including two years in rural Australia. She spent most of her public school career in the Poway Unified School District in southern California, where she retired as the director of professional development. A former teacher, teacher coach, principal, and central office administrator, Janet was able to meet the interests and needs of teachers, administrators, and support staff alike on topics ranging from assessment and effective grading to professional learning communities to team building, and more.

In retirement, Janet has presented at conferences, conducted professional workshops, and consulted with school districts throughout North America. Most recently, she has worked closely with Austin Buffum and Mike Mattos to co-create both the content of RTI at Work and the design of RTI at Work professional development offerings. Based on her range of experiences, she has made contributions to assessment, collaborative teamwork, leadership development, and facilitation of adult learning.

From her first teaching job to the leadership she demonstrates currently, Janet has always kept her focus on student learning. She passionately believes that in order for students to learn at their highest levels, the adults who serve them must be learning too.

To book Austin Buffum, Mike Mattos, or Janet Malone for professional development, contact pd@SolutionTree.com.

Introduction

> In a global economy where the most valuable skill you can sell is your knowledge, a good education is no longer just a pathway to opportunity—it is a prerequisite.
>
> **—Barack Obama**

This book is about doing the right work. Success in school is the factor that most directly predicts the length and quality of students' lives. A student that fails to succeed in our K–12 system is three times more likely to be unemployed, sixty-three times more likely to be incarcerated, and on average, lives at least a decade shorter than a college graduate (Breslow, 2012; Tavernise, 2012). Like any other professionals who make life-altering decisions on behalf of those they serve, educators have a professional and ethical obligation to utilize practices proven to best ensure every student succeeds. The very definition of *profession* is a vocation that requires specialized training in the practices deemed most effective in the field ("profession," n.d.). When a preponderance of evidence proves that a particular process, protocol, or procedure is most effective, professionals are not merely invited to use it, but instead are expected to conform to these technical and ethical standards.

When it comes to how educators should respond when students struggle in school, the research and evidence in our field have never been more conclusive—response to intervention (RTI) is the right way to intervene. Also known as a multitiered system of supports (MTSS), RTI is a systematic process to ensure every student receives:

> The additional time and support needed to learn at high levels. RTI's underlying premise is that schools should not delay providing help for struggling students until they fall far enough behind to qualify for special education, but instead should provide timely, targeted, systematic

interventions to all students who demonstrate the need. (Buffum, Mattos, & Weber, 2012, p. xiii)

Traditionally, the RTI process is represented in the shape of a pyramid (see figure I.1).

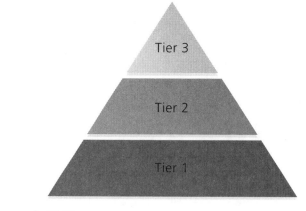

Source: Buffum et al., 2012.

FIGURE I.1: Traditional RTI pyramid.

The pyramid is commonly separated into tiers: Tier 1 represents core instruction, Tier 2 represents supplemental interventions, and Tier 3 represents intensive student supports. The pyramid is wide at the bottom to represent the instruction that all students receive. As students demonstrate the need for additional support, they receive increasingly more targeted and intensive help. Because timely supplemental interventions should address most student needs when they are first emerging, fewer students fall significantly below grade level and require the intensive services Tier 3 offers, creating the tapered shape of a pyramid.

> **RTI ranks in the top-three education practices proven to best increase student achievement.**

Based on his meta-analysis of more than eighty thousand studies relating to the factors inside and outside of school that impact student learning, researcher John Hattie (2009, 2012) finds that RTI ranks in the top-three education practices proven to best increase student achievement. When implemented well, RTI has an exceptional average yearly impact rate of 1.07 standard deviation (Hattie, 2012). To put this in perspective, consider the following.

- A one standard deviation (1.0) increase is typically associated with advancing student achievement within two to three years (Hattie, 2009).

- Based on longitudinal studies, the yearly typical impact rate of a classroom teacher's instruction ranges between 0.15 and 0.40 standard deviation growth (Hattie, 2009). This means a school that successfully implements RTI leverages a process that is considerably more effective than a school that leaves it up to individual, isolated teachers to meet students' instructional needs.

- The greatest home or environmental factor that impacts student learning is a family's economic status. Students that come from more affluent homes—defined as middle class or higher—gain a yearly academic benefit of 0.57 standard deviation growth per year (Hattie, 2009). This home support contributes to an achievement gap on standardized tests between affluent households and students of poverty that has grown more than 40 percent since the 1960s (Reardon, 2011), while the college graduation rate gap has increased more than 50 percent since the late 1980s (Bailey & Dynarski, 2011). RTI's impact rate of 1.07—more than twice as powerful as what some students might receive at home each night—provides educators a proven, powerful tool to close the United States' largest achievement gap.

Equally important, we know that a successful system of interventions must be built on a highly effective core instructional program, as interventions cannot make up for a toxic school culture, low student expectations, and poor initial instruction. Fortunately, our profession has near unanimous agreement on how to best structure a school to ensure student and adult learning.

Comprehensive study of the world's best-performing school systems finds that these systems function as professional learning communities (Barber, Chijioke, & Mourshed, 2010; Barber & Mourshed, 2007). Additionally, virtually all our professional organizations endorse PLCs (DuFour, 2016). When implemented well, the PLC process is the best way to build the learning-focused culture, collaborative structures, instructional focus, and assessment information necessary to successfully respond when students don't learn.

At a time in which our students' lives depend on educators utilizing practices proven to be most effective, should we allow professional educators to disregard this overwhelming evidence and cling to outdated procedures? Would this be acceptable in any other profession? Imagine if you are diagnosed with a life-threatening illness, and you ask your doctor to identify your best course of action. In response, your doctor says, "There is a treatment process that, based on over eighty thousand studies, is the most effective way to cure your illness. It is proven to be multiple times more powerful than traditional treatments used throughout most of the past century. Additionally, the most successful hospitals in the world utilize this practice, and virtually all our medical organizations endorse this treatment."

How would you respond? "When can we start?"

Now imagine if your doctor knows of this near unanimous professional consensus on the best possible treatment of your illness, yet disregards it and utilizes a less effective, outdated procedure. You would be outraged. We would consider such actions as professional malpractice, profoundly unethical, and grounds for removal from the field. Knowing what we know today about how to best respond when students struggle, there is no debate: implementing RTI within a professional learning community framework is the right work.

If RTI Works, Why Is There Still an Achievement Gap?

> Knowing what we know today about how to best respond when students struggle, there is no debate: implementing RTI within a professional learning community framework is the right work.

In fall 2015, the following headline appeared on *Education Week*'s front page: "Study: RTI Practice Falls Short of Promise" (Sparks, 2015). The research, which the National Center for Education Evaluation and Regional Assistance conducted, studies the yearly reading progress of over twenty thousand grades 1–3 students. It finds that first graders who received reading interventions actually did worse than identical peers who did not receive the RTI support. More troubling, students who were already in special education or older than average for their grade performed "particularly poorly if they received interventions" (Sparks, 2015, p. 1).

Yet, when you dig deeper, the researchers find that the implementation practices at a majority of the participating schools were misaligned to the guiding principles of RTI, including the following.

▸ Sixty-nine percent of schools in the impact sample offered at least some intervention services *during* Tier 1 core instruction. As noted, "In such schools, intervention may have displaced instruction time and replaced some small-group or other instruction services with intervention services. As a result, reading intervention services may have been different from, but not necessarily supplemental to, core reading instruction" (Balu et al., 2015, p. ES-11). A basic tenet of RTI is that we should provide interventions *in addition* to effective Tier 1 core instruction, not in place of it. When students miss new critical grade-level core curriculum to receive interventions, it is akin to having students take one step forward (improvement in a remedial skill), while taking one step back (missing a new essential grade-level skill).

▸ The study finds that "even in schools using the more traditional model of providing intervention services only to readers below grade level, classroom teachers played an additional role and provided intervention services to 37 percent of those groups in Grade 1" (Balu et al., 2015, p. ES-11). RTI advocates that staff members with a higher level of expertise in a student's target area of need should be the ones providing the interventions. While a classroom teacher might meet these qualifications, it would be unrealistic to expect that same teacher to always have more effective ways to reteach this skill to the same students who did not learn it the first time. Our experience is that teachers don't save their best instructional practices for Tier 2 interventions. More often, teachers provide students with the same pedagogies from core instruction, only in a smaller group setting.

When interviewed about this study, coauthor Fred Doolittle states, "We don't want to have people say that these findings say these schools aren't doing RTI right; this turns out to be what RTI looks like when it plays out in daily life" (as cited in Sparks, 2015, p. 1). We strongly disagree with his interpretation.

To apply this conclusion to a similar situation, we know that there is tremendous consensus in the medical field regarding the best ways to lose weight in a healthy and effective way. According to the Cleveland Clinic (n.d.), "To lose weight, you must eat fewer calories or burn up more calories than you need. The best way to lose weight is to do both." Translated into practice, this means the best diets should include eating better and regular exercise. Armed with this knowledge, millions of Americans each year commit to diets based on these principles, yet more than 90 percent of their efforts fail (Rodriguez, 2010). Should we assume then that the current research behind losing weight is at fault? Should medical researchers conclude, "We don't want to hear that people aren't dieting right—this turns out to be what eating fewer calories and burning up more calories looks like when it plays out in daily life."

In reality, and as the Cleveland Clinic (n.d.) makes note of, the reason why most people don't lose weight is because they briefly commit to eating somewhat better and increasing their exercise but ultimately fail to make these practices part of their ongoing lifestyle. Likewise, many schools are committing to some disjointed efforts at interventions but are failing to fully commit to the collaborative, learning-focused PLC lifestyle required to ensure every student's success.

Common Missteps When Implementing RTI

While we disagree with Doolittle's interpretation of the findings, unfortunately, the study's results—that many schools are failing to see the gains in student achievement that RTI can provide when implemented well—did not surprise us. We have directly led the RTI process as site and district practitioners and have subsequently assisted hundreds of schools around the world. Throughout our travels, we have found that many site educators, district administrators, and state policymakers misinterpret key concepts, skip critical steps, look for shortcuts, and fail to discontinue traditional practices that are counterproductive to the RTI process. In addition to the two RTI implementation mistakes from the study (Sparks, 2015), nine other common missteps include the following.

1. Viewing RTI primarily as a process to identify students for special education

2. Viewing RTI as a regular education process

3. Building interventions on an ineffective core instructional program

4. Failing to create a guaranteed and viable curriculum

5. Using mismatched and misused assessments

6. Relying too heavily on purchased intervention programs

7. Perpetuating ineffective interventions

8. Focusing too much on what the staff cannot directly influence

9. Assuming some students are incapable of learning at high levels due to innate cognitive ability or environmental conditions

Viewing RTI Primarily as a Process to Identify Students for Special Education

There is an important *secondary* benefit of RTI—educators can use it as a process to identify students with learning disabilities. When all students have access to essential grade-level curriculum, highly effective initial teaching, and targeted interventions when needed, a vast majority of them succeed. If a student does not respond to these

There is an important *secondary* benefit of RTI—educators can use it as a process to identify students with learning disabilities.

proven practices, it can indicate a potential learning disability and would justify a comprehensive evaluation of the student's unique learning needs.

Unfortunately, many educators too quickly assume that a student's failure in core instruction means he or she has a disability (Prasse, n.d.). When educators begin the RTI process assuming that a student's struggles are likely due to a potential learning disability, then they usually view the tiers as the mandatory steps to achieve special education placement. Rigid time lines and laborious documentation then drive the process, and special education placement is the predetermined outcome.

Even if the RTI process worked perfectly to identify students with learning disabilities, what great benefit would we expect this qualification to provide these students? An objective analysis of special education's impact since the passage of the Education for All Handicapped Children Act in 1975 concludes that it has not only failed to close student achievement gaps but has actually been detrimental to achieving this outcome.

The graduation rate for students with special needs was 61 percent in 2014—almost 20 percent lower than for regular education students (Diament, 2014). Students with special needs are underrepresented in postsecondary education (Samuels, 2010) but overrepresented in prison. It is estimated that at least one-third and up to 70 percent of those incarcerated received special education services in school (Mader & Butrymowicz, 2014). These statistics are not meant to condemn special education teachers' heroic efforts. Instead, it demonstrates the limitations of legislation that was never designed to ensure that students with special needs actually learn but to simply allow them to attend school. Based on these results, viewing RTI as merely a new way to qualify a student for traditional special education services is nothing more than creating a new pathway to educational purgatory.

Viewing RTI as a Regular Education Process

Instead of viewing RTI as a process to qualify students for special education, some go to the opposite extreme and see a multitiered system of supports as a way to stop the over-identification of students for special education. While this goal is noble, the unintended consequence is usually detrimental to both regular and special education students. For example, policymakers in one southwestern state dictate that Tier 3 can only serve special education students. This means that regular education staff alone must serve students who need intensive remediation in foundational skills but do not have an identified learning disability.

Often categorical dollars fund the best-trained faculty in areas like reading remediation, language acquisition, and behavior support, which would then deny regular education students access to their expertise. It is unrealistic to expect content-credentialed teachers to have the training equivalent of a reading specialist or school psychologist. This is why federal law acknowledges this need and allows early intervening services, in which a percentage of a district's special education resources can be used in preventive ways for students who demonstrate the need for these services but don't have a disability (Individuals With Disabilities Education Improvement Act [IDEIA], 2004).

Creating this artificial divide between regular and special education staff also hurts special education students. Special education teachers cannot be content experts in every subject at every grade level. Yet many individualized education programs (IEPs) assign special education staff to provide supplemental interventions in multiple content areas. To implement RTI effectively, we cannot view it as regular education or special education. Instead, educators should base interventions on each student's individual needs, and assign staff based on who is best trained to meet each need. We are not suggesting that schools should discontinue special education services altogether, or that educators can disregard student IEPs. What we are suggesting is that special education law now advocates for providing schools much more flexibility to meet all students' needs. But taking advantage of this requires schools to rethink the way regular and special education have worked for years.

Building Interventions on an Ineffective Core Instructional Program

A school with weak and ineffective teaching will not solve its problems by creating a system of timely interventions for students. Eventually, the number of students it is attempting to support will crush that system. Interventions cannot make up for a core instructional program functioning in teacher isolation, a culture of "my students and your students," tracking students by perceived ability and demographic expectations, assessing students with archaic grading practices, and expecting parents and special education to be the primary solution for struggling students. This is why our approach to RTI works best in schools that function as a PLC. The PLC at Work process focuses and unites all the school's practices toward one mission: to ensure high levels of learning for every student. As long as we view RTI as an appendage to a school's traditional instructional program, instead of an integral part of a school's collaborative efforts to ensure all students succeed, a school's intervention efforts will most likely be ineffective (DuFour, 2015).

Failing to Create a Guaranteed and Viable Curriculum

To learn at high levels, students must have access to essential grade-level curriculum each year. Every student might not leave each school year having mastered *every* grade-level standard, but every student must master the learning outcomes the school or district has deemed indispensable for future success. Anything less, and the student is on a trajectory to drop out of school.

Working collaboratively as a PLC, educators must create a guaranteed and viable curriculum grade by grade, course by course, and unit by unit that represents the skills, content knowledge, and behaviors every student must master to achieve this goal. Equally important, they must ensure students have access to this essential, grade-level curriculum as part of their Tier 1 core instructional program. With the rare exception of those few students who have profound disabilities, there should be no track of core instruction that focuses exclusively on below-grade-level skills.

> Tragically, many schools assume their most at-risk students are incapable of learning at grade level.

Tragically, many schools assume their most at-risk students are incapable of learning at grade level and, instead, replace these students' core instruction with Tier 3 remedial coursework. If a student receives below-grade-level instruction all day, where will he or she end up at the end of the year? Below grade level, of course. Educators must provide Tier 3 interventions *in addition* to Tier 1 essential grade-level curriculum, not in place of it.

Using Mismatched and Misused Assessments

Interventions are most effective when they target a student's specific learning needs. This requires assessment data that can identify the specific standard, learning target, skill, or behavior that a student lacks. Unfortunately, many schools use broad indicators to drive their interventions, including report card grades, state or provincial assessments, district benchmark results, or universal screening scores. The National Center for Education Evaluation and Regional Assistance's study validates this common implementation mistake. It finds that most schools' RTI implementation is fairly rigid, using a single test to identify students for Tier 2 and a standard set of interventions once they get there (as cited in Sparks, 2015). These assessments usually measure multiple standards and then report a student's results in a single composite score. While this information can be helpful in identifying the students who need additional help, it is insufficient for assigning students with specific interventions.

Relying Too Heavily on Purchased Intervention Programs

No Child Left Behind (NCLB) and IDEIA advocate using interventions based on "research that involves the application of rigorous, systematic, and objective procedures to obtain reliable and valid knowledge relevant to educational activities and programs" (IDEIA, 2004). As a result, some districts have created lists of approved interventions that constitute the only programs their schools can use which, in turn, restricts a school's ability to creatively meet each student's individual needs. Furthermore, outside of primary reading, a limited number of scientifically research-based interventions is available for each subject and grade level.

Some schools and districts have fallen into the trap of searching for the perfect product to buy that will help all their struggling readers, writers, or mathematics students. For example, a school might purchase a Tier 3 reading intervention program and then place all its struggling readers into it. The problem is that at-risk readers don't all struggle for the same reason, so there is no one program that addresses every student's unique needs. Some very good, scientific research-based products are available that can become powerful, targeted tools in a school's intervention toolbox—but there is no silver bullet solution for all struggling students. Improving student achievement requires job-embedded, ongoing processes, not disjointed programs.

Perpetuating Ineffective Interventions

A system of interventions can only be as effective as the individual interventions it comprises. When we work with schools, we often have them list their current site interventions. At practically every school, the list includes remedial support classes of varying types, study hall opportunities, summer school, retention, and special education—interventions that research concludes are generally ineffective (Buffum et al., 2012; Hattie, 2009). For example, the research on retention shows that it does not promote higher levels of learning, close achievement gaps, or increase an at-risk student's odds of future success in school. The most comprehensive meta-analysis on retention finds that being retained one year almost doubles a student's likelihood of dropping out, while being retained twice almost guarantees it (Hattie, 2009). In spite of this conclusive evidence, schools continue to use retention as an intervention for their most at-risk students.

Educators must provide interventions *in addition* to Tier 1 essential grade-level curriculum, not in place of it.

When it comes to interventions, giving at-risk students more of what is not working is rarely the answer. Common sense tells us this, yet many schools continue to build their systems of interventions with practices that don't work, have never worked, and have no promise of getting better results the following year (Buffum et al., 2012).

Focusing Too Much on What the Staff Cannot Directly Influence

When planning interventions for struggling students, many schools spend an inordinate amount of time identifying and discussing factors that they cannot directly change. These topics include a student's home environment, a lack of parental support, the pressure of preparing students for high-stakes state or provincial assessments, and ill-conceived district, state or provincial, and federal education policies. While these concerns are real and might be impacting both the student and the site educators, they are rarely the primary reason why a student has not learned specific essential learning outcomes. Similar schools are facing the same obstacles but nevertheless are reaching record levels of student achievement. This demonstrates that these external obstacles are undeniable hurdles but should not become insurmountable obstacles to improving student learning.

Assuming Some Students Are Incapable of Learning at High Levels Due to Innate Cognitive Ability or Environmental Conditions

Virtually all educators believe their students can learn, but many think that how much a student can learn varies depending on his or her innate abilities and demographic background. They might assume students from economically disadvantaged homes—who are more likely to be minority students and English learners—are less capable than peers that come from more advantaged households. They rarely express their beliefs formally in the school's mission statement or policies, but they carry out these beliefs in school practice every day. We know that a student's ethnicity, native language, and economic status do not reduce the student's innate capacity to learn, yet minority students, English learners, and economically disadvantaged students are disproportionately represented in special education (Brantlinger, 2006; Ferri & Connor, 2006; Skiba, Poloni-Staudinger, Gallini, Simmons, & Feggins-Azziz, 2006; Skiba et al., 2008) and under-represented in gifted and honors programs (Donovan & Cross, 2002). It is unlikely an intervention will be effective when educators begin with the assumption that some students can't achieve in the first place.

Undoubtedly, educators are not making these mistakes purposely. The hard work, dedication, and personal sacrifice individual educators display daily in support of their students continually inspire us. Because RTI practices represent a seismic shift in how schools have traditionally functioned, it would be naïve to think that the level of change required to do it well would be a smooth, seamless process. It is not enough to commit to doing the right work; we must do the right work *right* to secure the benefits that RTI is proven to provide.

> When it comes to interventions, giving at-risk students more of what is not working is rarely the answer.

The Right Work *Right*

If you want to cook a delicious meal, it requires more than a proven recipe and the right ingredients. These conditions are necessary but are not sufficient. The recipe must be prepared with a high level of cooking skill. Similarly, unlocking the potential power of RTI requires more than state guidelines, site resources, and a dedicated school staff—schools must implement RTI at a very high level. That is the purpose of this book—to walk you through *exactly* how to create a highly effective, multitiered system of supports within the framework of the PLC at Work process.

The first sentence in Mike and Austin's first book, *Pyramid Response to Intervention: RTI, Professional Learning Communities, and How to Respond When Kids Don't Learn* (Buffum, Mattos, & Weber, 2009), states, "This book is written for practitioners by practitioners" (p. 1). We did not create PLCs, RTI, or MTSS. We are educators who collaborate with our colleagues to successfully turn this powerful research into daily practice. Our schools are not immune to the misinterpretations and missteps previously described. In fact, we have hit just about every possible pothole and speedbump on our journey. But because we stay committed to the PLC process, these mistakes help us develop the simplified approaches, practical processes, and proven tools needed to dramatically increase student learning.

Our work is further enriched and refined through our collaboration with schools around the world. The recommendations in this book are grounded in research, and equally important, have been tested, revised, and validated in the real-world conditions that educators face daily. Most important, this book is designed to help schools avoid and overcome the most common implementation missteps.

RTI is as much a way of thinking as it is a process of doing. Our fear in writing an implementation book is that readers will interpret it as a checklist of tasks. *There are both important guiding principles that drive the work and essential actions to do for RTI to work.* But within these parameters, each school must be flexible regarding how to implement these practices to best meet the unique needs of the students they serve with the resources available. Additionally, schools must work within the laws and regulations of their district, state or province, and country. Understanding the right thinking empowers educators to be true to the process but flexible in implementation. To this end, this book is designed to develop two types of outcomes.

1. *Guiding principles* that serve as a framework for the right thinking

2. *Essential actions* that transform this thinking into specific steps

Both are critical and will help educators do the right work right. Research and theory alone won't help a single student unless we transform them into action. Educators rarely embrace and effectively implement new practices when they don't understand *why* they are doing them.

Because being a professional learning community is the foundation of our approach to RTI, understanding the PLC at Work process is necessary to apply our recommendations and practices. At its core, three big ideas and four critical questions guide the PLC at Work process.

The Three Big Ideas That Drive the Work of PLCs

We call our approach RTI *at Work* because we firmly believe that the best way to ensure high levels of learning for both students and educators is for schools or districts to function as a professional learning community. The essential characteristics of our approach to RTI perfectly align with the fundamental elements of the overarching PLC at Work process. RTI at Work is built on a proven research base of best practices and is a tool to assist PLC schools in achieving their mission to ensure high levels of student learning.

> Research and theory alone won't help a single student unless we transform them into action.

The PLC at Work process requires educators to work collaboratively to:

▸ Learn together about the practices, policies, procedures, and beliefs that best ensure student learning

▸ Apply what they are learning

▸ Use evidence of student learning to evaluate, revise, and celebrate their collective efforts to improve student achievement

These outcomes are captured in the three big ideas of the PLC at Work process: (1) a focus on learning, (2) a collaborative culture, and (3) a results orientation.

A Focus on Learning

A PLC school's core mission is not simply to ensure that all students are *taught* but also that they actually *learn*. As Richard DuFour, Rebecca DuFour, Robert Eaker, Thomas W. Many, and Mike Mattos (2016) state in the PLC handbook *Learning by Doing*:

> The first (and the biggest) of the big ideas is based on the premise that *the fundamental purpose of the school is to ensure that all students learn at high levels (grade level or higher)*. This focus on and commitment to the learning of each student is the very essence of a *learning community*. (p. 11)

In previous books, we refer to this concept as *collective responsibility*—a shared belief that the primary responsibility of each member of the organization is to ensure high levels of learning for every child.

This seismic shift from a focus on teaching to a focus on learning requires far more than rewriting a school's mission statement or creating a catchy "learning for all" motto to put on the school's letterhead. This commitment to ensure student learning unites and focuses the collaborative efforts of the staff and serves as the organization's "north star" when making decisions. The school's policies, practices, and procedures are guided by the question, Will this help more students learn at higher levels?

As stated in *Learning by Doing*:

> The members of a PLC create and are guided by a clear and compelling vision of what the organization must become in order to help all students learn. They make collective commitments clarifying what each member

will do to create such an organization, and they use results-oriented goals to mark their progress. Members work together to clarify exactly what each student must learn, monitor each student's learning on a timely basis, provide systematic interventions that ensure students receive additional time and support for learning when they struggle, and extend their learning when students have already mastered the intended outcomes. (DuFour et al., 2016, p. 11)

Creating consensus and commitment to becoming a learning-focused school or district is an essential prerequisite to successful RTI implementation. Likewise, any school already committed to the PLC process would heartily embrace RTI as an essential tool in achieving their commitment to guarantee every student's success.

A Collaborative Culture

The second big idea is a commitment to creating a collaborative culture. Because no teacher can possibly possess all the knowledge, skills, time, and resources needed to ensure high levels of learning for all his or her students, educators at a PLC school work collaboratively and take collective responsibility for student success. Instead of allowing individual teachers to work in isolation, teacher teams become the fundamental structure of the school. Collaboration does not happen by invitation or chance; instead, frequent team time is embedded into the contractual day.

Creating collaborative teacher teams will not improve student learning unless their efforts focus on the *right work*. To this end, teacher collaboration in the PLC at Work process is guided by four critical questions:

1. What knowledge, skills, and dispositions should every student acquire as a result of this unit, this course, or this grade level?

2. How will we know when each student has acquired the essential knowledge and skills?

3. How will we respond when some students do not learn?

4. How will we extend the learning for students who are already proficient? (DuFour et al., 2016, p. 36)

Question 1 requires teachers of the same course or grade level to collectively determine what they expect all their students to know and be able to do. After all, a school cannot possibly create a systematic, collective response when students do not learn if individual teachers focus on different essential learning standards. By identifying essential standards, teacher teams can analyze, prioritize, and otherwise unpack standards of what is most essential for students to know. We refer to this process as *concentrated instruction*—a systematic process of identifying essential knowledge, skills, and behaviors that all students must master to learn at high levels and determining the specific learning needs for each child to get there.

Because the school is committed to all students learning these essential standards, teams must be prepared to identify students who require additional time and support. This process is captured in the third big idea.

A Results Orientation

The third big idea focuses on evidence of student learning. In order to assess their effectiveness in ensuring all students learn, educators must use "evidence of learning to inform and improve their professional practice and respond to individual students who need intervention and enrichment" (DuFour et al., 2016, p. 12).

After identifying the knowledge and skills that all students must learn, collaborative teams focus on the second critical question: How will we know when each student has acquired the essential knowledge and skills? Educators functioning as a PLC must assess their efforts to achieve high levels of learning for all students based on concrete results rather than good intentions.

Student assessment information constitutes the "life blood" of an effective system of interventions; teachers use it to identify students in need of additional time and support and to confirm which core instructional strategies are most effective in meeting students' needs. We refer to this process as *convergent assessment*—an ongoing process of collectively analyzing targeted evidence to determine the specific learning needs of each child and the effectiveness of the instruction the child receives in meeting these needs.

By answering the first two critical questions, the school is now prepared to successfully intervene for students who need extra help mastering essential curriculum and to extend the learning for students that have. These two outcomes are captured in critical questions 3 and 4.

3. How will we respond when some students do not learn?

4. How will we extend the learning for students who are already proficient?

We define a school's systematic response to answering these two questions as *certain access*—"a systematic process that guarantees every student will receive the time and support needed to learn at high levels" (Buffum et al., 2012, p. 10).

Because RTI is proven to be the best way to intervene when students need additional time and support, schools that function as a PLC should not view RTI as a new initiative but instead, as deepening their current intervention practices. For schools that have not embraced PLC practices, RTI might seem like a nearly impossible undertaking. Trying to implement RTI without creating a school culture and structure that aligns with PLC practices is like trying to build a house starting with the roof—without a proper foundation, no structure can stand. RTI is an essential piece of the puzzle to ensure student success—PLC *is* the puzzle.

The Design of This Book

The goal of this book is to dig deeply into critical questions 3 and 4 of the PLC at Work process (DuFour et al., 2016):

3. How will we respond when some students do not learn?

4. How will we extend the learning for students who are already proficient?

Undoubtedly, answering these questions requires a school to address the first two critical questions regarding curriculum and assessment and also to consider the cultural beliefs and collaborative structures it requires to collectively respond when students need additional time and support. While this book addresses these foundational PLC building blocks—especially in the chapters that focus on creating a strong Tier 1 core instructional program—it is insufficient in creating a deep understanding of the entire PLC at Work process.

This book is modeled after the handbook for the PLC at Work process, *Learning by Doing, Third Edition* (DuFour et al., 2016). We do not intend to replace this invaluable resource but instead, complement it. We purposefully align our critical concepts, essential actions, and vocabulary to this resource. Additionally, where appropriate, we reference chapters and tools in *Learning by Doing* that will help support and extend our RTI recommendations. We highly recommend that this book's readers also read and reference *Learning by Doing*.

Taking Action is divided into three parts. Part one includes chapters 2–4 and focuses on the essential actions necessary to build a highly effective Tier 1 core instructional program. Chapter 2 addresses how to create a schoolwide culture of collective responsibility and how to form the collaborative teams necessary to guide the RTI process. Chapter 3 digs deeply into the essential work of teacher collaborative teams at Tier 1, while chapter 4 describes the schoolwide responsibilities of site leadership.

Part two of the book targets Tier 2 interventions. Chapter 5 reviews how teacher teams should lead supplemental interventions for students who need additional time and support to learn team-identified essential standards. Chapter 6 describes the schoolwide actions of the site leadership team at Tier 2, including scheduling time for supplemental help during the school day and how to utilize site support staff to lead supplemental behavior interventions.

Part three, chapters 7 and 8, addresses the schoolwide essential actions needed to plan and target Tier 3 interventions for students who need intensive remediation. Chapter 7 examines the essential responsibilities of the site leadership team, while chapter 8 focuses on the formation and tasks of the school's intervention team.

Each chapter focuses on a specific part of the RTI at Work pyramid, which is highlighted so you can see how each part relates to the whole. Within each chapter, we also describe the specific essential actions schools must take to create a highly effective system of interventions. Consider for a moment the meaning of the word *essential*. When something is essential, it is so important to the whole that the whole cannot survive without it. The analogy we like to use is this: Is your arm essential to your whole body? Can you cut it off and live? Yes, so then it is not essential. It's very useful but not essential. Now, is your heart essential? Yes. Every other part of your body can be perfectly healthy, but if your heart stops working, everything else soon follows. We are not suggesting that the specific steps we present at each tier are the *only* beneficial actions a school can take to improve student learning. Other elements (like arms) are good too. This book focuses on the absolutely essential elements—the hearts—that, if we skip any one of them, will ultimately kill the effectiveness of the overall system of interventions. Many of these essential elements are the practices a school must be tight about in the PLC at Work process.

For each essential action, we clearly and concisely describe the specific outcome and who should take lead responsibility to ensure that it happens. Similar to *Learning by Doing* (DuFour et al., 2016), we then address the following elements.

- **Here's why:** We provide the research, evidence, and rationale behind the recommended action.

- **Here's how:** We provide a step-by-step process to successfully implement the essential element.

- **Helpful tools:** We provide tools needed to support the implementation process.

- **Coaching tips:** We provide reminders, ideas, and strategies for engaging and supporting educators in learning by doing. Based on the belief that staff members should solve their own most complex problems, it is essential to create a culture in which the adults effectively collaborate and learn together. These tips are meant to assist leadership team members as catalysts of change—promoting inquiry into current practices and, in turn, working to create an environment conducive to growth for teachers and students alike.

While we designed the content of this book to sequentially address each tier of the RTI process, you do not have to read the book sequentially. We want this book to be an ongoing resource, so we have written each chapter so it can stand alone. This design required us to repeat some key ideas more than once in the book, when specific content was relevant to multiple steps in the PLC and RTI processes. So, as you read the book, if you have a déjà vu moment and think, "I've read that idea already," you're right. We hope this repetition also helps solidify and reinforce key concepts.

Finally, while we designed this book to specifically address and help you avoid the most common RTI implementation mistakes, we know this to be true—you are going to make mistakes. We tell stories about our own mistakes on the journey to teach specific points in the book. These mistakes were unintentional but ultimately critical to our subsequent improvement.

However, one mistake is a sure death knell to the process—failing to put what you learn into action. This book is about taking action. The most powerful research—and the best of intentions—will not help a single student at your school unless you transform it from ideas into effort. To start our journey, it is important to lay out a vision of the road ahead. Visually, we capture this with our RTI at Work pyramid, the focus of chapter 1.

CHAPTER 1

The RTI at Work Pyramid

Where there is no vision, there is no hope.

—George Washington Carver

The use of graphic organizers is nothing new in education. Using a symbolic image, such as a Venn diagram, to compare and contrast two items or ideas, can be a powerful tool to visually capture and guide thinking. The use of a pyramid shape to represent a multitiered system of supports is designed to be just that—a graphic organizer. But just as a Venn diagram would be useless to students who don't understand the thinking represented by two interlocking circles, providing schools with a blank pyramid to build a site intervention program would be useless without ensuring that those using the tool understand the thinking behind it.

We find the traditional RTI pyramid both a blessing and a curse. When interpreted properly, it is a powerful visual that can organize and guide a school intervention program and processes. But as we mentioned in the introduction, we find that many schools, districts, and states have misinterpreted the pyramid diagram to represent a pathway to special education, which in turn can lead to practices counterproductive to a school's goal of ensuring every student's success.

We have carefully rethought and revised the traditional RTI pyramid. We refer to our visual framework as the RTI at Work pyramid. See figure 1.1 (page 18).

We call it the RTI *at Work* pyramid because, as mentioned in the introduction, our recommendations leverage research-based processed to ensure student learning—PLCs and RTI.

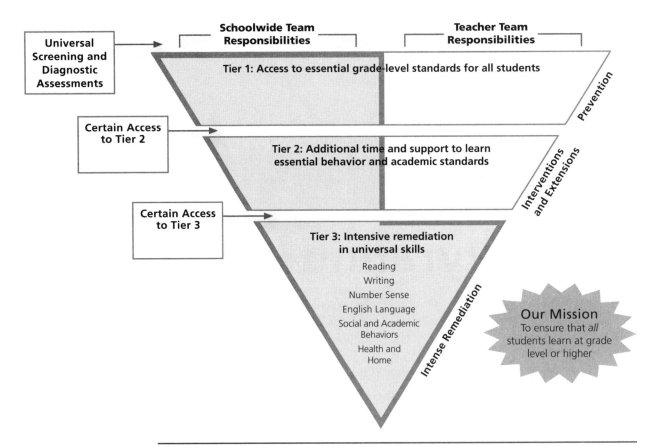

FIGURE 1.1: The RTI at Work pyramid.

Because the RTI at Work pyramid serves as this book's culminating activity, let's dig deeper into the guiding principles behind the design.

Why Is the RTI at Work Pyramid Upside Down?

While we are not the first educators to invert the traditional RTI pyramid (Brown-Chidsey & Steege, 2005; Deno, 1970), our reason for this design is in response to a common misinterpretation of the traditional RTI pyramid, which we addressed in the introduction—that RTI is primarily a new way to qualify students for special education. States, provinces, and school districts visually reinforce this conclusion when they place special education at the top of the pyramid, as illustrated in figure 1.2.

This incorrect application is understandable, as the traditional pyramid seems to focus a school's intervention system toward one point: special education. Subsequently, schools then view each tier as a required step that they must try to document prior to placing students into traditional special education services. Tragically, this approach tends to become a self-fulfilling prophecy because the organization starts interventions with protocols designed to screen and document students for this potential outcome.

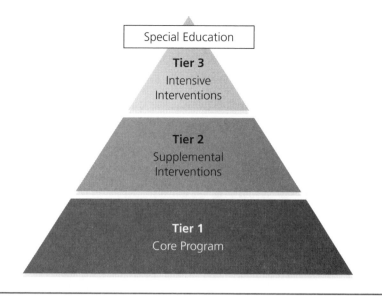

FIGURE 1.2: RTI pyramid with special education at the top.

To challenge this detrimental view of the traditional pyramid, we intentionally inverted the RTI at Work pyramid, visually focusing a school's interventions on a single point—the individual student. See figure 1.3.

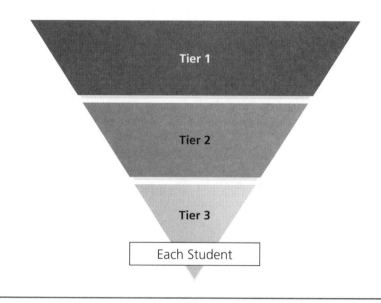

FIGURE 1.3: Inverted RTI at Work pyramid.

With this approach, the school begins the intervention process assuming that every student is capable of learning at high levels, regardless of his or her home environment, ethnicity, or native language. Because every student does not learn the same way or at the same speed, or enter school with the same prior access to learning, the school builds tiers of additional support to ensure every student's success. The school does not view these tiers as a pathway to traditional special education but instead as an ongoing process to dig deeper into students' individual needs.

The school begins the intervention process assuming that every student is capable of learning at high levels, regardless of his or her home environment, ethnicity, or native language.

What Are the Three Tiers of the RTI at Work Pyramid?

RTI has two defining characteristics. It is *multitiered* and *systematic*. Additionally, a multitiered system of interventions addresses four outcomes.

1. If the ultimate goal of a learning-focused school is to ensure every student ends each year having acquired the essential skills, knowledge, and behaviors required for success at the next grade level, then all students must have access to essential grade-level curriculum as part of their core instruction.

2. At the end of every unit of study, some students will need additional time and support to master this essential grade-level curriculum.

3. Some students enter each school year lacking skills they should have mastered in prior years—skills such as foundational reading, writing, number sense, and English language. These students require intensive interventions in these areas to succeed.

4. Some students require all three tiers to learn at high levels.

The RTI at Work pyramid has three tiers to visually represent these characteristics and outcomes. The widest part of the pyramid represents the school's core instruction program. The purpose of this tier—Tier 1—is to provide *all* students access to essential grade-level curriculum and effective initial teaching. See figure 1.4.

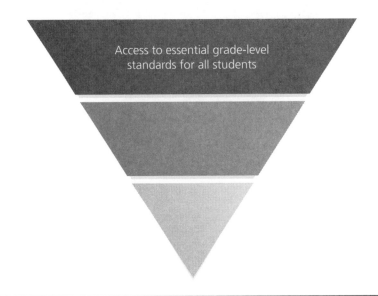

Access to essential grade-level standards for all students

FIGURE 1.4: Core instruction program.

Many traditional RTI approaches advocate that the key to Tier 1 is effective first instruction. We don't disagree with this, but this teaching must include instruction on the skills, knowledge, and behaviors that a student must acquire during the current year to be prepared for the following year. Unfortunately, many schools deem their most at-risk students incapable of learning grade-level curriculum, so they pull out these students and place them in Tier 3 interventions that replace core instruction with remedial coursework. So, even if the initial teaching is done well, if a student's core instruction is focused on below-grade-level standards, then he or she will learn well below grade level.

If the fundamental purpose of RTI is to ensure all students learn at high levels—grade level or better each year—then we must teach students at grade level. Every student might not leave each school year having mastered *every* grade-level standard, but he or she must master the learning outcomes deemed indispensable for future success.

There is a point in every unit of study when most students demonstrate mastery of the unit's essential learning outcomes, and the teacher needs to proceed to the next topic. But because some students may not master the essential curriculum by the end of the unit, the school must dedicate time to provide these students additional support to master this essential grade-level curriculum *without missing critical new core instruction*. This supplemental help to master grade-level curriculum is the purpose of the second tier—Tier 2—in the RTI at Work pyramid. See figure 1.5.

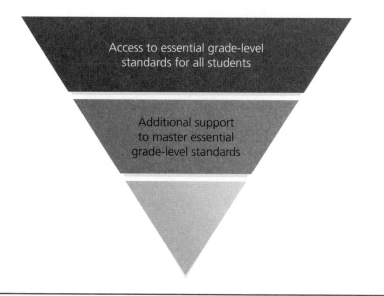

Access to essential grade-level
standards for all students

Additional support
to master essential
grade-level standards

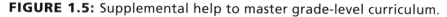

FIGURE 1.5: Supplemental help to master grade-level curriculum.

This is a critical point—the defining characteristics of Tier 2 are not the size of the intervention group or the duration of the intervention. Instead, it is defined by the targeted learning outcomes. Supplemental help should focus on providing targeted students with the additional time and support needed to master the specific skills, knowledge, and behaviors identified at Tier 1 to be absolutely essential for a student's future success. Classroom teacher teams should be actively involved at Tier 2, as these outcomes directly relate to their areas of expertise. Because supplemental interventions are focused on very specific learning targets, placement into Tier 2 interventions must be timely, targeted, flexible, and most often guided by team-created common assessments aligned to grade-level essential standards.

> The defining characteristics of Tier 2 are not the size of the intervention group or the duration of the intervention.

If a school provides students access to essential grade-level curriculum and effective initial teaching during Tier 1 core instruction, and targeted supplemental academic and behavioral help in meeting these standards at Tier 2, then most students should be succeeding.

However, there inevitably will be a number of students who enter each school year lacking the foundational skills needed to learn at high levels. These universal skills of learning include the ability to:

1. Decode and comprehend grade-level text

2. Write effectively

3. Apply number sense

4. Comprehend the English language (or the school's primary language)

5. Consistently demonstrate social and academic behaviors

6. Overcome complications due to health or home

> If a student is significantly behind in just one of these universal skills, he or she will struggle in virtually every grade level, course, and subject.

As you may have noticed, these skills are listed inside Tier 3 on our RTI at Work pyramid. They represent much more than a student needing help in a specific learning standard; instead, they represent a series of skills that enable a student to comprehend instruction, access information, demonstrate understanding, and behave appropriately in a school setting. If a student is significantly behind in just one of these universal skills, he or she will struggle in virtually every grade level, course, and subject. And usually a school's most at-risk students are behind in more than one area. Therefore, for students who need intensive remediation in foundational skills, the school must have a plan to provide this level of assistance *without denying these students access to essential grade-level curriculum.* This is the purpose of Tier 3. See figure 1.6.

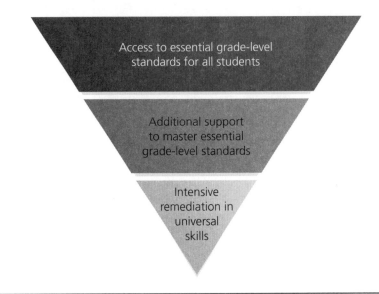

FIGURE 1.6: Intensive remediation in foundational skills.

Because students develop universal skills over time, targeted students should receive this intensive remediation as part of their instructional day. Also, only a school's most highly trained staff in the students' targeted areas of need should provide these interventions.

Last and most important, some students need all three tiers to learn at high levels—this is why it is called a multitiered system of supports. Schools don't just move students from tier to tier. Instead, the tiers are cumulative . . . value added! All students need effective initial teaching on essential grade-level standards at Tier 1. In addition to Tier 1, some students need supplemental time and support in meeting essential grade-level standards at Tier 2. In addition to Tier 1 and Tier 2, some students need intensive help in learning essential outcomes from previous years. Students in need of Tier 3 intensive help in remedial skills most likely struggle with new essential grade-level curriculum the first time it is taught. This means these students need Tier 2 and Tier 3, all without missing new essential instruction at Tier 1.

Individual teachers cannot effectively provide this level of support in their classrooms. We tried this model for many years—it was called a one-room schoolhouse. Instead, it requires a schoolwide, collective, collaborative, coordinated, all-hands-on-deck mentality. This is why structuring a school to function as a PLC is the key to effectively implementing RTI.

> **Structuring a school to function as a PLC is the key to effectively implementing RTI.**

Why Is the RTI at Work Pyramid Split?

Another misinterpretation of RTI occurs when schools view Tier 1 as the classroom teachers' responsibility, and interventions as solely the interventionist staff's responsibility, such as instructional aides, categorical-funded teachers, and the special education department. This approach means some classroom teachers assume that when students require help after initial teaching, their job is to send them to someone else. According to Buffum and colleagues (2012), this practice can overwhelm site intervention teams and resources, especially at schools with a large number of at-risk students:

> In response to this problem, many districts dictate that classroom teachers cannot refer a student for schoolwide interventions until they can document a set of predetermined interventions that must first be tried in the classroom. This mandate places the initial responsibility of Tier 2 interventions with classroom teachers exclusively. The problem with this approach is that every student does not struggle for the same reason. As previously discussed, the reasons why students struggle can vary from just needing a little extra practice on a new concept, to lacking necessary prerequisite skills, to requiring assistance with English language, to having attendance and behavior issues. It is unlikely that each teacher has all the skills and time needed to effectively meet all of these needs. This approach fails students *and* educators.
>
> The answer lies not in determining who is responsible for intervening when students don't learn after core instruction—classroom teachers *or*

the school's intervention resources—but in determining the lead responsibilities of each specific staff member. To visually capture this thinking, we have divided the RTI at Work pyramid into two distinct areas of responsibility: interventions led by collaborative teacher teams and interventions led by the schoolwide teams. (p. 12)

The upper-right portion of the pyramid in Tier 1 and Tier 2 represents responsibilities that collaborative teacher teams should lead. See figure 1.7.

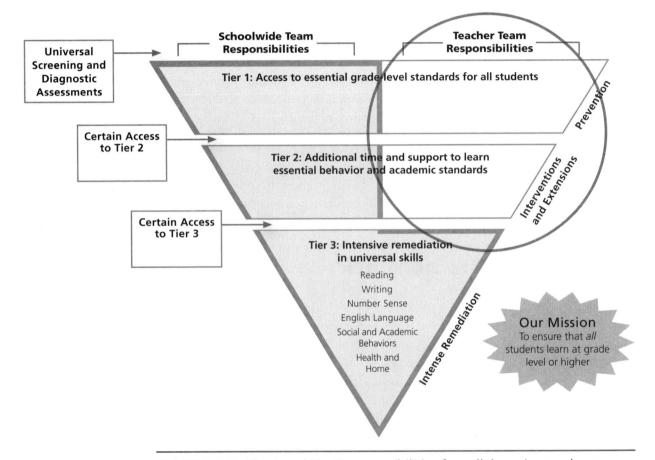

FIGURE 1.7: Tier 1 and Tier 2 responsibilities for collaborative teacher teams.

By collaborative teacher teams, we mean teams of educators who share essential learning outcomes for their students—the structure advocated for in the PLC at Work process. At the elementary level, they are most likely grade-level teams, while at the secondary level, they are content and course specific. This book clearly identifies the essential actions for which teacher teams should take lead responsibility at Tiers 1 and 2. These outcomes directly relate to the expertise, training, and job-embedded responsibilities of classroom teachers.

The left side of the RTI at Work pyramid at Tiers 1, 2, and 3 represents processes that must be coordinated across the entire school. See figure 1.8.

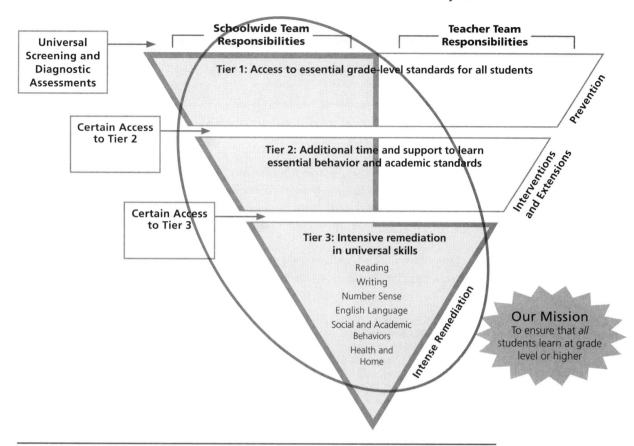

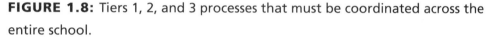

FIGURE 1.8: Tiers 1, 2, and 3 processes that must be coordinated across the entire school.

The essential actions in this portion of the pyramid represent decisions that must be coordinated across the entire school, and thus should not be left up to each grade level, department, or administration to make in isolation. An example is creating a master schedule that makes it possible for targeted students to receive all three tiers of supports. For this portion of the pyramid, schoolwide teams—including a site leadership team and intervention team—take lead responsibility for carrying out essential actions. This book clearly defines these teams and their exact responsibilities.

We use the phrases *lead responsibility* or *take the lead* often in this book. Do not equate *lead* responsibility to mean *sole* responsibility. For example, we might recommend that a third-grade teacher team take lead responsibility for planning Tier 2 interventions that reteach third-grade essential standards. We are not suggesting that third-grade teachers—and these teachers alone—are responsible for this outcome. Could they utilize instructional aides, special education staff, peer tutors, and parent volunteers to help provide interventions for these students who need additional time and support in mastering third-grade essential curriculum? Of course. But to ensure something happens, the buck must stop with specific people. It makes sense that the third-grade team is the best group on campus to know the specific learning needs of each third-grade student and would thus be the logical choice for taking lead responsibility to plan these interventions.

What Do the Boxes Represent?

Every school has interventions, but very few have systematic interventions. A school has a systematic intervention process when it can promise every parent that it does not matter which teacher his or her child is assigned to, as every student receives the additional time and support needed to learn at high levels (Buffum et al., 2012).

> The first step of any intervention is identifying students who need help.

Failure to create a timely, systematic process to identify students in need of additional help makes the school's interventions an education lottery that leaves the question of intervention up to each teacher to resolve. The first step of any intervention is identifying students who need help. How can a school help students if it is ignorant of students' struggles?

The boxes down the left side of the pyramid represent the processes a school uses to identify students for Tier 2 and Tier 3 assistance. See figure 1.9.

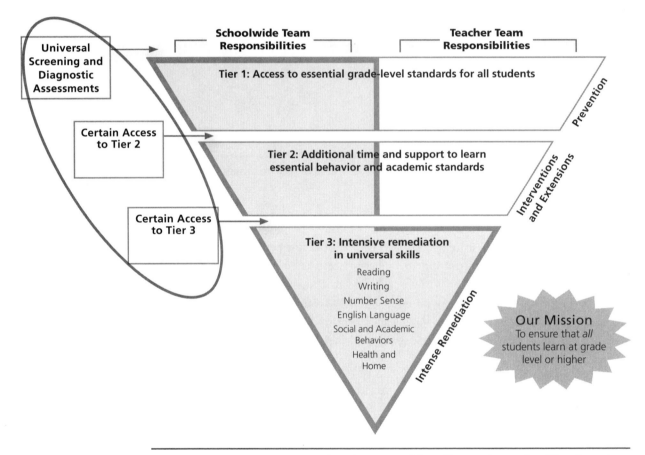

FIGURE 1.9: Processes a school uses to identify students for Tier 2 and Tier 3 assistance.

A systematic identification process not only identifies which students need interventions but also utilizes the right kinds of information to best target each student's needs at each tier. Throughout this book, we clearly define the roles and uses of universal screeners, formative assessments, and diagnostic tools in the RTI process.

What Is the Role of Special Education?

If there were no labels in education—regular education, special education, Title I, English learner (EL), gifted, accelerated—how would a school target students for interventions? Wouldn't it be based on students who have the same needs? For example:

▶ Students struggling with consonant-vowel-consonant (CVC) blends

▶ Students having difficulty multiplying exponents

▶ Students lacking organizational skills to keep track of assignments

So, wouldn't it make sense to group students by need and not by a label for school funding purposes?

And how would a school determine which staff members should lead each of these interventions? Wouldn't it be based on who has training and expertise in teaching CVC blends, algebra, or organizational skills? Although this approach is clearly logical, it is often not the norm, as many schools instead group students by labels tied to funding sources. Such decisions are justified with the claim, "But the law does not allow us the flexibility to group students by need."

As referenced earlier, the federal reauthorization of IDEIA in 2004 promotes early intervention services, which allows districts to use a percentage of special education resources to support students not currently in special education. We are not suggesting that there are no limitations on how to use the skills of special education staff, but whenever possible, school resources should be allocated based on a student's need, not his or her label.

As discussed earlier, RTI is based on a multitiered system of interventions delivered by both general and special education teachers and staff. However, what exactly is an intervention?

What Is an Intervention?

An *intervention* is anything a school does above and beyond what all students receive to help certain students succeed academically. If all students receive a particular instructional practice or service, it is part of the school's core instructional program. But if the school provides a specific practice, program, or service to some students, it is an intervention. Intervention and remediation are not merely provided for academic skills. Behavior, attendance, and health services can be interventions as well as enrichment for students who have already mastered essential grade-level standards.

> An *intervention* is anything a school does above and beyond what all students receive to help certain students succeed academically.

Beyond this broad definition of the term *intervention*, we make some further distinctions. When interventions occur during Tier 1 core instruction, we call them *preventions*. This captures the thinking in the phrase, "The best intervention is prevention." We don't want to wait until the summative test to find out which students need more help. Instead, we are constantly assessing which students could benefit from a quick clarification or reteaching.

As noted, when, despite the preventions received during Tier 1 core instruction, some students do not demonstrate proficiency on essential standards our summative assessments measure, we continue to provide them with additional help. This is Tier 2 intervention—a little more help with what we just finished studying. The teacher must now move on to the next unit, but because these are essential standards, students continue to receive Tier 2 interventions until they achieve mastery.

When the causes of students' struggles are rooted in a lack of skills and knowledge from previous years of study, we call efforts to fill in this gap Tier 3 remediation. These are not skills and knowledge from the last lesson the teacher taught; they are from previous years—many times, from several years before. We capture this thinking in figure 1.10.

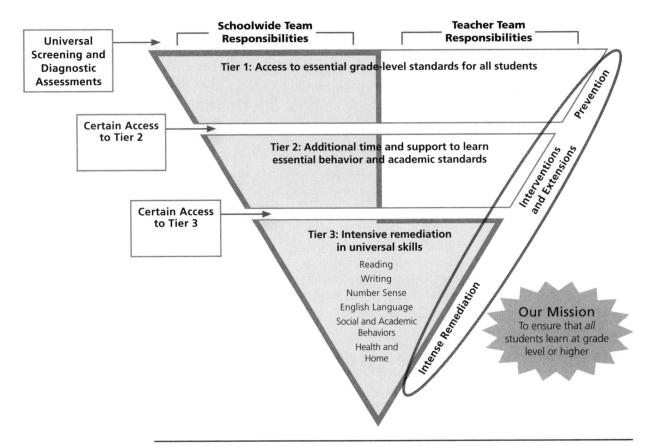

FIGURE 1.10: Skills and knowledge from previous years of study.

Just as there are interventions for students who are struggling, there is a need for extensions for students who need more challenge.

Extension is when students are stretched beyond essential grade-level curriculum or levels of proficiency.

What Is Extension?

Extension is when students are stretched beyond essential grade-level curriculum or levels of proficiency. We can achieve this outcome in many different ways, including the following.

▶ Ask students to demonstrate mastery of essential standards at a level beyond what is deemed grade-level proficient. For example, many schools applying a four-point rubric to a grade-level writing prompt deem a score of 3 as grade-level proficient. Stretching students beyond to a score of 4 would be an example of extended learning.

▶ Give students access to more of the required grade-level curriculum deemed important but not essential.

▶ Teach students above-grade-level curriculum, such as advanced placement (AP) classes.

Interventions should not be focused exclusively on supporting struggling students, nor should RTI come at the cost of students already learning at or above grade level. RTI is about providing every student with the differentiated time and support needed to ensure he or she learns at the highest levels possible. If a school is going to build flexible time, support, and collaboration into its school week, it can apply these efforts to support students in advanced coursework as well. The fourth critical question of the PLC at Work process captures this outcome, "How will we extend the learning for students who are already proficient?" (DuFour et al., 2016, p. 36).

In addition to extensions, students should have access to subjects and activities that provide enrichment.

What Is Enrichment?

There is an important difference between *enrichment* and *extension*. We define *enrichment* as students having access to the subjects that specials or electives teachers traditionally teach, such as music, art, drama, applied technology, and physical education. We strongly believe that this curriculum is essential. These subjects often teach essential core curriculum through different modalities. Also, students usually view these subjects as the fun part of school.

When we pull students from enrichment to receive extra help in core curriculum, interventions turn into a punishment. Subsequently, a student's motivation and attitude can suffer. Finally, there is an equity issue. Often, the students who need interventions come from economically disadvantaged homes. For many of these students, the only way they will learn a musical instrument or use advanced technology is at school. For these reasons, students should not be denied access to enrichment because they need additional time and support in core subjects.

> We define *enrichment* as students having access to the subjects that specials or electives teachers traditionally teach.

Conclusion

As captured in the title, this book is about *taking action*. Using the RTI at Work pyramid as our road map, we can now dig deeper into each tier and the essential actions schools must take to ensure every student succeeds. By the end of this book, if you complete each task, you will have completed an RTI at Work pyramid for your school. In the next three chapters, we begin by focusing on Tier 1.

PART ONE

TIER 1 ESSENTIAL ACTIONS

CHAPTER 2

A Culture of Collective Responsibility

A small body of determined spirits, fired by an unquench-
able faith in their mission, can alter the course of history.

—Mahatma Gandhi

RTI is not an end in itself but a means to an end. It is a tool. Consider that for a moment: *a tool*. You can use a hammer to help build a home for a family—what a positive, productive purpose. However, you can use the same hammer to tear a house down. A tool is only as effective as the hands that are guiding it and the purpose for which it is used.

We have seen many schools and districts approach RTI as an end in itself, viewing it as a mandate that must be implemented. When this happens, they see the critical elements of the process as steps on an implementation checklist—as actions to complete to achieve compliance. As the top-down legislation of No Child Left Behind proves, compliance-driven reform efforts rarely create the deep levels of commitment and ownership necessary to truly transform an organization.

Why should a school commit to the RTI process? What is the purpose of the RTI tool? The first big idea of the PLC at Work process captures the answer to these questions—a focus on learning. See the highlighted piece of the RTI at Work pyramid in figure 2.1 (page 34). Richard DuFour, Rebecca DuFour, Robert Eaker, Thomas W. Many, and Mike Mattos (2016) state it this way:

> A focus on learning is a PLC's commitment to making student learning the fundamental purpose of the school or district. It means that schools assess every policy, practice, and procedure with these questions: Will doing this lead to higher levels of learning for our students? Are we willing to revise or discontinue actions that fail to increase student learning? (p. 7)

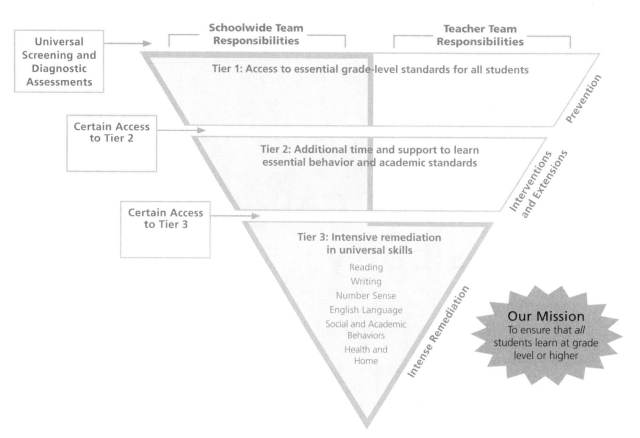

FIGURE 2.1: Focus on creating a culture of collective responsibility.

A school or district claiming that its mission is to ensure student learning is much more than a hopeful wish or a catchy motto on the organization's letterhead. An organization's mission:

▶ States its fundamental purpose

▶ Guides decisions and actions

▶ Provides a path, framework, and context that the organization uses to formulate strategies

In other words, a school or district's mission serves as both a sacred promise to those it serves and the organization's highest priority when making decisions. It represents what is non-negotiable—what the school will not compromise.

Because the purpose of RTI is to ensure high levels of learning for every student, then one would expect educators to enthusiastically embrace the RTI process. Would any educator be against proven practices that help all students succeed? Have some schools and districts adopted a mission statement in conflict with this goal? We have had the honor of working with schools across the globe, and we have never found mission statements that sound like the following.

▶ Our mission is to ensure that *most* students succeed.

▶ Our mission is to maintain a bell-shaped curve of student achievement.

▶ Our mission is to use students' perceived genetic ability and home demographics to rank, sort, and track them.

Instead, what we see in school mission statements are the words *each*, *every*, and *all*, such as:

▶ We will focus on *each* student's needs.

▶ We will maximize *every* student's potential.

▶ We are committed to the success of *all* students.

When the mission ensures student success, RTI is the perfect tool to achieve this goal.

Sadly, our experience is that many schools and districts struggle with implementing RTI because what they claim in their public mission statement conflicts with what they advocate for in the privacy of the staff lounge, faculty meeting, or district cabinet meeting. Propose to a school staff that they actually commit to practices aligned to their mission of ensuring that all students learn at high levels, and we find that many educators begin to hedge on two words: *ensure* and *all*. Some claim it is unfair to hold educators responsible for student learning when so many factors outside of school impact each student's academic success. Others state that it is a teacher's job to teach and a student's job to learn. Still others assume that some students are incapable of learning rigorous academic outcomes. The underlining point in these concerns is this: some educators neither believe in, nor support, a mission that claims all students will succeed.

If the purpose of RTI is to ensure that all students learn at high levels, but a critical number of staff does not believe it is fair and reasonable to commit to this purpose, then it would be unrealistic to expect educators to embrace the practices required to achieve this outcome. Likewise, if the reason why PLC members collaborate is to ensure every student's success, but a majority of the staff is unwilling to commit to this outcome, then team meetings are likely to digress and lose focus.

A successful journey does not begin with taking a first step but by facing the right direction (Buffum et al., 2012). Likewise, transforming a school or district does not start with implementing a sequence of tasks but with clarifying the organization's direction—its fundamental purpose. This chapter focuses on how an organization builds agreement on a mission of collective responsibility and what foundational conditions must be in place to successfully build a multitiered system of supports to achieve this outcome. The five essential actions we discuss are:

1. Establish a guiding coalition.

2. Build a culture of collective responsibility.

3. Form collaborative teacher teams.

4. Create time for collaboration.

5. Commit to team norms.

In this chapter, we explore each of these essential actions required to build the right school culture and collaborative structures that serve as the foundation of an effective system of interventions.

> When the mission ensures student success, RTI is the perfect tool to achieve this goal.

Action 1

Establish a Guiding Coalition

> Leading by example is perhaps the purest form of leadership and the one over which each of us has the most control. You can lead only where you will go.
>
> **—Roland Barth**

Creating a culture built around the concept of *every* student succeeding represents a major shift in thinking for many schools. In his book *Leading Change*, John Kotter (1996) asserts that such shifts in thinking (cultural change) often fail due to the lack of what he calls a "guiding coalition" (p. 52).

We recommend that a school's leadership team serve as the site's guiding coalition. Because of this recommendation, we use two terms—(1) *leadership team* and (2) *guiding coalition*—which are interchangeable throughout this book. To achieve this goal, many schools need to redesign or repurpose their existing leadership team, as we find that most site leadership teams rarely function as a guiding coalition dedicated to ensuring high levels of learning for all students. Instead, traditional leadership teams, at the site or district level, often focus exclusively on managing the school's day-to-day operations. RTI represents an almost overwhelming level of change compared to how schools have functioned for more than two hundred years. We know that even slight levels of change can be hard for people. Unless the right team leads the RTI process—a team that focuses its efforts on the right work—the anxiety and inevitable obstacles inherent in this level of change will overwhelm the best organization's intentions.

Here's Why

To transform an organization, Kotter (2007) states:

> No one person, no matter how competent, is capable of single-handedly developing the right vision, communicating it to vast numbers of people, eliminating all the key obstacles, generating short-term wins, leading and managing dozens of change projects, and anchoring new approaches deep in an organization's culture. . . . Putting together the right coalition of people to lead a change initiative is critical to its success.

In his book *Good to Great: Why Some Companies Make the Leap . . . and Others Don't*, Jim Collins (2001) similarly asserts that the first step to implementing successful change is to "get the right people on the bus" (p. 41). Collins (2001) says, "If we get the right people on the bus, the right people in the right seats, and the wrong people off the bus, then we'll figure out how to take it someplace great" (p. 41). The right people don't need to be closely managed or constantly fired up. Rather, they are capable, self-motivated, and eager to take responsibility for creating something great.

We find it both fascinating and tragic that many schools give more careful consideration to forming their varsity football coaching staff or school social committee than to forming the best possible school guiding coalition. Random practices, such as the following, often determine positions on the school leadership team.

- ▸ **Seniority:** "I should be department chair because I have been here the longest."

- ▸ **Novice:** "Make the rookie do it. Pay your dues, kid!"

- ▸ **Rotation:** "It's Sally's turn to be grade-level leader."

- ▸ **Default:** "Bill is the only person who applied."

Forming an effective guiding coalition is unlikely to happen serendipitously. It takes carefully considering both the essential tasks that the leadership must accomplish and the research behind effective leadership.

Here's How

In selecting the right people for an effective guiding coalition, it is important to consider the essential tasks that this team will take responsibility for in the RTI at Work process. They include:

- Build consensus for the school's mission of collective responsibility.

- Create a master schedule that provides sufficient time for team collaboration, core instruction, supplemental interventions, and intensive interventions.

- Coordinate schoolwide human resources to best support core instruction and interventions, including the site counselor, psychologist, speech and language pathologist, special education teacher, librarian, health services staff, subject specialists, instructional aides, and another classified staff.

- Allocate the school's fiscal resources to best support core instruction and interventions, including school categorical funding.

- Assist with articulating essential learning outcomes across grade levels and subjects.

- Lead the school's universal screening efforts to identify students in need of Tier 3 intensive interventions before they fail.

- Lead the school's efforts at Tier 1 for schoolwide behavior expectations, including attendance policies and awards and recognitions.

- Ensure all students have access to grade-level core instruction.

- Ensure that sufficient, effective resources are available to provide Tier 2 interventions for students in need of supplemental support in motivation, attendance, and behavior.

- Ensure that sufficient, effective resources are available to provide Tier 3 interventions for students in need of intensive support in the universal skills of reading, writing, number sense, English language, motivation, attendance, and behavior.

- Continually monitor schoolwide evidence of student learning. (Buffum et al., 2012, p. 36)

In addition to administrative representation, the guiding coalition should have teacher representatives from each collaborative teacher team because many of the outcomes listed relate to supporting and monitoring these teams' work. At the elementary level, this most likely will be grade-level leaders; at the secondary level, this mostly likely will be department or course-level leaders. Additionally, representation from classified and support staff will help the leadership team best allocate schoolwide resources to support the school's system of interventions.

Traditionally, school leadership teams have included representation from administration, teachers, and support staff. But beyond just departmental representation, Kotter (1996) states a successful guiding coalition must comprise four essential types of power.

1. **Positional power:** These individuals have a certain level of defined authority because of their title or office. For example, schools afford the principal the ability to make certain decisions because of the defined responsibilities of this position. Kotter (1996) says that if a guiding coalition does not have enough positional power, it will not have the authority to carry out essential actions. In other words, are enough key players on board so those who disagree cannot easily block progress?

2. **Expertise:** When reviewing the previous list of essential tasks, what types of expertise must the leadership team possess to successfully achieve these outcomes? For example, because RTI requires coordinating data about specific students, we have found that having at least one member with a deep level of expertise in the school's education technology can be very helpful.

3. **Credibility:** Anyone with expertise in an organization knows that some individuals influence and sway decision making more than others. Some of these individuals use this credibility to advocate for keeping the status quo, while others can use their influence to build support for a new change initiative. It is critical that a guiding coalition has sufficient levels of credibility with those it is trying to convince. An important question to ask is, Does our leadership team have enough people with credibility that its recommendations and decisions will be taken seriously, especially by those staff members who we most need to convince?

4. **Leadership ability:** Leaders have the ability to convincingly articulate a position, unite others toward a common goal, build trust with others, and respectfully confront actions that are not aligned to the school's mission. If a guiding coalition lacks members with leadership ability, it is unlikely that the best-laid plans will be implemented successfully. Even if the school's principal possesses leadership ability, it would be unwise to always make the principal the spokesperson for the leadership team. When

> It is critical that a guiding coalition has sufficient levels of credibility with those it is trying to convince.

administrators always introduce new ideas, staff members often view them as top-down directives. Identifying other members—especially teacher leaders—with leadership ability is a powerful asset for an effective guiding coalition. The right question to ask is, "Does the group include enough proven leaders to be able to drive the change process?"

So, an effective leadership team must be comprised of people who possess strong positional power, broad expertise, and high credibility with their peers. Moreover, it is important that the guiding coalition is comprised of people who have strong leadership skills and not just the ability to organize and manage programs. In other words, the guiding coalition, along with the school administration, acts as a change agent relative to the mission and vision of the school.

While the previous examples focus on creating a school leadership team, we should apply these same principles to forming a leadership team to guide *districtwide* RTI implementation. Building a broad base of expertise, including representation from each school, special and regular education, classified support staff, the teachers' union, district and site administration, parents, and community resources, is important to the team's success.

As important as getting the "right people on the bus" is to establishing an effective leadership team, it is equally important to establish a culture of collective responsibility within the team itself. In other words, each individual on the leadership team must see him- or herself as a leader whose role it is to participate in, model, and inspire a similar culture in the school as a whole. The team's work, therefore, must consistently have a dual focus—*internal* attention to how members are working together and *external* attention to coaching and inspiring others.

To begin, the team must discuss and agree on its purpose—to unite and coordinate the school's collective efforts to help every student succeed and to allocate the school's resources to best achieve this goal. It is also important to identify any nonpurposes—topics that will be off limits during team meetings, such as complaining about students, parents, or staff members. Once the team clearly understands and agrees to its purpose, it is then essential to reach consensus on team tasks, desired outcomes for each meeting, team norms, and each team member's roles and responsibilities. The following tools and tips can help in this process.

Helpful Tools

The following tools will help you accomplish the work for this essential action.

▸ **"Building a School Leadership Team" (page 41):** This activity is designed to help a principal or administrative team create an effective school leadership team.

▸ **"Team Charter" (page 42):** Use this form to organize and set norms for your leadership team.

▸ **"Meeting Agenda Template" (page 44):** Use this template to record the meeting agenda for your leadership team.

Coaching Tips

As stated previously, once the right people are on the schoolwide leadership team, it is essential for the team to embrace the importance of *doing* the work, not just leading the work. In other words, team members must establish and *live* a culture of collective responsibility among themselves in order to model, inform, and establish a similar culture in the school as a whole.

An effective way to get started is to create a team charter, a document that outlines the foundations on which to base all team interactions and work. All team members must participate in the dialogue and discussions that result in consensus on the document itself. Once they reach agreement, all members sign and date the charter. As work progresses, the team might need to revisit, revise, or supplement the charter to meet its needs.

The success of the leadership team goes hand in hand with the success of its meetings. Every time the leadership team meets, there must be a clear path to action (goals and tasks), attention to culture building (collaborative work, norms, and all members' equal participation), exchange of information (structured conversations to ensure shared understanding), and tangible action steps.

> The most productive meetings often have fewer topics, which, in turn, allow for all members to have greater participation.

A carefully planned and skillfully facilitated meeting agenda is the key to success. High-performance teams consistently use an agenda template, such as the "Meeting Agenda Template" (page 44). Using a consistent agenda template ensures that each meeting begins with an overview of purpose, desired outcomes, and tasks to be accomplished, along with team member roles and approximate time needed for each task. Remember, *less is more*. The most productive meetings often have fewer topics, which, in turn, allow for all members to have greater participation.

Each meeting must also conclude with consistency—reviewing tasks the team completed and decisions it made, clarifying team members' responsibilities to accomplish before the next meeting, evaluating the meeting's effectiveness, and brainstorming a list of topics to include on the next meeting agenda. Team members should compile and share notes after each meeting. This responsibility can be assigned to a specific team member or shared among team members. Assigning additional team member roles, such as facilitator, timer, or public recorder may also help team meetings run more smoothly.

Once the leadership team establishes the foundational steps outlined in this section, its work broadens to include ongoing attention to its own team culture and productivity as well as developing a similar culture in the school as a whole. Team members must model the purpose and beliefs of the leadership team both formally and informally. Daily conversations and interactions with colleagues, in addition to team and faculty meetings, are the most influential building blocks for changing culture. Gandhi (2017) said it best, "You must be the change you wish to see in the world." Teachers, staff, and leaders can also be the change they want to see in their schools.

Building a School Leadership Team

This activity is designed to help a principal or administrative team create an effective school leadership team.

First, list the names of the current members who you might consider to be your guiding coalition. If no such group currently exists, list the potential members who come to mind.

_____   _____

_____   _____

_____   _____

_____   _____

_____   _____

Then consider the following personal characteristics that will impact your team's success. Write the name of each team member under any characteristic that applies (a person may be listed under more than one). Eliminate any person from your list who possesses none of these characteristics. Note that it is recommended that a member of each teacher team be on the leadership team. Does your team have the necessary balance?

Position Power	Expertise
_____ _____ _____ _____	_____ _____ _____ _____
Ask: Are enough key players on board so that those left out cannot easily block progress?	Ask: Are the various points of view—in terms of discipline, work experience, and so on—relevant to the task at hand adequately represented so that informed, intelligent decisions will be made?
Credibility	**Leadership**
_____ _____ _____ _____	_____ _____ _____ _____
Ask: Does the group have enough people with good reputations that its recommendations and decisions will be taken seriously?	Ask: Does the group include enough proven leaders to be able to drive the change process?

Source: Buffum, A., Mattos, M., & Weber, C. (2012). Simplifying response to intervention: Four essential guiding principles. Bloomington, IN: Solution Tree Press.

Team Charter

Use this form to organize and establish norms for your leadership team.

Team: _____   Date: _____

Team members: _____
_____
_____
_____

Team members' strengths: _____
_____
_____
_____

Team purpose: _____
_____
_____
_____

Team nonpurposes or purposes: _____
_____
_____
_____

Team norms or guidelines: _____
_____
_____
_____

Team tasks: _____

_____

_____

_____

Team questions or concerns: _____

_____

_____

_____

Signatures: _____   Date: _____

_____   _____

_____   _____

_____   _____

Meeting Agenda Template

Agenda: _____

Purpose:

Desired outcomes:

We will have the following by the end of this meeting.

Meeting Agenda			
What (content)	**How (process)**	**Who (facilitator)**	**Time (estimated minutes)**

Action 2

Build a Culture of Collective Responsibility

> Our experience verifies that the possibilities are unlimited once a dedicated school staff goes in search of research and best practices to advance their shared vision of learning for all. However, until they embrace the possibility that all children can learn, the obstacles and barriers they will find are virtually endless and will seem insurmountable.
>
> **—Larry Lezotte**

The schoolwide leadership team's first and most important task is to establish what we refer to as a *culture of collective responsibility*. Kent Peterson and Terrence Deal define school culture as the norms, values, rituals, beliefs, symbols, and ceremonies that produce a school persona (Deal & Peterson, 1999).

Working from the premise that the purpose of establishing a system of interventions is to ensure all students learn at high levels, there must be consensus among and between staff on two fundamental assumptions.

1. **Educators assume primary responsibility to ensure high levels of learning for every student:** As Buffum et al. (2012) state, "While parental, societal, and economic forces impact student learning, the actions of the educators will ultimately determine each child's mastery of the essential academic skills, knowledge, and behaviors needed for future success in school" (p. 16).

2. **Educators assume that all students can learn at high levels:** We define *high* levels of learning as "high school *plus*," connoting every student will graduate from high school with the skills and knowledge to continue to learn. To compete in the 21st century global marketplace, "students must continue to learn beyond high school, and there are many paths for that learning, including trade schools, internships, community colleges, and universities. To achieve this outcome, students must master essential grade-level curriculum each year" (Buffum et al., 2012, p. 16).

Many schools want to hedge on the word *ensure*, and instead commit to a mission that states it is their job to provide their students the *opportunity* to learn. It is virtually impossible for RTI to succeed within this school culture, as the very purpose of RTI is to provide students additional time and support when they don't succeed after initial teaching. Buffum and colleagues (2012) write that an *opportunity to learn* school believes:

> Its responsibility for student learning ends once the child has been given the chance to learn the first time. But a learning-focused school understands that the school was not built so that teachers have a place to

teach—it was built so that the children of the community have a place to learn. Learning-focused schools embrace RTI, as it is a proven process to help them achieve their mission. (p. 18)

As referenced in the introduction, research proves that RTI is twice as powerful as any single environmental factor that can impact student success (Bailey & Dynarski, 2011; Hattie, 2009, 2012; Reardon, 2011). Until educators stop blaming factors outside of school for why failing students have not learned essential academic curriculum, and instead look internally at what they can control to ensure this outcome, it is unlikely they will fully commit to the RTI process.

The second essential assumption required to create a culture of collective responsibility is for educators to assume that all students can learn at high levels.

When we ask educators to commit to a mission of ensuring that *all* students learn at high levels, a reasonable concern is this: What about students with disabilities? Isn't it unfair to commit to a mission of learning for all when some students lack the cognitive ability to achieve this outcome?

Undeniably, there is a very small percentage of students with profound cognitive disabilities that make it impossible for them to learn the higher-level-thinking skills required for postsecondary education. In the United States, we understand their limitations and would not expect these individuals to become self-sufficient, independent adults. We are not suggesting that these students cannot learn or that schools do not have a responsibility for their education. While almost all students must transition to postsecondary education to succeed in the global economy, these students are not expected to compete in this environment, so their curriculum in school might not meet our criteria of high school plus.

So when we ask educators to assume all students can learn at high levels, we should define *all* as any student who can or might be an independent adult someday. This reasonable definition means that most students currently in special education must learn at high levels too. These students are not going to receive modified rent someday, accommodated bills, or an IEP at work. These students can and must leave the K–12 system with the skills needed to succeed in postsecondary education and in life.

Regardless of this reality, many educators refuse to assume that all students can learn at high levels because, beyond students with profound disabilities, they believe that some students lack the ability to learn rigorous curriculum. These educators often point to students with IQ scores that are above the threshold of profound disabilities but much lower than the average. Yet we know that IQ testing is an imperfect science that was not designed to definitively predict a child's future academic limitations. Also, IQ testing has been legally determined to be culturally biased (Powers, Hagans-Murillo, & Restori, 2004).

While working with schools, we hear some educators claim that the law of averages—the distribution of the bell-shaped curve—proves that we must always expect some students to be below average. We should not be surprised that many educators feel this way, since these assumptions are the foundation of our traditional school system. Because the traditional U.S. K–12 system was preparing students for a farm-and-factory-driven economy, people assumed that only a small percentage of students

> **Research proves that RTI is twice as powerful as any single environmental factor that can impact student success.**

> **Students can and must leave the K–12 system with the skills needed to succeed in postsecondary education and in life.**

would learn beyond grammar school. Therefore, schools did not expect all students to learn at high levels. Instead, they ranked and sorted students on a bell-shaped curve, which identified those few expected to reach higher education. In this kind of system, it is reasonable to expect that "a few people will excel, most will be satisfactory or average, and a few will fail" (Fendler & Muzaffar, 2008, p. 63). Yet Benjamin Bloom (1971) states:

> The normal curve is not sacred. It describes the outcome of a random process. Since education is a purposeful activity in which we seek to have the students learn what we teach, the achievement distribution should be very different from the normal curve if our instruction is effective. In fact, our educational efforts may be said to be unsuccessful to the extent that student achievement is normally distributed. (p. 49)

RTI is the purposeful activity that can flatten the bell-shaped curve and ensure all students succeed.

And most tragically, some educators tell us that a trained teacher can spot students who just don't have it—the capacity to learn at high levels. Overwhelming evidence would prove otherwise. We know that a student's ethnicity, native language, and economic status do not reduce his or her capacity for learning. Yet, across the United States, minority students, non-native language learners, and economically disadvantaged students are disproportionately represented in special education (Brantlinger, 2006; Ferri & Connor, 2006; Skiba et al., 2006, 2008) and underrepresented in gifted and honors programs (Donovan & Cross, 2002).

Why are these students being over-identified as learning disabled? Some educators assume these students are less capable, and these inaccurate judgments often become a self-fulfilling prophecy for their students (Buffum et al., 2012). Educators typically view students who enter school with a head start from their home environment as being capable of learning at high levels, and they are subsequently placed in more rigorous coursework, taught at advanced levels, expected to achieve, and thus are much more likely to learn at this level. Conversely, students perceived as being incapable of learning at high levels are placed in below-grade-level curriculum, taught at remedial levels, expected to achieve at lower levels, and to no one's surprise, most likely learn at low levels. These outcomes falsely confirm the school's initial assumptions and reinforce the misgiving some educators have to committing to a mission of learning for all.

We could make a convincing argument that, regardless of how effective a school's system of interventions, it is possible that some students might face cognitive challenges or environmental factors that prove beyond a school's ability to overcome. But here is the critical point: to start the journey, we must accept primary responsibility for what we can control—student mastery of academic skills, knowledge, and dispositions—and assume that each student is capable of achieving these outcomes, regardless of his or her demographic background. Consider the alternative. If a school is unwilling to commit to the word *all*, then educators are, by default, accepting a mission that *most* students will succeed, but undoubtedly, some students are always going to fail. In other words, the school believes there will always be educational "collateral damage," regardless of the school's policies and practices. If staff are unwilling

RTI is the purposeful activity that can flatten the bell-shaped curve and ensure all students succeed.

to commit to a mission that embraces the words *ensure* and *all*, they are unlikely to fully commit to the RTI at Work process.

Here's Why

In his book *Transforming School Culture*, Anthony Muhammad (2018) describes two types of school-reform efforts: *technical changes* and *cultural changes*. Technical changes are made of tools such as a school's master schedule, instructional materials, and policies. Obviously, creating a multitiered system of supports requires a significant amount of technical change. Cultural changes are shifts in the norms, values, assumptions, and collective beliefs of an organization. Substantial cultural change must precede technical change. Muhammad (2018) argues that technical changes "are definitely necessary to effect improvement in student performance, but they produce very few positive results when people who do not believe in the intended outcome of the change use them" (pp. 22–23). For the technical steps of RTI to work, we must execute them within a culture of high expectations for both educators and students.

To measure its organization's current culture, the leadership team should consider what would happen at its school if an educator asks, "Our school mission says we are committed to *all* students learning at high levels. Currently, we know that some students are failing. What are we going to do to fix this problem?"

Will the faculty meet the question with resistance? Will it create a faculty debate? Will this person be ostracized, or will it be a rallying cry for self-reflection and improvement? If this question creates significant staff division, this indicates that the school's culture misaligns to RTI's goals. Change the setting for this question. What if someone raises this concern in a district cabinet meeting? How would central office leadership respond?

Here's How

> What they have to give, not what they expect to receive, is what attracts educators to this field.

Unfortunately, a learning-focused school culture is not a reality in most schools. Through our work at sites struggling to implement RTI, schools often acknowledge that they lack a shared commitment. But then they ask the wrong question: How do we get buy-in from our staff? We don't care for the term *buy-in* because it conveys the wrong connotation. RTI helps students, and the concern that staff won't *buy into it* suggests that educators are resisting because they want to know what is in it for *them*. But there is hardly an educator who does not work with the best interest of students in mind. What they have to give, not what they expect to receive, is what attracts educators to this field.

We suggest the correct term is *ownership*: how does a school create a sense of staff ownership of the RTI process, especially in light of the cultural hurdles this chapter describes? We cannot achieve cultural change through force or coercion (Muhammad, 2018). Rational adults resist change for many reasons, and experienced educators often raise legitimate concerns regarding the professional conditions and personal commitments needed to make RTI work. Complex problems require multiple solutions.

Establishing this kind of culture requires much thought and planning by the leadership team, beginning with discussing the critical questions outlined in the reproducible "Creating Consensus for a Culture of Collective Responsibility" (page 53). The leadership team's initial work is also summarized in the following four steps. In considering the challenges of leading change, it is important to recognize that long-lasting and substantial change does not happen overnight. Rather, it is more of a one-thousand-step journey, with each step carefully and intentionally planned. As Michael Fullan (1994) points out, "Leading change is a planned journey into uncharted waters with a leaky boat and a mutinous crew."

1. **Assess the current reality:** It is difficult to map a successful journey if team members are unsure of the school's current location. In this case, it is critical to determine the staff's current culture to ensure all students learn. Muhammad (2018) recommends using data to create a catalyst for change in an inspirational way. We have found that many successful schools don't look solely at data such as the percentage of students below proficient on state assessments or the number of students reading below grade level. Instead, these schools connect data to individual students—instead of telling teachers that 12 percent of the school's students are below proficient in reading, they connect those numbers with a list of specific students who make up the 12 percent. These connections resonate with why we joined the profession—to help children.

2. **Provide a compelling case for change:** Too often, we describe what needs to be done without first providing a compelling reason *why* the alteration is necessary to introduce change initiatives. In his study of educational *fundamentalists*—members who actively fight change, Muhammad (2018) finds that many resist because no one provides them with a clear rationale for change. If school leadership cannot provide a compelling *why*, the staff won't care about the *what*. Agreeing on the need for change results from assessing and confronting current reality, celebrating what is right, identifying areas for growth, and learning together about new possibilities through research and dialogue.

   Mike Mattos created a video titled *Timebomb* (2017), which offers a vision of what happens to students who don't succeed in school. It can be helpful at building a sense of urgency regarding committing to systematic interventions. (Visit www.solutiontree.com/products/timebomb.html to find out more information about the video.)

3. **Create a doable plan:** The most compelling reason for change is irrelevant if the staff view the goal as impossible. It is critical that staff receive a doable plan that defines specific responsibilities and includes the resources needed to meet these expectations. If teachers view RTI as a demand requiring them to work beyond their current contractual hours, they have a legitimate right to resist.

> Most people
> become committed
> to a process once
> they see that it
> works, not before.

4. **Build staff consensus:** Most people become committed to a process once they see that it works, not before. This creates an interesting dilemma: Schools can't start until they build consensus, but they never get true commitment until they start. Consequently, taking months and months planning for change and getting everyone to feel ownership in the process follows the law of diminishing returns. If schools wait for everyone to get on board before starting, the train never leaves the station. What it takes to start is consensus—everyone has had a say, the will of the group has emerged, and it is evident, even to those who disagree (DuFour et al., 2016).

To build consensus on the plan, people tend to come to the same conclusions when they base their decisions on the same facts. Regrettably, many schools average opinions to make decisions. Because every staff member enters the RTI discussion with different prior experiences, priorities, and perspectives, it is often difficult to reach consensus. More often than not, the loudest and most aggressive voices win, and those resistant to change are usually the most vocal in this debate process; Muhammad's (2018) research finds that fundamentalists are usually the most aggressive at stating their beliefs.

By contrast, team members in a PLC build shared knowledge instead of averaging opinions to arrive at consensus on vital questions. They engage in collective inquiry into best practices (DuFour et al., 2016). The leadership team should serve as the lead learners. They must dig deeply into the areas of focus, identify powerful research and relevant information, and determine the best format for sharing this information with the staff.

Reaching true consensus begins with a shared understanding of what consensus actually represents. To get there requires time, trust building, structured conversations, and consistent monitoring along the way.

Helpful Tools

The following tools will help you accomplish the work for this essential action.

▶ **Chapter 2 of *Learning by Doing* (DuFour et al., 2016), "Defining a Clear and Compelling Purpose":** This chapter focuses on the how to create the four pillars of the PLC process: common mission, vision, values, and goals.

▶ **"Creating Consensus for a Culture of Collective Responsibility" (page 53):** The leadership team can use this tool to help build consensus regarding a school mission to ensure high levels of learning for all students.

▶ **"Creating Consensus Survey" (for the leadership team) (page 54):** The leadership team can use this tool to self-assess its readiness to building consensus and leading change.

▶ **"Forces at Work" (page 55):** Once the leadership team has self-assessed its current readiness, it can use this tool to identify its strengths, areas of weakness, and specific action steps for moving forward.

- ▶ **"Simplifying RTI Culture Survey" (for the entire staff) (page 56):** All staff can use this tool to provide the leadership team with a more accurate picture of current cultural beliefs and norms.

- ▶ **"Building Consensus for Change and Bell Schedule Chart" (page 57):** This tool provides an example of how one school successfully surveyed and achieved consensus.

Coaching Tips

At its most fundamental level, the task of creating consensus for cultural change is all about building shared knowledge and understanding. As the leadership team works through and discusses the questions included on the reproducible "Creating Consensus for a Culture of Collective Responsibility" (page 53), it's important to structure and facilitate the same discussions with the entire staff. Cultural change happens when all staff members reveal their beliefs and assumptions, read research, confront the current reality, explore the possibilities of a new vision for their work, and hear each other's thoughts and opinions. It is not enough for the leadership team to have these powerful discussions only amongst its members.

Building shared knowledge takes time, consistency of message, and multiple opportunities for dialogue. Team members must pay attention to both written and verbal communication, including emails, bulletins, meeting notes, one-on-one conversations, team and department meetings, and whole-staff meetings. It is also important to ensure that all stakeholders are included—administrators, counselors, instructional staff, support staff, parents and, when appropriate, students.

As the leadership team engages in this work, it may choose to use the reproducible "Creating Consensus Survey" (page 54) to formatively assess its progress. The reproducible "Forces at Work" (page 55) is useful for ensuring discussions include evidence and data as their basis, not just opinions. It also helps the team develop a prioritized to-do list of next steps.

The most challenging steps in creating cultural change are those at the beginning and the end, in which team members explore assumptions and beliefs in a nonthreatening way and reach consensus about the proposed change.

Many tools are available for structuring and facilitating a discussion about assumptions and beliefs. The bottom line is that teams cannot ignore this step. The likelihood of reaching consensus on shared assumptions and beliefs is almost nil without first uncovering and discussing current beliefs.

As conversations take place, it is important for the leadership team to check progress toward consensus. A tool such as the reproducible "Simplifying RTI Culture Survey" (page 56) is one way to "dipstick" along the way. You can use it more than once, as long as enough time and conversation take place between uses to show change.

Lastly, a common obstacle to cultural change is a lack of common understanding of consensus and lack of a clear tool or strategy to demonstrate consensus. Sharing the example highlighted in the reproducible "Building Consensus for Change and Bell

Schedule Chart" (page 57) is one way to ensure everyone has a common definition of *consensus* and a common vision of knowing how and when the school achieves it.

> Culture is a dynamic and amoeba-like social organism that requires constant nurturing and care.

Beware! The work described in this section—Action 2: Build a Culture of Collective Responsibility—never ends! It is something that the schoolwide leadership team must attend to in its own meetings, as well as each and every day on an ongoing basis. Culture is a dynamic and amoeba-like social organism that requires constant nurturing and care.

Creating Consensus for a Culture of Collective Responsibility

A culture of collective responsibility is based on two fundamental beliefs:

1. The first assumption is that we, as educators, must accept responsibility to ensure high levels of learning for every student. While parental, societal, and economic forces impact student learning, the actions of the educators will ultimately determine each child's success in school.

2. The second assumption is that all students can learn at high levels. We define *high* levels of learning as *high school plus*, meaning every student will graduate from high school with the skills and knowledge required to continue to learn. To compete in the global marketplace of the 21st century, students must continue to learn beyond high school, and there are many paths for that learning, including trade schools, internships, community colleges, and universities.

Discussing the following critical questions will assist the school leadership team in creating consensus for a culture of collective responsibility aligned with these beliefs.

1. **How will we provide a compelling case for change?** For someone to change, they first must see a compelling reason to change. In other words, one must show why there is a need to change. Raising test scores or meeting district, state, or federal mandates hardly meets this goal. Instead, look to paint a picture of what adulthood will likely look like for students who don't succeed in school.

2. **What must we do differently?** Besides a compelling reason to change, one must also provide a doable plan. The noblest cause is useless if the changes required are seen as unrealistic. Staff members want a clear picture of exactly what changes are necessary to achieve learning for all students.

3. **How do we know these changes will work?** Having experienced the pendulum of school change for the past decades, many educators are skeptical of change processes. What evidence is available to demonstrate the validity of the recommended changes? (Besides the research quoted in *Simplifying Response to Intervention*, the website www.allthingsplc.info has dozens of schools and hundreds of pages of research validating the elements of PLCs and RTI.)

4. **What concerns do we expect, especially from staff members traditionally against change?** The leadership team should brainstorm the concerns staff members will have regarding the recommended changes. What will be the leadership's response to these concerns?

5. **What is the best setting or structure for the conversations needed to create consensus?** One of the leadership team's greatest leverage points is its ability to determine the location, structure, and timing of the conversations to create staff consensus. All stakeholders must have a voice in the process, but not necessarily in the same meeting. Sometimes the feelings of the silent majority can be drowned out by the aggressive opinions of a loud minority resistant to change. Consider a series of meetings with teams, grade levels, or departments. Also, set clear norms for the meeting, as professional, respectful dialogue is essential.

6. **How will we know if we have reached consensus?** Remember, it does not take 100 percent approval to get started; it takes consensus. Consensus is reached when all stakeholders have had a say and the will of the group has emerged and is evident, even to those who disagree. Consider how many key people will be needed to create the tipping point necessary for consensus.

In the end, true commitment comes when people see that the changes work. So the key is to build consensus, then get started doing the work. You will never get commitment until you start doing the work, but you cannot start until you get consensus.

Source: Adapted from Buffum, A., Mattos, M., & Weber, C. (2012). Simplifying response to intervention: Four essential guiding principles. *Bloomington, IN: Solution Tree Press.*

Creating Consensus Survey

A culture of collective responsibility is based on two fundamental beliefs.

1. The first assumption is that we as educators must accept responsibility to ensure high levels of learning for every student. While parental, societal, and economic forces impact student learning, the actions of educators ultimately determine each student's success in school.

2. The second assumption is that all students can learn at high levels. We define high levels of learning as *high school plus*, meaning every student graduates from high school with skills and knowledge required to continue to learn. To compete in the 21st century global marketplace, students must continue to learn beyond high school. There are many paths for learning, including trade schools, internships, community colleges, and universities.

Collective Responsibility Survey

1 = Never   2 = Seldom   3 = Sometimes   4 = Often   5 = Always, or almost always

Statement	5	4	3	2	1
1. We show teachers why there is a need for change. This need is not primarily tied to raising test scores or meeting district, state, and federal mandates. The need for change is tied to what the future looks like for students who do not succeed in school.					
2. In addition to providing compelling reasons to change, we make change doable. Our plans for change are realistic and scaffolded.					
3. We provide teachers with evidence that demonstrates the validity of recommended changes. We acknowledge that teachers are rightfully skeptical of change processes due to constant swings of the pendulum.					
4. We anticipate concerns staff members have regarding proposed change and prepare our responses in advance.					
5. We create a series of meetings and opportunities for staff to express their opinions. We are careful to structure meetings in a way that encourages professional dialogue rather than allowing a few voices to dominate.					
6. We define consensus so that it does not require 100 percent approval to get change started. The tipping point is reached when the will of the group is evident, even to those who still oppose it.					

Source: Adapted from Buffum, A., Mattos, M., & Weber, C. (2012). Simplifying response to intervention: Four essential guiding principles. Bloomington, IN: Solution Tree Press.

Forces at Work

Based on these critical questions, consider the forces in your team's favor and those working against you. Then, create a to-do list of next steps.

Critical Questions to Consider	Forces in Our Favor	Forces Working Against Us	Next Steps to Effectively Address These Questions
How will we provide a compelling case for change? ❏ Quantitative evidence ❏ Qualitative evidence			
What must we do differently? How doable is our plan? ❏ Clarity of changes needed ❏ Skills and resources needed to support change			
How do we know these changes will work? ❏ Research ❏ Experience			
What concerns do we expect, especially from staff members who are traditionally against change? ❏ Staff concerns ❏ Leadership response			
What is the best setting or structure for the conversations needed to create consensus? ❏ Meetings ❏ Clear norms			
How will we know if we have reached consensus? ❏ Evidence of consensus ❏ Implementation			

Simplifying RTI Culture Survey

Answer the following questions with the number scale.

1 = Never   2 = Seldom   3 = Sometimes   4 = Often   5 = Always, or almost always

Question	5	4	3	2	1
1. Our school supports and appreciates staff sharing new ideas.					
2. When something at our school is not working, our staff predict and prevent rather than react and repair.					
3. Our school schedule includes frequent collaboration opportunities for teachers as well as staff.					
4. Staff use team time to work as collaborative teams rather than as separate individuals.					
5. Our teams write norms or commitments that govern their work with each other, and they review and revise norms as needed.					
6. Our school enjoys a rich and robust tradition of rituals and celebrations that honor the work of teams as well as individuals.					
7. It is evident that learning for all is our core purpose as a school.					
8. Our staff believe that all students are capable of learning at high levels.					
9. Our staff believe that what we do can overcome the effects of poverty, language barriers, and poor parenting.					
10. Our staff believe that it is our responsibility to help all students become successful, even if the cause of challenges originates outside of school.					

Building Consensus for Change and Bell Schedule Chart

Voices: I understand the current attached proposal, and my voice and opinion have been clearly heard and represented through this process. (Please circle the statement that reflects your position.)

I Veto	**I Strongly Disagree**	**I Agree**	**I Strongly Agree**
I have never seen the proposal.	I have many unanswered questions. I had no opportunity to express my views.	I was heard. I understand. I had the opportunity to express my views.	All my views and opinions were heard. All questions were answered.

- -

Proposal: It is proposed that XYZ School adopt the following mission statement reflecting its commitment to ensure high levels of learning for all students.

_____

_____

Please circle the statement that reflects your position on this mission statement.

I Veto	**I Disagree**	**I Have Reservations**	**I Support It**	**I'm In**	**"You Had Me at Hello" (Absolutely)**
It's not good for students. Do not pursue.	It's not the best way. Let's keep trying.	But I'll support the will of the people.	Let's get moving.	I'll promote this proposal. I'll help.	I'll champion this proposal. I'll lead.

- -

Consensus: It's clear to me that the will of this school has emerged regarding this proposal. The staff have given a mandate to adopt this mission statement effective _____ (deadline).

Please circle the following statement that best reflects your position.

- I see clear disagreement, which communicates to me *not* to move ahead with this proposal.

- I see reservations, but the overall will of the group to move forward is evident.

- It is clearly the will of this staff to move forward with this proposal.

Action 3

Form Collaborative Teacher Teams

Alone we can do so little, together we can do so much.

—Helen Keller

Achieving a learning-focused mission requires more than the belief that all students can learn at high levels—it also requires collaborative structures and tools to achieve this goal. In addition to the school leadership team, collaborative teacher teams form the engine that drives a school's PLC and RTI efforts. Collaborative teacher teams comprise educators who share essential curriculum and thus, take collective responsibility for students learning their common essential learning outcomes.

Because the uniting characteristic of teacher teams is shared learning outcomes, the most common and preferred structures would be grade-level teams at the elementary level and course-based teams at the secondary level. It is likely that every school has singleton educators, who are the only people teaching a specific grade, course, or subject. When this is the case, the following structures can be effective ways to form teams.

▶ **Vertical teams:** Vertical teams share common learning outcomes developed across consecutive years of school. Examples include a K–2 primary team at the elementary level or a high school language arts team at the secondary level. While grade-level standards are not identical from kindergarten to second grade, they have several essential skills in common, such as phonemic awareness and number sense, with increasing rigor over time. Students develop these skills across all three grades. Likewise, a high school language arts team does not share identical content standards but does share essential skills such as persuasive writing or analytical reading. Vertical teams can also ensure that prerequisite skills are taught in sequence. This team structure often works best at smaller schools, where there may only be one teacher who teaches a particular grade level, subject, or course.

▶ **Interdisciplinary teams:** Interdisciplinary teams are comprised of teachers who teach different subjects. While interdisciplinary teams do not share content standards, they can focus their team efforts on shared essential skills. For example, an interdisciplinary team can focus on the college-ready skills David Conley (2007) recommends, including:

  ▶ Performing analytical reading and discussion

  ▶ Demonstrating persuasive writing

  ▶ Drawing inferences and conclusions from texts

  ▶ Analyzing conflicting source documents

  ▶ Supporting arguments with evidence

  ▶ Solving complex problems with no obvious answer

These essential learning standards are not subject specific—instead, each teacher on the interdisciplinary team can use his or her unique subject content as the vehicle to teaching these higher-level-thinking skills. The team can clearly define these common learning outcomes, discuss effective Tier 1 core instruction, develop common rubrics to assess these skills, and respond collectively when students need additional help. This approach can work especially well at smaller secondary schools.

▶ **Regional and electronic teams:** It is possible that the previous teaming options might not work for a specific faculty member. When this is the case, it is unlikely that this educator is the only person in the district, county, region, state or province, or country who teaches that curriculum content. Forming collaborative teams beyond the site is an option. This collaboration most likely requires virtual team meetings.

There are some significant limitations for vertical teams and regional or electronic teams. One of the most important outcomes of teacher teams is the ability to compare results on common assessments to determine instructional effectiveness. (We explore this process more deeply in the next chapter.) For this process to work best, teachers must compare assessment results on similar students, on the same standard, measured by the same assessment. On a vertical team, students are not similar, as one teacher will have older students who might score higher on a common assessment due to more experience instead of better core instruction.

A significant drawback to regional and electronic teams is that team members work on different campuses, and thus can't share students for interventions. One potential solution to these drawbacks is to have teachers on a vertical team also be part of an electronic grade-level team, and have members on an electronic team also be part of a site team that shares common students. This dual structure allows for both comparing results on common assessments and sharing common students for interventions.

While there are numerous ways to structure teacher collaborative teams, all these structures have one characteristic in common—if the purpose of school collaboration is to improve student learning, then team members must share student-learning outcomes. Ronald Gallimore and colleagues (2009) find that "successful teams need to set and share goals to work on that are immediately applicable to student learning. Without such goals, teams will drift toward superficial discussions and truncated efforts" (p. 549). These common learning goals are what unite and focus each teacher team's work. This focus on learning ensures that teacher teams are able to fulfill the vision of collective responsibility.

Here's Why

It is a universal truth that no one teacher has all the skills, knowledge, and time necessary to meet the needs of all students assigned to his or her classes. There is no evidence that having teachers work in isolation is an effective way to enhance student or teacher success.

> Teachers must compare assessment results on similar students, on the same standard, measured by the same assessment.

> There is no evidence that having teachers work in isolation is an effective way to enhance student or teacher success.

In the book *Concise Answers to Frequently Asked Questions About Professional Learning Communities at Work*, the authors provide five significant reasons why educators need time to collaborate (Mattos, DuFour, DuFour, Eaker, & Many, 2016):

1. Leaders in most professions consider time collaborating with colleagues as essential to success. As professionals, educators benefit from the expertise and collective efforts of a team. Collaboration is not a frill; it is an essential element of best practice.

2. The research supporting collaboration is extensive. The collaborative team is the fundamental building block of a learning organization, and the link between a collaborative culture and improving schools is well established.

3. U.S. educators have been criticized because their students do not score as well as Asian students on international tests. The fact is, Japanese teachers spend much less time in front of students in the classroom than U.S. teachers (Mehta, 2013). In Japan, a teacher working with colleagues to perfect a lesson or review student work is engaged in highly productive activities that improve student achievement (Mehta, 2013).

4. Lou Gerstner (1995), the former chairman of IBM, was asked if he felt the key to improving U.S. schools was simply extending the time teachers spent in the classroom. In response, Gerstner pointed out in the U.S. education system, one of every four students fails to finish school (he or she drops out). Furthermore, many of those who do complete school are incapable of doing what school is designed to ensure they can do. Gerstner claimed that if IBM discovered one of every four of its computers failed to reach the end of the assembly line, and many of those that did could not do what they were designed to do, IBM would not solve the problem by running the assembly line for a longer period of time. They would have teams get together to collaborate and find more effective ways to achieve the intended objective.

5. Finally, organizations show their priorities by how they use their resources. In a school, time is one of the most important resources. Knowing the strong correlation between meaningful collaboration and improved student achievement, any board of education should be willing to provide this precious resource.

> The degree to which teachers depend on one another, interdependently, to help all students learn at high levels largely determines that school's success.

The degree to which teachers depend on one another, interdependently, to help all students learn at high levels largely determines that school's success.

Here's How

The expectation for teachers to meet with colleagues, either in grade-level or department meetings, is nothing new in education. Yet, at most schools, these meetings rarely lead to increased student learning. This is because the act of meeting does not mean teachers are collaborating. They aren't doing the right work. As we emphasized previously, this book is about *doing the right work right*. Buffum and colleagues (2012) state:

The responsibilities of each teacher team in the RTI process are:

- Clearly define essential student learning outcomes

- Provide effective Tier 1 core instruction

- Assess student learning and the effectiveness of instruction

- Identify students in need of additional time and support

- Take primary responsibility for Tier 2 supplemental interventions for students who have failed to master the team's identified essential standards (p. 33)

The key to team success lies in the development of *systematic processes*—foundational structures that promote consistency, honest communication, respect, and mutual accountability within each team. Tools and strategies, such as those listed and explained later in this chapter, are critical to establishing such processes. It's the leadership team's responsibility to not only facilitate dialogue and promote the development of a shared understanding of collaboration but also to *live* this work, thus modeling what it looks and sounds like to be a high-performing collaborative team.

Helpful Tools

The following tools will help you accomplish the work for this essential action.

- ▶ **Chapter 3 of *Learning by Doing* (DuFour et al., 2016), "Building the Collaborative Culture of a Professional Learning Community":** This chapter discusses different structures to create collaborative teams that share essential learning outcomes, including options for educators who are the only people on campus who teach their particular grade, course, or curriculum.

- ▶ **"Are We a Group or a Team?" (page 63):** This activity facilitates powerful dialogue about both the *what* and the *why* of collaboration. You can use the chart of team descriptors generated in this activity as the foundation for self-assessment and goal setting for moving from group work to *teamwork*. In addition, many books and articles are available for shared reading and dialogue, including *The Handbook for SMART School Teams* (Conzemius & O'Neill, 2014), *Learning by Doing* (DuFour et al., 2016), and *Collaborative Teams That Transform Schools* (Marzano, Heflebower, Hoegh, Warrick, & Grift, 2016).

- ▶ **"Stages of Team Development" (page 64):** This form highlights the stages that all groups go through to transition from being a group of individuals to a cooperative group and, finally, to becoming a high-performing collaborative team.

- ▶ **"Team Action-Planning Template" (page 66):** Teacher teams can use this template to ensure that their collaborative goals and tasks are based on data rather than opinions.

- ▶ **"The Trust on Our Team Survey" (page 67):** This survey helps the leadership team assess the current level of trust among team members.

Coaching Tips

We find that, when asked, almost all teachers report that they are working together collaboratively. The fact is, however, very few of these groups are actually engaged in true collaboration, and therefore, they have little chance of producing powerful results.

You can invest time in activities that ensure a shared understanding of the differences between cooperation (groups) and collaboration (teams) to avoid this scenario. Once you reach consensus on the definition of *collaboration*, you might consider writing a charter of collaboration that all staff members sign as a symbol of support and commitment to active participation.

All the tools in this section are useful for helping team members understand themselves and how to work together as a team. Understanding where each group is in the process allows the leadership team to make better decisions about tools and strategies to help each group progress to the next stage of development.

Most important, it is the leadership team's responsibility to not only facilitate dialogue and promote the development of a shared understanding of collaboration but also to *live* this work, thus modeling what it looks and sounds like to be a high-performing collaborative team.

Are We a Group or a Team?

Complete the following ten steps to understand the differences between cooperation and collaboration.

1. Give the following directions to teams: "I will show you a triangle graphic comprised of twenty-five randomly placed capital letters (twenty-five out of twenty-six—none repeated). You have ten seconds to study the triangle, and you may *not* write during those ten seconds. When I remove the triangle, record as much as you can remember. Score your work based on the number of correct letters in the correct location on the triangle."

2. Show the first triangle for ten seconds, and then remove it from view (see the sample triangles).

3. When everyone is finished looking, show the triangle again. Have individuals score their recordings and find the average for their table team. Report out and chart the averages.

4. Using the same data, direct teams to determine their team score by compiling their individual results into a team total—there is still a total of twenty-five possible, so each letter only counts once, even if all team members got it correct. But every letter counts, even if only one member got it correct. Report out and record team scores. Point out the positive impact of cooperating—more heads are better than one.

5. Give the following directions to teams: "I will now show you a new triangle—same format, different letter placement. You have ten seconds to view it. The difference this time is that you only need to create one triangle as a team, and you will have one minute to figure out how you want to do it."

6. Monitor planning time (one minute). Give a cue, show the second triangle for ten seconds, and then remove it from view. Tell teams to compile their recordings for their team triangle.

```
        F
      K P D
    V A G T O
  E Q I L C W J
M U B R Y H N X S
```

7. Once everyone is finished, show the second triangle again. Have teams determine their team scores—report out and chart.

8. Ask participants to look at data and point out the significant gains between team totals and team results. Ask them to briefly talk about how and why their teams improved. Ask for individuals to share and chart their responses. Be sure to probe for ideas such as: clear, common goal; clear individual expectations; individual strengths factoring into work division; data used for reflection and improvement; trust; accountability to teammates; communication; and strategies for sharing.

9. Once you chart all responses, ask participants to reflect on a team that they currently work with and answer *yes* or *no* to each question you are about to pose. Using the charted responses, ask a question based on each response. For example, "Does your team have a clear, common goal?"

10. Finally, suggest that the responses on the chart reflect the differences between cooperative teams and collaborative teams to conclude the activity. Highlight the potential of increasing student achievement (getting results no one is able to get when working alone or in cooperative groups) when educators understand and commit to true collaboration.

Stages of Team Development

While the process of developing a professional learning team may feel uniquely personal, there are certain stages of development common across teams. By understanding that these stages exist—and by describing both the challenges and opportunities inherent in each stage—school leaders can improve the chances of success for every learning team. Use the following quick reference guide to evaluate the stages of team development in your building and to identify practical strategies for offering support.

Characteristics of Stage	Strategies for Offering Support
Stage: Filling the Time	
• Teams ask, "What is it exactly that we're supposed to do together?" • Meetings can ramble. • Frustration levels can be high. • Activities are simple and scattered rather than a part of a coherent plan for improvement.	❑ Set clear work expectations. ❑ Define specific tasks for teams to complete (for example, identifying essential objectives or developing common assessments). ❑ Provide sample agendas and sets of norms to help define work.
Stage: Sharing Personal Practices	
• Teamwork focuses on sharing instructional practices or resources. • A self-imposed standardization of instruction appears. • Less-experienced colleagues benefit from the planning acumen of colleagues. • Teams delegate planning responsibilities.	❑ Require teams to come to consensus around issues related to curriculum, assessment, or instruction. ❑ Require teams to develop shared minilessons delivered by all teachers. ❑ Structure efforts to use student learning data in the planning process. ❑ Ask questions that require data analysis to answer.
Stage: Developing Common Assessments	
• Teachers begin to wrestle with the question, "What does mastery look like?" • Emotional conversations around the characteristics of quality instruction and the importance of individual objectives emerge. • Pedagogical controversy is common.	❑ Provide teams with additional training in interpersonal skills and conflict management. ❑ Moderate or mediate initial conversations around common assessments to model strategies for joint decision making. ❑ Ensure that teams have had training in how to best develop effective common assessments. ❑ Create a library of sample assessments from which teams can draw.

page 1 of 2

Stage: Analyzing Student Learning

• Teams begin to ask, "Are students learning what they are supposed to be learning?" • Teams shift attention from a focus on teaching to a focus on learning. • Teams need technical and emotional support. • Teachers publicly face student learning results. • Teachers can be defensive in the face of unyielding evidence. • Teachers can grow competitive.	❏ Provide tools and structures for effective data analysis. ❏ Repurpose positions to hire teachers trained in data analysis to support teams new to working with assessment results. ❏ Emphasize a separation of *person* from *practice*. ❏ Model a data-oriented approach by sharing results that reflect on the work of practitioners beyond the classroom (for example, by principals, counselors, and instructional resource teachers).

Stage: Differentiating Follow-Up

• Teachers begin responding instructionally to student data. • Teams take collective action rather than responding to results as individuals. • Principals no longer direct team development. Instead, they serve as collaborative partners in conversations about learning.	❏ Ask provocative questions about instructional practices and levels of student mastery. ❏ Demonstrate flexibility as teams pursue novel approaches to enrichment and remediation. ❏ Provide concrete ways to support differentiation. ❏ Identify relevant professional development opportunities; allocate funds to after-school tutoring programs. ❏ Redesign positions to focus additional human resources on struggling students.

Stage: Reflecting on Instruction

• Teams begin to ask, "What instructional practices are most effective with our students?" • Learning is connected back to teaching. • Practitioners engage in deep reflection about instruction. • Action research and lesson study are used to document the most effective instructional strategies for a school's student population.	❏ Facilitate a team's efforts to study the teaching-learning connection. ❏ Create opportunities for teachers to observe one another teaching. ❏ Provide release time for teams to complete independent projects. ❏ Facilitate opportunities for cross-team conversations to spread practices and perspectives across an entire school. ❏ Celebrate and publicize the findings of team studies.

Source: Adapted from Graham, P., & Ferriter, W. M. (2010). Building a Professional Learning Community at Work: A guide to the first year. *Bloomington, IN: Solution Tree Press.*

Team Action-Planning Template

For novice learning teams, the decision to collectively analyze student learning data does not come naturally. To ensure that your team incorporates the analysis of student learning data into its work, include explicit references to data in any team action planning documents. By doing so, you will constantly reinforce the message that data are important. Use the sample action-planning template below as a guide.

Your Team: _____
1. What is your area of focus? Please identify both general content area and specific curricular objectives, and any appropriate student subgroups.
2. Why did you pick this area of focus? What data did you use in making your decision?
3. What is your SMART goal for this area of focus?
4. How will you regularly assess progress toward this goal? How will you respond to the results of these assessments? In your answer, please include the following elements. • Use of common assessments • Plans for analyzing data from common assessments • Plans for making team-based instructional adjustments based on assessment data • Clear timelines
5. What additional skills might your team need to accomplish the goal? What professional learning opportunities or resources would help your team acquire these skills?

Source: Adapted from Graham, P., & Ferriter, W. M. (2010). Building a Professional Learning Community at Work: A guide to the first year. *Bloomington, IN: Solution Tree Press.*

The Trust on Our Team Survey

This survey is designed to collect information about the levels of trust on our learning team. For each of the descriptors below, please indicate the extent to which you agree or disagree with each statement by circling one of the three letters (D, N, A), and the level of importance that you place on each indicator by circling one of the three numbers (1, 2, 3).

D = Disagree   N = Neutral   A = Agree

1 = Very important   2 = Somewhat important   3 = Not important

My colleagues willingly share their materials, resources, and ideas with me.	D	N	A	1	2	3
I feel welcome in my colleagues' classrooms before and after school.	D	N	A	1	2	3
I feel welcome in my colleagues' classrooms during their instructional periods.	D	N	A	1	2	3
I feel comfortable with my colleagues in my room during my instructional periods.	D	N	A	1	2	3
I believe that my colleagues have good intentions in their interactions with me.	D	N	A	1	2	3
I believe that my colleagues have good intentions in their interactions with students.	D	N	A	1	2	3
I know that I can count on my colleagues.	D	N	A	1	2	3
I believe that my colleagues are honest.	D	N	A	1	2	3
I am not afraid to share student learning results with my colleagues.	D	N	A	1	2	3
I believe that my colleagues are competent and capable teachers.	D	N	A	1	2	3
I believe that I can learn from my colleagues.	D	N	A	1	2	3
I believe that everyone on my team makes meaningful contributions to our work.	D	N	A	1	2	3
I believe that everyone on my team is pulling in the same direction.	D	N	A	1	2	3
Our team celebrates the personal and professional successes of individual members.	D	N	A	1	2	3
Our team celebrates our collective accomplishments.	D	N	A	1	2	3
I look forward to the time that I spend with my colleagues.	D	N	A	1	2	3
Final Thoughts: On the back of this page, please describe the kind of support you think your team would need in order to improve the overall levels of trust between teachers.						

Source: Adapted from Graham, P., & Ferriter, W. M. (2010). Building a Professional Learning Community at Work: A guide to the first year. *Bloomington, IN: Solution Tree Press.*

Action 4

Create Time for Collaboration

Until we can manage time, we can manage nothing else.

—Peter F. Drucker

"At its core, RTI is about creating a collective response when students need additional support, rather than leaving this response up to each individual teacher. This process is predicated on the staff having the time necessary to work together" (Buffum et al., 2012, p. 39). The school leadership team, working within the district and state or province contractual agreements and regulations, must lead the process of creating sufficient collaborative time for each team. At a minimum, this collaborative time should meet the following criteria.

▸ **Frequency:** We recommend that teacher teams and the site intervention team meet at least once a week. The leadership team should meet at least twice a month.

▸ **Duration:** Each weekly meeting should be approximately one hour in length. If the meetings are bimonthly, then it's best to dedicate at least ninety minutes.

▸ **Attendance:** Participation must be *mandatory*. Collaboration by invitation does not work.

Buffum and colleagues (2012) state:

> Considering that the professional learning communities process is endorsed by virtually every national teacher professional association, it is difficult to understand why a teaching professional would desire or expect the *right* work in isolation. More importantly, if a teacher is allowed to opt out of team collaboration, then that teacher's students will not benefit from the collective skills and expertise of the entire team. If the purpose of collective responsibility is to ensure that all students learn at high levels, then allowing any teacher to work in isolation would be unacceptable. (p. 40)

Here's Why

There is both a practical and an ethical reason why collaboration time is a prerequisite condition for a successful system of interventions. As we mentioned previously in this chapter, convincing staff members to commit to a mission of collective responsibility requires the leadership team to offer a doable plan. If ensuring high levels of student learning requires staff to work beyond contract hours, staff members have the right to refuse to participate. Any proposal that violates contractual agreements or education law is doomed to fail.

But even if district and site leaders had the authority to unilaterally require teachers to work longer hours to provide student interventions, it would be ethically wrong to do so. It is morally bankrupt to force teachers to make a choice between meeting the needs of their students at school and their children at home, or between making teaching their career or their entire life. It is possible to do the essential work of the RTI process within the contractual hours of the workday.

Here's How

Some districts use early dismissal or late-start days for students to provide teachers with collaboration time while students are off campus. In many communities, however, changing school schedules is not an option because of busing issues, custodial care, budget constraints, or state or province mandates regarding instructional minutes each day. Therefore, the leadership team must be creative in finding ways to provide time for teachers to collaborate while students are at school, without increasing costs or losing significant amounts of instructional time.

Our discussion here of the critical components of effective collaboration is intended as an overview of the process. To dig deeper into PLC practices and structures for collaboration, we highly recommend the book *Learning by Doing* (DuFour et al., 2016). We consider this book the "PLC manual," as it goes in depth into every aspect of the PLC process and provides the tools necessary to support these outcomes.

Occasionally, we encounter schools that claim to be stumped in their efforts to find the time necessary for collaboration. We find this perplexing, as the average teacher is paid to be on campus six to seven hours a day, totaling thirty to forty hours a week. Is it really impossible to carve out sixty minutes of meeting time from a thirty-five-hour work week? More often than not, the problem is that the school is trying to find extra time while keeping the current schedule unaltered. Very few schools have extra time in their schedule—that is, time that is currently unallocated to any particular purpose. For this reason, the task is not to find time for collaboration but rather to make collaborative time a priority.

Helpful Tools

The following tools will help you accomplish the work for this essential action.

- **Chapter 3 of *Learning by Doing* (DuFour et al., 2016), "Building the Collaborative Culture of a Professional Learning Community":** This chapter provides multiple options regarding how schools and districts create collaborative teams without needing added funding for lengthening the teacher contractual work week.

- **"Team Collaboration Time: Planning Guide and Schedule" (page 71):** The leadership team can use this tool to plan team collaboration time.

> It is possible to do the essential work of the RTI process within the contractual hours of the workday.

> The task is not to find time for collaboration but rather to make collaborative time a priority.

Coaching Tips

The key tip to keep in mind here is to involve teachers in each and every step of creating time for collaboration. This includes building a shared understanding of *why* collaborative time is essential, *where* to find the time within the school day, and *how* to use that time. That said, the following are several strategies to consider for involving teachers in the process of creating time for collaboration.

- ▶ Incorporate reading and dialogue into faculty meetings about professional articles that focus on the importance of collaboration.

- ▶ Create a teacher-led task force to explore options for creating time during the school day. This might entail research, visitation of other schools, or attendance at professional conferences focused on teacher collaboration.

- ▶ Ensure teachers understand the difference between *collaboration* (a systematic process in which people work together on a single, shared goal) and *coblaboration* (people meeting with no structures or processes for sharing knowledge, solving problems, or creating new ideas), *cooperation* (people meeting to accomplish individual, yet common goals), or other forms of *collaboration lite* (any process with superficial levels of collaborative implementation). Professional reading and role play may be helpful.

- ▶ Model collaboration in faculty meetings by agreeing on the purpose and non-purpose of meetings, brainstorming and setting meeting norms, reviewing norms regularly, and holding each other accountable to the norms.

- ▶ Identify clear expectations for the products you will create as a team during collaboration time.

- ▶ Use a consensus decision-making process for establishing the schedule for collaboration time.

The more teachers are involved in understanding, developing, and supporting the creation of collaborative time, the more likely they are to use that time well.

Team Collaboration Time: Planning Guide and Schedule

Collaborative time is essential to the PLC and RTI processes. Without it, the work is virtually impossible. It is the leadership team's responsibility to ensure frequent collaboration for schoolwide and teacher teams. This time should be:

- **Frequent**—Each team should meet weekly, or once every other week at a minimum.

- **Scheduled**—Meetings should last at least forty-five to sixty minutes per week.

- **Embedded**—Time must be embedded in the professional and contractual work week.

Site Collaboration Schedule

Schoolwide Teams	Time and Day	Location
Leadership team		
Intervention team		
Teacher Teams	Time and Day	Location

Action 5

Commit to Team Norms

> Gettin' good players is easy. Gettin' 'em to play together is the hard part.
>
> **—Casey Stengel**

We cannot overemphasize the importance of setting team norms—or collective commitments—to guide professional behavior while collaborating. True collaboration often requires staff members to have difficult conversations and to trust colleagues with their students. People can feel vulnerable discussing the best ways to meet students' needs or the current reality of what is not working. For this reason, teams must set collective commitments regarding how they are going to act and interact with each other. Unfortunately, some schools struggle with building a collaborative culture because personal conflicts prevent the team from functioning efficiently.

Teams must set collective commitments regarding how they are going to act and interact with each other.

Team norms should address three types of outcomes.

1. **Procedural meeting expectations** to address such things as meeting attendance, punctuality, preparedness, division of labor, and the follow-through of team decisions

2. **Behavioral expectations** to explain how the team makes decisions and addresses disagreements between team members

3. **Protocols** to successfully address when team norms are violated

Here's Why

Collaborative teacher teams form the engine that drives RTI. Team meetings, in turn, provide the vehicle within which the engine can thrive, and team norms ensure that both the engine and the vehicle function at maximum productivity.

Robert Garmston and Bruce Wellman (2009) remind us, "Meeting success is influenced more by the collaborative norms of the group than by the knowledge or skill of the group's facilitator" (p. 56). In other words, when team members develop norms to which they hold themselves accountable, they make better use of meeting time, maintain their focus on student learning challenges, confront conflicts more effectively, and produce greater results.

Garmston and Wellman (2009) also point out that professional communication is at the heart of getting work done in schools. With that in mind, additional experts also highlight the importance of establishing team norms.

▶ Business writer Patrick Lencioni (2002) says, "Having clear norms gives teams a huge advantage when it comes to ensuring the exchange of good ideas" (p. 43).

▶ Susan Sparks (2008) shares, "They [norms] help us take risks, work through issues, and communicate well" (p. 45).

Here's How

There are many ways for teams to create and enforce their norms. Fundamental to any process a team might choose are the following six key considerations.

1. Team members understand the purpose of their meetings. Ensuring that all team members have a clear, shared understanding of why they are meeting helps the rationale for establishing team norms gain leverage. Asking the question, "How do we need to work together to accomplish our goals?" is much more substantive than "How do we need to behave?"

2. All team members need to participate in brainstorming, clarifying, and reaching agreement on team norms. Without full participation in the process, it is unlikely that members will be willing to hold themselves or others accountable to the norms.

3. Team norms need to include a commitment to confronting behaviors that violate the norms. Teams often identify and agree on a specific signal as a norm check that causes everyone to stop and self-assess his or her own behavior. For example, a middle school leadership team printed its norms on a bright pink bookmark and agreed to raise a pink flag whenever anyone noticed a norm being violated. Instead of pointing it at an individual, someone simply raised the bookmark in the air as a signal to everyone.

4. Make the norms visible at all meetings once your team agrees to the norms. To accomplish this, you can post norms on a chart or table tent or include them on each meeting agenda.

5. Review team norms at each meeting. A single norm might be highlighted at the beginning of each meeting, or individual members can take turns highlighting a norm that he or she believes to be in place and suggesting a norm for reflection and improvement.

6. Assess team norms for celebration or revision at least twice a year. Team members can respond to an individual survey to assess how well the team is living its norms or participate in a group assessment during a team meeting to do this. For example, give each team member a set of red and green dots. Have them post the dots on a charted list of the norms (green for *in place* and red for *needs improvement*). Once they post all the dots, team members can discuss which norms are working well and should stay as they are and which ones need to be reinforced or revised.

Helpful Tools

The following tools will help you accomplish the work for this essential action.

▶ **Chapter 2 of *Learning by Doing* (DuFour et al., 2016), "Defining a Clear and Compelling Purpose":** This chapter provides research regarding the importance of team norms and specifics on how to create and enforce these collective commitments.

▶ **"Steps for Establishing Team Norms" (page 76):** Teams can use this reproducible to follow a step-by-step process to establish team norms and behaviors.

▶ **"Sample Team Norms" (page 77):** This sheet provides sample norms to help teams understand the types of behaviors to address when establishing team norms of their own.

Coaching Tips

Schools and teams need to embrace the concept of *go slow to go fast*.

Most important, schools and teams need to embrace the concept of *go slow to go fast*. One of the biggest mistakes teams can make is to ignore how essential it is to develop norms. Yes, it takes time to establish norms, but the payoff occurs when teams become more efficient and productive because they have clearly articulated their collective commitment to working together.

Based on many experiences with multiple teams, two additional tips stand out.

1. Clarify why the team is meeting and what it seeks to accomplish through collaboration. As noted previously, this allows the conversation to center on *how we need to work together to accomplish our goals* rather than *how we need to behave*. Working together to accomplish goals feels more professional than simply setting rules for behavior.

2. Have members reflect on the behaviors they are willing to commit to as individuals to begin the brainstorming process. For example:

   • Pose an open-ended question such as, "How can I best support my team and the accomplishment of our goals?" Ask each person to silently record a brief list of the behaviors that he or she needs to bring to each team meeting.

   • Following that, pose an additional question, "What do I need from my teammates to help us accomplish our goals?" Each person draws a line under his or her first brainstormed list and then adds behaviors he or she needs from others.

- After completing the written brainstorming (without talking), a facilitator collects and charts ideas from members' initial list of personal behaviors. Challenge members to share only those behaviors from their own lists that are not already noted on the chart.

- Review and clarify the list, and then ask members to offer any additional behaviors they identified as *needs from others*. Often, there are very few additions, thus reinforcing the idea that team norms start with individual commitments.

A team's first efforts at developing norms are often quite simplistic. This is normal. As team members strengthen their collaborative skills and begin to experience success, team members' norms typically strengthen and begin to go beyond surface behaviors. As an example, a high school English team was into its third year as a team before members became ready to identify "Check your ego at the door!" as a norm that they could all agree and commit to.

Of course, challenges are always part of this process. Educators often ask us this question regarding RTI and collaborative teams: "How do you deal with a staff member who refuses to commit to this work?" Once reluctant staff members learn the compelling reasons to change and receive a doable plan and every opportunity to succeed, then they have no professional, logical, or ethical justification to resist the proposed changes a majority of the staff deems necessary for the welfare of their students. By this point, they have neither the right to stop the plan from proceeding nor the option of refusing to participate. Leaders must be willing to confront these resisters and demand that they meet their responsibilities to the collective school efforts. Failure to do so empowers resisters to continue their destructive ways and damage trust with the majority of staff members who support the changes.

While the school administration must take the lead in confronting hardcore resistant members, our experience is that the greatest coercive pressure comes from peers who are willing to take a stand. At most schools, a silent majority is willing to change, and an aggressive minority does whatever it takes to stop change. Many of these extreme resisters mistakenly believe that they speak for the majority of the staff, because they share their combatant opinions in the staff lounge every day, and their peers sit silently and don't say a word. That silence seemingly condones the comments and emboldens resisters. The individual actions of each staff member shape the collective culture of an entire school. Unless the silent majority begins to have some courageous conversations with the aggressive minority holding their school hostage, it is difficult to truly transform the school's culture.

The individual actions of each staff member shape the collective culture of an entire school.

Steps for Establishing Team Norms

As a team, use the following five steps to establish behaviors for your team to operate under. These are the standards you must commit to accomplish your goals.

1. Discuss and agree on your team's purpose, goals, and desired products.

2. Post the question, "How do we need to work together in order to accomplish our goals?"

   a. Individually, brainstorm or record responses to "What do I need to do to ensure my team's success?"

   b. Underline the responses, and then individually brainstorm and record responses to "What do I need from my teammates in order to best contribute to my team's success?"

3. Collect and publicly record responses from all team members, beginning with individual needs and adding needs from others to complete the list.

4. Clarify, prioritize, and narrow the list to five to eight norms.

5. Reach consensus on the norms. Confirm commitment to norms from all members, and agree to give feedback.

6. Post norms, review them, and assess their use frequently. Modify as needed and agreed to.

Sample Team Norms

> ## NORMS
> Standards of behavior we commit to in order to accomplish our goals

The following are sample team norms.

1. Be honest and share what you think and feel.

2. Participate in the conversation. It is your responsibility to get your voice in the room.

3. Focus on the task.

4. Think creatively and comprehensively.

5. Treat one another as equals.

6. Listen and hear one another's viewpoints—one's perspective is one's truth.

7. Ensure equal airtime for all participants.

8. Come to meetings ready to work and learn.

9. Honor time limits and commitments.

Source: Adapted from Malone, J. (2006, August 17). Are we a group or a team? 2006 Getting Results Conference—The impact of one, the power of many *[Handout]. Accessed at http://results.ocde.us/downloads/JMalone-Group_Team_Handout.pdf on April 17, 2017.*

Conclusion

Anthony Muhammad (2018) uses a gardening analogy to describe the complementary relationship between school structure and school culture. Proven practices are like good seeds, while a healthy school culture is good soil. Planting good seeds in toxic, barren ground stunts and kills off the heartiest plants. Likewise, the powerful practices of PLCs and RTI wither and die in a school culture of isolation, negativity, and low expectations. Many schools and districts spend hours planning the schedules, assessments, and timelines that support successful RTI implementation but fail to properly prepare the soil before planting the seeds of RTI.

The five essential actions in this chapter are not recommendations or suggestions; they are "hearts"—the necessities. Beyond the research provided throughout this chapter, common sense would dictate that a highly effective system of interventions requires effective leadership, a learning-focused school culture, high-performing teams, and a commitment to adult behaviors that foster trust and mutual accountability. In the next chapter, we focus on the essential actions of collaborative teams at Tier 1.

CHAPTER 3

Tier 1 Teacher Team Essential Actions

> Why [does] knowledge of what needs to be done frequently fail to result in actions or behaviors consistent with that knowledge?
>
> **—Jeffrey Pfeffer and Robert I. Sutton**

In this chapter, we focus on the top-right portion of the RTI at Work pyramid (see figure 3.1, page 80). Again, we want to stress that this pyramid is merely a graphic organizer designed to guide thinking. Let us reconsider what this portion of the pyramid visually represents.

- ▶ This portion is part of Tier 1, which represents what *all* students receive. Any action or outcome the team places in this box is going to be part of the core instructional program for every student.

- ▶ Because it's on the right side of the pyramid, the portion represents outcomes the school's collaborative teacher teams lead. The essential actions in this chapter directly relate to the core instruction for each grade level or course a school offers, so the teachers who teach these classes have the best training and are in a position to take lead responsibility.

We believe this portion of the pyramid—and the essential actions that collaborative teams must successfully achieve at Tier 1—are the most important to a school's ability to create a highly effective system of interventions. Teacher teams are the engines that drive the entire RTI process. If teacher teams sputter, so will the school's efforts to achieve its mission of high levels of learning for all students.

> If teacher teams sputter, so will the school's efforts to achieve its mission of high levels of learning for all students.

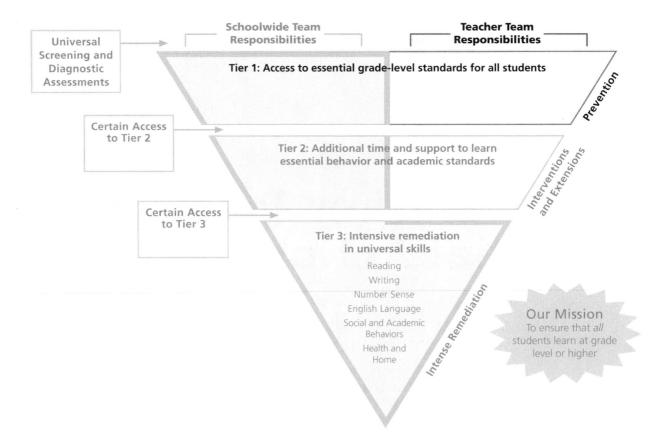

FIGURE 3.1: Focus on Tier 1 teacher team essential actions.

Besides forming the right teams, allocating frequent meeting times, and committing to norms of behavior, it is critical that teacher teams focus their efforts on the right work. In this chapter, we discuss the essential actions and responsibilities of collaborative teacher teams that provide the foundation of RTI academic content and skills.

These five essential actions are:

1. Identify essential standards for each grade level or course, unit by unit

2. Create an essential standards unit plan

3. Implement the team teaching-assessing cycle

4. Give common end-of-unit assessment for essential standards

5. Identify students for Tier 2 support by student, standard, and learning target

To align this book more closely with the common language of the PLC at Work process, we will use the term *common end-of-unit assessment* rather than *common summative assessment*. Here's why: For some educators, the term *summative* mistakenly signals the end of the learning process—a time to record grades and move instruction on. We use the term *end-of-unit* to remove any doubt that although the assessment comes at the end of a period of instruction, it does not mean that learning stops. Rather, teachers use the information the assessment gathers to help students who are still struggling to master essentials and to extend the learning for those students who demonstrate mastery of the essential standards.

Additionally, DuFour et al. (2016) remind us that team-developed common formative and end-of-unit assessments are most powerful as elements of a balanced assessment system for monitoring student learning. Such a system also includes assessments individual teachers create and use in their own classrooms on a regular basis; end-of-course or year summative assessments teacher or district teams create; and occasional district, state, or provincial benchmark assessments. All play a role in monitoring and improving student learning.

Because Tier 1 represents what all students receive in their core instruction, we must consider the outcomes placed here on a school's pyramid as promises to every student. A school cannot invite teacher participation in these activities or hope that they are actually carried out in core instruction. Instead, teacher teams must deliver these activities, which also must be supported with school resources, monitored frequently, and celebrated often. As discussed in chapter 2, the school leadership team should organize faculty into collaborative teacher teams in which team members share essential learning outcomes. Equally important, team members dedicate time each week to meet and collaborate.

Schools also must empower and support teacher teams to make the critical decisions around these promises and learning outcomes. Without teacher teams committing to these promises, they become merely possibilities, depending on which teacher a student has been assigned to. As Stephen R. Covey (1989) states, "Without involvement, there is no commitment. Mark it down, asterisk it, circle it, underline it. No involvement, no commitment" (p. 143).

> Schools also must empower and support teacher teams to make the critical decisions around these promises and learning outcomes.

This chapter may represent a sort of "handwashing" example for you and your school. What does washing hands have to do with RTI? Consider how a hospital lowered its infection rate from 11 percent to 0 percent. As a result of this effort, in two years, the hospital prevented eight deaths and saved approximately two million dollars. If you are wondering what this breakthrough protocol might have been—the hospital simply and continuously reminded all staff to wash their hands (Sickbert-Bennett et al., 2016). Like washing your hands, this will not be the first time you have heard or read about the ideas we discuss here, such as the need to create a guaranteed and viable curriculum or the use of common formative assessments. Indeed, you may already consider these things done. However, as the Pfeffer and Sutton quote at the start of this chapter so perfectly states, *knowing* and *doing* are different concepts!

Action 1

Identify Essential Standards for Each Grade Level or Course

> Things which matter most must never be at the mercy of things which matter least.
>
> **—Goethe**

The mission of a learning-focused school is to *ensure* that *all* students learn at high levels. We defined *high levels of learning* as grade level or better, so essential standards represent the absolutely essential knowledge, skills, and behaviors every student must acquire to succeed in the next unit, semester, year, and course—and ultimately, in life.

We know it is folly to expect all students to master every standard that district or state or provincial curricular guides determine we are required to teach—that would be impossible. There are some standards we teach each year that are *nice to know*— that is, if a student does not master it this year, it will not cripple his or her chances for future success. But we know some standards are absolutely *have to know* learning outcomes. They represent content and skills that keep a student from progressing in that subject if he or she doesn't master them.

For example, ask kindergarten teachers, "Is letter recognition important for your students to learn?" They would chuckle at this ridiculous question. In our work with schools throughout the United States, we have never heard a single kindergarten teacher respond to that question with this answer: "Letters, shmetters . . . who cares if kids know their letters?" Kindergarten teachers know that letter recognition is absolutely essential to a student's future success in reading, in first grade, in all future subjects, and in life.

However, are *all* the kindergarten English language arts (ELA) standards essential? Of course not. In California, another required kindergarten ELA standard is the Common Core's, "With prompting and support, name the author and illustrator of a story and define the role of each in telling the story" (RL.K.6; National Governors Association Center for Best Practices and Council of Chief State School Officers [NGA & CCSSO], 2010).

Will a kindergartener make it in first grade if he or she can't yet name the illustrator of the book the class is reading? Probably. So, identifying these absolutely essential learning outcomes—year by year, subject by subject, and unit by unit—is a critical first step in focusing a school's core instruction and intervention processes. Yet, like handwashing in a hospital, while the need to create a guaranteed and viable curriculum is obvious, achieving this outcome at most schools has proven elusive at best.

Rather than focus on how a team might cover content (for example, a copy of the state or provincial standards, district pacing guide, or curriculum map), we believe each collaborative teacher team must receive the time to examine such materials and then decide what skills and concepts are essential and thus, what every student must master. In other words, identifying essential standards means clarifying what each student must *learn*, not simply what we will *teach* and when we will teach it.

While we believe that the district and state or province have a role to play in this discussion, teacher teams must ultimately commit to what they will prioritize, teach, reteach, and intervene about with students. Without the teacher teams' involvement and the resulting ownership that comes from that involvement, the implemented curriculum and intended curriculum are seldom the same.

Here's Why

The research supporting the need to identify essential standards, and the importance of engaging every teacher in the identification process, is compelling and conclusive. In their book, *Concise Answers to Frequently Asked Questions About Professional Learning Communities at Work*, Mattos et al. (2016) argue:

Merely providing teachers with a copy of the state standards for their grade level does not ensure all students will have access to a guaranteed curriculum that can be taught in the amount of time available for teaching. Teachers may ignore the standards, assign different priorities to the standards, vary dramatically in how much time they devote to the standards, have huge discrepancies in what the standard looks like in terms of student work, and possess significant differences in their ability to teach the standards. (p. 17)

After analyzing more than eight hundred meta-analyses involving millions of students, Hattie (2009) says:

Teachers need to know the learning intentions and success criteria of their lessons, know how well they are attaining these criteria, and know where to go next in light of the criteria of: "Where are you going?" "How are you going?" and "Where to next?" (p. 239)

Carol Ann Tomlinson and Jay McTighe (2006) state that the first step in curriculum development is to:

Identify desired results. What should students know, understand and be able to do? What content is worthy of understanding? What 'enduring' understandings are desired? What essential questions will be explored? [This step] calls for clarity about priorities. (pp. 27–28)

More emphatically, Robert J. Marzano, Phil Warrick, and Julia A. Simms (2014) proclaim a high-reliability school provides students with a guaranteed and viable curriculum focused on enhancing student learning. The Marzano High Reliability Schools™ framework, based on forty years of education research, defines five progressive levels of performance that a school must master to become a high-reliability school—where all students learn the content and skills they need for success in college, careers, and beyond.

The curriculum is focused enough that it can be adequately addressed in the time available to teachers. All students have the opportunity to learn the critical content of the curriculum. Individual teachers do not have the option to disregard or replace content that has been designated as essential (Marzano et al., 2014).

While a preponderance of the education research, conventional wisdom, and common sense would tell us that creating a guaranteed and viable curriculum increases student learning, few schools and districts have fully committed to it. Instead, most have settled for shortcuts in the process or have actually promoted practices that are counterproductive to this goal. For example:

► The district office hand-selects a few teachers to produce lists of essential or *power* standards. The school distributes these standards to all teachers with the explanation that these documents are teacher created. Since all teachers were not involved in the selection and prioritization process, they have little ownership or commitment to the list. Heidi Hayes Jacobs (2001) reminds us that most district-curriculum guides are "well-intended but fundamentally fictional accounts of what students actually learn" (p. 20).

▶ The district office asks teachers to prioritize standards but do nothing more than place a checkmark next to standards they believe are important for students to learn. This approach does little to create clarity around what the standards actually mean. Because standards are often written in a way that leaves a great deal of room for interpretation, teachers need to give more than a head shake when making critical decisions about student learning. Mike Schmoker (2011) puts it this way: "And though the national standards for language arts are better than the state standards they would replace, there are still too many of them, and many are poorly and confusingly written" (p. 41).

> We must recognize that the system will never be systematic until teacher teams are clear on what each student must master.

If we are to build a solid foundation of essential skills and knowledge in students at Tier 1, we must be crystal clear what those skills and knowledge are. If we plan to build a schoolwide system of supports for students when they struggle to learn, we must recognize that the system will never be systematic until teacher teams are clear on what each student must master. If not, schools will reteach different things and send students for Tier 2 interventions for different reasons, while experiencing large numbers of students falling so far behind that they require Tier 3 interventions. Schools suffer this frustrating fate simply because they never gain clarity on what they want each student to learn.

Here's How

In chapter 4 of *Simplifying Response to Intervention* (Buffum et al., 2012), the authors give detailed advice on how teacher teams might go about prioritizing and selecting what all students must learn from a particular unit of study or during a particular time period (such as a trimester or quarter). For example, Douglas Reeves (2002) offers three lenses teachers might apply to this discussion of what is essential for students to learn.

1. **Endurance:** Will this standard provide students with knowledge and skills that are valuable beyond a single test date?

2. **Leverage:** Will it provide knowledge and skills that are valuable in multiple disciplines?

3. **Readiness:** Will it provide students with knowledge and skills essential for success in the next grade or level of instruction?

We ask teams to use the reproducible "Criteria for Selecting Essential Standards" (page 87) to guide their discussions around prioritizing standards. We also suggest using the reproducible "Essential Standards Chart" (page 88) to provide further clarity about the essential standards the team selects. (Visit **go.SolutionTree.com/RTIatWork** to download the free reproducibles in this book.) Rather than simply placing a checkmark next to a standard deemed essential, we want to be certain teams do the following five things.

1. Simplify the wording of the standard.

2. Agree on the level of rigor required (and give an example of that rigor).

3. Identify the prerequisite skills and vocabulary needed for students to be successful in mastering the standard.

4. Agree in general on when to teach the standard and how to most accurately assess it at the end of the unit.

5. Determine how to meaningfully extend and enrich learning for students who demonstrate early in the unit that they already have mastered the standard.

We believe that this kind of discussion leads teams to a deeper understanding of what they are expecting all their students to learn and a deeper commitment to be sure every student learns it.

Helpful Tools

The following tools will help you accomplish the work for this essential action.

▸ **Chapter 5 of *Learning by Doing* (DuFour et al., 2016), "Establishing a Focus on Learning":** This chapter provides foundational content knowledge as well as tools that can help schools accomplish the action steps outlined in this section.

▸ **"Criteria for Selecting Essential Standards" (page 87):** Teams can use this tool to guide their discussions regarding the determination of essential standards.

▸ **"Essential Standards Chart" (page 88):** Teams can use this chart to bring greater clarity to understanding the essential standards they expect students to learn.

Coaching Tips

As teams begin this work, it is worthwhile to remind them of Patrick Lencioni's (2002) quote, "If everything is important, then nothing is" (p. 106). So true, and so challenging to accomplish! To agree on what is truly essential for students to learn requires time, structure, patience, and courage. Not only do teachers need to be prepared to speak up for their own views, but they also need to keep an open mind and truly listen to their colleagues. The leadership team's role, then, is to provide a balance of support and accountability.

First, teams need to designate time to do the work. Generally speaking, two approaches have proven to be successful.

> The leadership team's role, then, is to provide a balance of support and accountability.

1. **Provide large chunks of student-free time (a day or two) before the school year begins:** This allows teachers to create a draft of their agreed-on essentials for an entire semester or more. As they teach each instructional unit, teachers should discuss and re-evaluate this draft with the goal of having a completed essential standards chart for the entire year at the time school ends.

2. **Discuss and identify essentials one unit at a time:** In this case, teams set aside at least one team meeting several weeks prior to the beginning of each

instructional unit to complete their essential standards chart. By the end of the year, the team is then ready to reflect on the year, as a whole, and evaluate its work to be sure the essentials it identified sequence appropriately and best support student success.

No matter which approach they use, teams must consistently review and re-evaluate their decisions to ensure that their essential standards chart represents what is most important for their students to learn and, therefore, the "mountains teachers are willing to die on" in support of student learning.

As teams do this work, two questions we hear are: (1) "How many essential standards should we select?" and (2) "If the standard is not essential, does that mean we don't teach it at all?" Our response to the first question is both a gift (no one right answer) and a challenge (no one right answer!). In other words, teams must find their own right answer—enough standards to ensure students master what is most important, but few enough standards to allow teachers and students to truly focus their work. Regarding the second question, if the team doesn't identify a standard as essential, it does not mean that teachers ignore it. Rather, individual teachers should continue to teach and assess each standard. Standards not included on the essential standards chart, however, are not the focus of their collaborative teamwork, common assessments, and team-provided interventions.

As teams seek consensus, we cannot stress the importance of using a structured tool and process enough. The essential standards chart is the tool, but teachers must determine how to best complete it together. That said, not all the work takes place during team meetings. Teams are most productive when they divvy up the work and come to each meeting with individual recommendations for review, rather than starting each meeting with a blank slate.

Finally, don't forget the value of vertical articulation and celebration. It is time well spent to designate faculty meeting time, two to three times per year, for teams to share their work with each other, check for continuity between grade levels and subject areas, and to cheer each other on. According to an ancient Chinese proverb, "The journey of a thousand miles begins with a single step." Celebrate every step!

Criteria for Selecting Essential Standards

In the following space, list those standards from your grade-level or course-alike team that meet the criteria of endurance, leverage, and readiness for the next level, as defined here.

In *The Leader's Guide to Standards*, Douglas Reeves (2002) outlines three criteria for selecting essential standards.

1. **Endurance:** Will this standard provide students with knowledge and skills that are valuable beyond a single test date?

2. **Leverage:** Will this standard provide knowledge and skills that are valuable in multiple disciplines?

3. **Readiness:** Will this standard provide students with essential knowledge and skills essential for success in the next grade or level of instruction?

_____

_____

_____

_____

_____

_____

_____

_____

_____

_____

_____

_____

_____

Source: Adapted from Buffum, A., & Mattos, M. (2014, May). Criteria for selecting essential standards. *Presented at the Simplifying Response to Intervention Workshop, Prince George, British Columbia.*

Reeves, D. B. (2002). The leader's guide to standards: A blueprint for educational equity and excellence. *San Francisco: Jossey-Bass.*

Essential Standards Chart

Working in collaborative teams, examine all relevant documents, Common Core standards, state standards, and district power standards, and then apply the criteria of endurance, leverage, and readiness to determine which standards are essential for all students to master. Remember, *less is more.* For each standard selected, complete the remaining columns. Complete this chart by the second or third week of each instructional period (semester).

		What Is It We Expect Students to Learn?			Team Members	
Grade	Subject	Semester				
Description of Standard	Example of Rigor	Prerequisite Skills	When Taught?	Common Summative Assessment	Extension Standards	
What is the essential standard to be learned? Describe in student-friendly vocabulary.	What does proficient student work look like? Provide an example or description.	What prior knowledge, skills, or vocabulary are needed for a student to master this standard?	When will this standard be taught?	What assessments will be used to measure student mastery?	What will we do when students have already learned this standard?	

Source: Adapted from Buffum, A., Mattos, M., & Weber, C. (2012). Simplifying response to intervention: Four essential guiding principles. Bloomington, IN: Solution Tree Press.

Action 2

Create an Essential Standards Unit Plan

The key is not to prioritize your schedule but to schedule your priorities.

—Stephen R. Covey

Once a team prioritizes and identifies essential standards, it needs to create a road map describing how it will get all students to the destination of mastery—not of everything—but of those standards it deemed as essential. We call this road map the *essential standards unit plan.*

In preparation for an upcoming unit of study, the team should discuss and agree on the essential learning outcomes. Then team members select the standard or standards from their essential standards chart that represent those essential learning outcomes.

At this point, teams are ready to map out a plan for ensuring all students master each essential standard. The four-step plan should include:

1. Identifying the overall nature of each standard—what it expects of students: mastering knowledge, applying knowledge, performing a task, or creating a product

2. Unwrapping the standard into learning targets and determining the more discrete building blocks that establish a foundation for successful mastery of the standard

3. Converting learning targets into student-friendly language

4. Creating or selecting assessments to use throughout the unit of study, both formative and summative, and agreeing on when to administer each assessment

As a result of the dialogue and decisions needed to complete these steps, the team creates an essential standards unit map. Even more important, team members are ready to share the learning targets with students, begin implementing instruction with collective clarity on the intended outcomes, and identify when and how they expect students to demonstrate progress.

Here's Why

As schools shift from a focus on teaching and coverage to a focus on learning and mastery, each step teams take to create an essential standards unit plan establishes a foundation for success. This is because:

- ▸ Understanding the overall nature of each essential standard helps teams better understand the component parts of the standard (learning targets)

▶ Identifying the type of learning standards and targets expected of students ensures that teams create or select appropriate assessments to accurately measure learning and assists them in providing feedback to students that promotes more learning

▶ Converting standards to student-friendly language and sharing them with the class invite students to actively partner with teachers in the learning journey

Students are better able to self-assess, set goals, and respond appropriately to feedback and evaluation. As curriculum and assessment specialists Jan Chappuis, Rick J. Stiggins, Steve Chappuis, and Judith A. Arter (2012) state, "Students can hit any target they can see and that holds still for them" (p. 42).

▶ Collaboratively creating and selecting assessments, for both formative and summative uses, ensures that teams collect the detailed, granular information needed to effectively monitor and support each student's learning

Teachers use assessment data to measure and report, as well as diagnose and improve, student learning. These assessments also provide the information critical to implementing an effective system of interventions.

> **The best intervention is prevention.**

In summary, it is important to remember that Tier 1 of RTI expects teachers and teams to understand how each student responds to instruction. The process of creating an essential standards unit plan positions teachers to not only react to student learning struggles, but more important, to proactively limit those struggles. This helps teachers to actualize the powerful premise: *The best intervention is prevention.*

Here's How

Creating an essential standards unit plan is truly the most important task for educators seeking to transform themselves into high-performing teams who take collective responsibility for high levels of student learning. Each step of the four-step process requires designated time, a shared understanding of the task, and commitment to collaborative work. Teams must complete the following four steps.

1. Analyze and discuss the type of learning each essential standard requires of students

2. Deconstruct each essential standard to identify the learning targets

3. Convert learning targets into student-friendly language

4. Collaboratively create or select assessments to administer throughout the unit of study and agree on when to administer them

Analyze and Discuss the Type of Learning Each Essential Standard Requires of Students

To begin the process, teams need to analyze and discuss the type of learning each essential standard requires of students. Chappuis, et al. (2012) recommend categorizing standards and learning targets as follows.

▶ **Knowledge:** Factual information, procedural knowledge, and conceptual understandings that provide the foundational content for all subjects

▶ **Reasoning:** Thought processes students utilize to solve problems and apply knowledge to new situations; *thinking skills*, such as inference, analysis, comparison, classification, evaluation, and synthesis

▶ **Performance skills:** Physical processes students must demonstrate in order for teachers to determine mastery; *doing skills* such as playing an instrument, kicking a ball, reading orally, speaking a language fluently, or using a ruler

▶ **Product:** Creation of a product, as stated in the standard, is the focus of the learning, such as works of art, written compositions, maps, and graphs

To identify the type of learning defined in an essential standard, first look at the verb or verbs. For example, a potential grade 9 Common Core ELA essential standard might be: *Write arguments to support claims in an analysis of substantive topics using valid reasoning and relevant and sufficient evidence* (NGA & CCSSO, 2010). By focusing on the action students are expected to take, *write*, teams can determine that the standard is expecting a written product and, therefore, categorize it as a product-based standard.

Deconstruct Each Essential Standard to Identify the Learning Targets

The next step in creating an essential standards unit plan is to deconstruct, or unwrap, each essential standard to identify the learning targets that underpin it. Teams review standards documents as well as bring their own knowledge of the content to this discussion. They categorize the learning targets according to the type of learning expected of students.

For example, consider the grade 9 Common Core ELA standard: *Write arguments to support claims in an analysis of substantive topics using valid reasoning and relevant and sufficient evidence* (NGA & CCSSO, 2010). The text in the standard points out several foundational learning targets: *supporting claims* (reasoning), *using valid reasoning* (reasoning), and *using relevant and sufficient evidence* (reasoning). Additionally, students need to know and understand the concepts of *valid, relevant,* and *sufficient* (knowledge). Of course, they also must be able to write legibly or word process on a computer efficiently (performance skills), and they must be able to combine all their knowledge, reasoning, and skills into a finished written essay (product). Reviewing standards documents and discussing their own performance expectations of students help teams add to this beginning list of learning.

Understanding the type of learning expected of students assists teachers in clarifying their expectations, selecting or creating assessments that most accurately measure the learning, and aligning instructional strategies to build success for students.

To complete the essential standards unit plan, teams begin by recording the learning targets they identified under the appropriate category headings in the top section of the unit plan (see figure 3.2, page 92).

Essential standards:		❏ Knowledge	❏ Performance skills
		❏ Reasoning	❏ Product
End-of-unit assessment:		When taught: Instructional days needed:	
Knowledge Targets	**Reasoning Targets**	**Performance Skills Targets**	**Product Targets**

FIGURE 3.2: Essential standards unit plan—categories.

Convert Learning Targets Into Student-Friendly Language

Once the team analyzes essential standards and deconstructs them into learning targets, the next step is to convert learning targets into student-friendly language. Teams must agree on the most important targets, and then identify any potentially unclear or confusing language within them. After teams agree on their own definitions of critical terms and concepts, they must reach consensus on learning target statements to share with their students. These statements often begin with *I can*.

To clarify, let's again return to the grade 9 Common Core ELA standard. One of its essential learning targets is *use relevant and sufficient evidence*. Keeping in mind that this is a ninth-grade standard, teachers might agree on the following definitions.

> **Teams must agree on the most important targets, and then identify any potentially unclear or confusing language within them.**

- ▶ **Relevant:** Important or related to the main topic

- ▶ **Sufficient:** As much as is needed, enough

In turn, the statement to share with students might be, *I can make a claim and use relevant and sufficient evidence to support it*. In student-friendly language, this means, *I can identify information important to my topic and include enough of it in my argument to convince readers that my claim is worthy of consideration*.

Once teachers have completed this process, both the original standards and the revised, they can share student-friendly *I can* statements with students. It is important to include the original terminology in the targets teams share with students, as well as the more student-friendly definition. This supports students in learning the academic language necessary for ultimate mastery of the standard.

> **Teams must point out, discuss, and evaluate student-friendly targets on a regular basis.**

Equally important, teams must point out, discuss, and evaluate student-friendly targets on a regular basis. This helps students "see" the target and recognize that it is "holding still" for them. In other words, the targets become a consistent part of instruction rather than constantly changing or moving.

Teams record student-friendly learning targets in the shaded section of the essential standards unit plan (see figure 3.3).

Essential standards:		❏ Knowledge	❏ Performance skills
		❏ Reasoning	❏ Product
End-of-unit assessment:		**When taught:**	
		Instructional days needed:	
Knowledge Targets	**Reasoning Targets**	**Performance Skills Targets**	**Product Targets**
Student-friendly learning targets:			

FIGURE 3.3: Essential standards unit plan—student-friendly learning targets.

Collaboratively Create or Select Assessments to Administer Throughout the Unit of Study and Agree on When to Administer Them

The final step in creating an essential standards unit plan is to collaboratively create or select assessments to administer throughout the unit of study and to agree on when to give each assessment. The good news is that teams already did half the work when developing the essential standards chart. They already identified the common end-of-unit assessment to use at the unit's conclusion.

As teams discuss what types of assessments to include in their road map, it is important to consider how to use each assessment, formatively or summatively, and which assessments to administer independently or in common. All team members must give common assessments, and they must use these data for collaborative analysis and response. Additionally, common assessments should address significant steps in the learning sequence; and teachers should give them at times when teams have already scheduled a team meeting for collaborative analysis and response. Independent assessments may address less critical targets; and individual teachers may create and use them, rather than the whole team.

It is also important to identify which learning targets might need extra instructional attention and what type of learning they require of students. There is not "one right answer" to the number of assessments needed in a unit plan. That said, all students can benefit from a minimum of one risk-free opportunity to demonstrate and revise their learning. We recommend, therefore, that teams include at least one common formative assessment during each unit of instruction.

Critically important to valid and reliable data is making sure that the assessment method provides the most accurate information about the learning targets teachers will assess.

- ▸ Teachers can effectively determine mastery of knowledge-based targets through the use of selected-response assessments (true-or-false statements, multiple-choice questions, matching, and fill-in-the-blank responses).

- ▸ Teachers can only partially determine mastery of reasoning targets with selected-response assessments. They can more accurately determine mastery with an extended written-response assessment.

- ▸ Teachers can only accurately measure mastery of performance skill–based targets or standards with performance-based assessments.

- ▸ Finally, teachers can assess the quality of the product itself to determine mastery of product-based targets or standards.

Once team members agree on the assessments, they must agree on when to administer them. This is most crucial for any common assessment. Finally, teams must clarify how each assessment assists students in progressing toward successful demonstration of mastery on the end-of-unit assessment. They should also consider strategies for involving students in the assessment process throughout the unit of study.

Teams record assessments in two places on the unit plan. They name and describe the end-of-unit assessment at the top of the plan and list and describe assessments administered throughout the unit on the bottom half of the plan (see figure 3.4).

Essential standards:		❏ Knowledge ❏ Reasoning	❏ Performance skills ❏ Product
End-of-unit assessment:		When taught: Instructional days needed:	
Knowledge Targets	Reasoning Targets	Performance Skills Targets	Product Targets
Student-friendly learning targets:			

Assessment	Connection to Standard	Student Involvement	Time Line
(Which target or targets are being assessed? How will the assessment be used? Is it a common or individual assessment?)	(How will this assessment set up students for successful mastery of the standard?)	(How will students engage in the assessment process?)	
1.			
2.			
3.			

FIGURE 3.4: Essential standards unit plan—assessments.

Once the team has completed the essential standards unit plan, they will have collective clarity on learning targets, student-friendly versions to share with students, and agreement on when and how to assess. As a result, students in each teacher's classroom benefit from equal access to the essential standards.

Helpful Tools

The following tools will help you accomplish the work for this essential action.

▶ **"Essential Standards Unit Plan" (page 97):** This reproducible provides a template for putting together an essential standards unit plan.

▶ **"Sample ELA Essential Standards Unit Plan" (page 98):** This reproducible provides a sample essential standards unit plan for English language arts.

▶ **"Sample Mathematics Essential Standards Unit Plan" (page 100):** This reproducible provides a sample essential standards unit plan for mathematics.

▶ **"Deconstructing Standards" (page 102):** Teams can use this template to deconstruct, or unwrap, each essential standard to identify the learning targets that underpin it.

▶ **"Student-Friendly Language" (page 103):** This tool can help teams convert learning targets into student-friendly language.

Coaching Tips

The best advice for supporting this challenging work is to remember how to eat an elephant: one bite at a time! The leadership team needs to teach, discuss, and practice each step of the plan in a whole-staff setting before assigning individual teams the task of completion. This allows time for teachers to ask questions and learn with and from each other. It may also be less overwhelming for teams to use the templates for individual steps of the process before they are required to complete the entire unit plan.

Once the leadership team teaches, discusses, and practices each step in a whole-staff setting, each team should set a date for completing an essential standards unit plan with standards of its own for an upcoming unit of study. To lend support and assist with facilitating the process, leadership team members should drop in on teams as they collaborate to complete each task. It may also be helpful to have teams bring finished products to staff meetings for sharing and problem solving with other teams.

In a perfect world, teams would have a full student-free day (or more) to learn together and try out this process. However, if teams must use their weekly collaboration time to work through the process, it is important to ensure teachers continue to give formative and end-of-unit assessments, even if they have not yet implemented other steps of the process. Teachers must not hold up or sacrifice student learning as they gain mastery of new tools and strategies.

In conclusion, participating in a step-by-step process that has been carefully taught, guided, and monitored means teachers are more likely to fully understand both the logistics of the work and each step's importance. They also can begin working much more independently and efficiently. As a wise man once said, "Go slow to go fast!"

> Teachers must not hold up or sacrifice student learning as they gain mastery of new tools and strategies.

Essential Standards Unit Plan

Use the four-step process (page 89) to complete the following plan.

Essential standard:			☐ Knowledge ☐ Reasoning		☐ Performance skills ☐ Product

End-of-unit assessment:

When taught:

Instructional days needed:

Knowledge Targets	Reasoning Targets	Performance Skills Targets	Product Targets

Student-friendly learning targets:

Assessment (Which target or targets are being assessed? How will the assessment be used? Is it a common or individual assessment?)	Connection to Standard (How will this assessment set up students for successful mastery of the standard?)	Student Involvement (How will students engage in the assessment process?)	Time Line
1.			
2.			
3.			

Sample ELA Essential Standards Unit Plan

This is a sample essential standards unit plan for grade 9 English language arts.

Essential standard: W.9–10.1—Write arguments to support claims in an analysis of substantive topics or texts, using valid reasoning and relevant and sufficient evidence.		☐ Knowledge ☐ Reasoning	☐ Performance skills ☑ Product
End-of-unit assessment: Read an article on a contentious topic, and write a persuasive essay that includes an analysis of the topic. Then, take a stand and defend it with relevant and sufficient evidence. A choice of several articles will be provided.		When taught: November Instructional days needed: Nineteen	

Knowledge Targets	Reasoning Targets	Performance Skills Targets	Product Targets
• Organize essay and paragraph. • Demonstrate basic writing mechanics.	• Analyze text for key ideas. • Explain reasoning for stance taken. • Identify and include relevant and sufficient evidence. • Select and use persuasive language. • Sequence written text in a cohesive and organized manner.	• Demonstrate word processing skills. • Demonstrate understanding and use of all steps in the writing process.	• Write an effective introductory sentence. • Craft a cohesive, well-organized, and mechanically correct paragraph, text analysis, and support of a claim. • Draft multiple-paragraph essay.

Student-friendly learning targets:

• I can analyze nonfiction text for key ideas.

• I can make a claim and use relevant and sufficient evidence to support it.

• I can organize and explain my ideas in writing.

• I can use correct spelling, punctuation, and grammar.

• I can explain my thinking and strategies.

page 1 of 2

Assessment	Connection to Standard	Student Involvement	Time Line
(Which target or targets are being assessed? How will the assessment be used? Is it a common or individual assessment?)	(How will this assessment set up students for successful mastery of the standard?)	(How will students engage in the assessment process?)	
1. Mascot persuasive paragraph (common formative, individual)	Students demonstrate baseline persuasive writing skills.	Students self-assess and set goals for improving persuasive writing skills.	Day three
2. Text analysis paragraph (formative and summative, individual)	Students practice comprehension and analysis of text, as well as paragraph organization.	Students self-assess and peer-assess the pretest and revise.	Day six: Rough draft Day eight: Final draft
3. Mechanics quiz and paragraph editing (summative, individual)	Students develop accurate use of mechanics and ability to self-edit.	Students analyze quiz results to identify growth targets.	Day ten
4. Practice essay (formative, individual and partner classes)	Students combine all skills in a finished product.	Students peer-assess and collaboratively score sample papers.	Days eleven through fifteen

Source of standard: National Governors Association Center for Best Practices & Council of Chief State School Officers. (2010). Common Core State Standards for English language arts and literacy in history/social studies, science, and technical subjects. Washington, DC: Authors. Accessed at www.corestandards.org/assets/CCSSI_ELA%20 Standards.pdf on February 24, 2017.

Sample Mathematics Essential Standards Unit Plan

This is a sample essential standards unit plan for grade 4 mathematics.

Essential standard: Student will represent multiplication of two-digit by three-digit numbers and describe how that representation connects to the related number sentence.

☐ Knowledge　　　☐ Performance skills
☑ Reasoning　　　☐ Product

End-of-unit assessment: Twenty-five-item test with five items: one digit × two to three digits, five items with two digits × two digits, five items with two digits × three digits, and ten points for problem solution with description

When taught: March

Instructional days needed: Sixteen

Knowledge Targets	Reasoning Targets	Performance Skills Targets	Product Targets
• Know basic facts 0–10. • Know and use several models to represent number sentences.	• Explain how the representation matches the number sentence. • Identify and explain strategies used to solve problems. • Compute multiple-digit problems accurately.		

Student-friendly learning targets:

• I can recall basic facts, 0–10, quickly and accurately.
• I can set up multiplication problems.
• I can use two ways to solve multiplication problems.
• I can use effective strategies to solve problems and find a workable solution.
• I can explain my thinking and strategies.

Assessment (Which target or targets are being assessed? How will the assessment be used? Is it a common or individual assessment?)	Connection to Standard (How will this assessment set up students for successful mastery of the standard?)	Student Involvement (How will students engage in the assessment process?)	Time Line
1. Ongoing daily quizzes of basic multiplication facts 0–10; one summative quiz—that the student chooses—per week (individual)	Students develop accurate and fluent recall of multiplication facts to successfully compute multiple-digit problems.	Students track daily progress and determine when they are ready for a summative quiz each week.	Ongoing, daily
2. Single digit × two to three digits using two different models and with explanation of models (formative and summative, common formative)	Students develop fluency with multiple algorithms and mathematical language to explain their thinking.	Students self-assess and peer-assess the pretest and make corrections.	Day three: Pretest (formative) Day six: Summative test
3. Two digits × two digits using different models and with explanation of models (formative and summative, individual)	Students develop fluency with multiple algorithms and mathematical language to explain their thinking with problems that have two-digit multipliers.	Students self-assess the pretest, make corrections, and set goals for the summative test.	Day nine: Formative Day twelve: Summative
4. Two-digit × three-digit numbers (mysterious multiplication) (formative, common)	Students use multiplication understanding to solve problems and identify workable solutions.	Students self-assess, select appropriate practice activities, and set goals for final summative test.	Day fourteen: Formative Day sixteen: Final summative

Deconstructing Standards

Use the following chart to deconstruct, or unwrap, each essential standard to identify the learning targets that underpin it.

Essential standards:
Types: knowledge, reasoning, performance skills, or product

Learning Targets
What are the knowledge, reasoning, performance skills, or product targets underpinning the standard?

Knowledge Targets	Reasoning Targets	Performance Skills Targets	Product Targets

Student-Friendly Language

Use the following chart to convert the learning targets into student-friendly language.

Essential standards:		
Words or Terms to Clarify	**Definition**	**Student-Friendly Language**

Action 3

Implement the Team Teaching-Assessing Cycle

> You don't have to be a genius or a visionary or even a college graduate to be successful. You just need a framework and a dream.
>
> **—Michael Dell**

After teams complete the planning steps described in actions 1 and 2, they are ready to breathe life into their plans. The team teaching-assessing cycle in figure 3.5 provides a graphic and conceptual framework for moving from theory to action. This section focuses on the following critical aspects of core instruction and formative assessment in the cycle while action 4 will focus on the remainder of the cycle.

▸ Introduce students to learning targets, and begin core instruction (including checks for understanding and differentiation).

▸ Give common formative assessment.

▸ Collaboratively analyze formative assessment results, provide mid-unit interventions, and continue or complete core instruction.

▸ Repeat for additional learning targets and subskills as needed.

Before highlighting key aspects of the cycle, it is worthwhile to point out that teams have already completed most of the work necessary to put the cycle in motion. They have already identified essential standards, unwrapped them into learning targets, converted the targets into student-friendly language, collaboratively created or selected assessments, and determined how they will use those assessments. The only missing piece is the development of instructional plans. With the clarity that comes from completing the previous steps, teachers will find that instructional planning, whether done individually or collaboratively, falls into place very quickly.

As teams begin to familiarize themselves with the team teaching-assessing cycle, it is important to focus attention on four impactful actions that will maximize the impact on student achievement.

1. Introduce learning targets to students on the first day of unit instruction, and continue to discuss and evaluate them throughout the unit.

2. Implement ongoing checks for understanding and give differentiated feedback to students through the use of exit slips, responders, questioning strategies, whiteboards, and so on.

3. Implement a minimum of one *common* formative assessment (CFA) for every essential standard, which includes collaborative analysis of results and a collective response to support additional student learning.

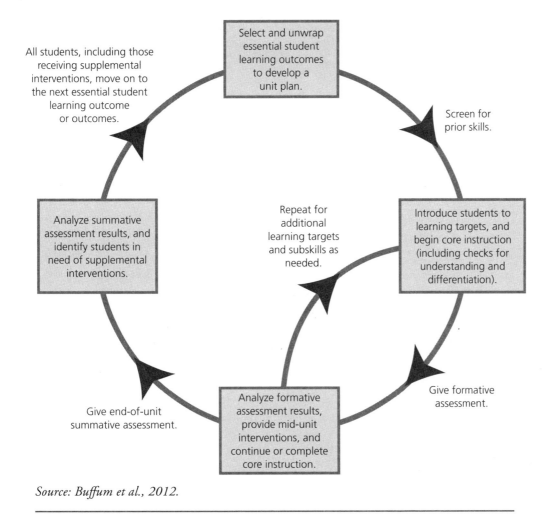

All students, including those receiving supplemental interventions, move on to the next essential student learning outcome or outcomes.

Select and unwrap essential student learning outcomes to develop a unit plan.

Screen for prior skills.

Analyze summative assessment results, and identify students in need of supplemental interventions.

Repeat for additional learning targets and subskills as needed.

Introduce students to learning targets, and begin core instruction (including checks for understanding and differentiation).

Analyze formative assessment results, provide mid-unit interventions, and continue or complete core instruction.

Give formative assessment.

Give end-of-unit summative assessment.

Source: Buffum et al., 2012.

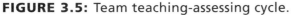

FIGURE 3.5: Team teaching-assessing cycle.

4. Though not stated in figure 3.5, schedule a day in the unit plan for responding to common formative assessment results prior to beginning unit instruction. This designated day for response should be no more than two days after administering the formative assessment in class.

These four actions help teachers begin to re-culture their classrooms from a focus on grading and evaluating to a focus on learning and facilitate greater engagement, and therefore, higher levels of student learning.

Here's Why

As teachers consider the team teaching-assessing cycle, they may question the value of having such a framework. Margot Fonteyn (AZQuotes, n.d.) responds best when she says:

> There is no way anything of value can be done without some framework. It might well be that the framework is discarded or the rules opposed; that is not important. What is essential is that they exist so that one knows when one is in opposition to them.

Working with the
team teaching-
assessing cycle
helps teams be
more productive
by providing a
common language
and process.

Working with the team teaching-assessing cycle helps teams be more productive by providing a common language and process. Teams can use it to identify where teachers are within the process and ensure that all team members are moving forward collectively as a group.

Teams might ask why these four actions are so important. Following is the answer to this question for each action.

1. **Why learning targets?** When students can "see" the targets they are trying to hit, have multipe opportunities to hit them, and receive frequent feedback on how they are doing relative to those targets, they are empowered to take responsibility for their own learning. Additionally, Hattie's (2009) exhaustive research concludes that the single most powerful strategy related to student learning is what he calls *self-reported grades*. Within a classroom setting, this means students understand what teachers expect of them (clear learning targets), set personal goals relative to the targets, and engage regularly in self-assessment to determine their progress and push themselves further.

2. **Why ongoing checks for understanding?** Gathering information from ongoing checks for understanding (exit slips, responders, whiteboards, questioning strategies, and so on) enables teachers to give frequent, meaningful, and differentiated feedback to students without having to wait for results from a team-developed common formative assessment.

3. **Why common formative assessment?** A minimum of one common formative assessment within a unit of instruction ensures students have at least one risk-free opportunity to test out their current understanding of the targets being assessed. It also ensures teams collaboratively analyze assessment results to determine how best to support high levels of learning for all students. Additionally, it provides each teacher with an opportunity to reflect on the effectiveness of his or her instruction and learn new strategies from colleagues.

4. **Why schedule time for response?** The biggest pushback to formalizing the use of formative assessments is often, "I don't have time to reteach!" To address this challenge, when teams schedule a day for responding to formative assessment results *before the beginning of the unit*, time for reteaching or extending learning is already available.

The team teaching-assessing cycle is the foundation of Tier 1 instruction. It is what makes RTI such a powerful approach to ensure high levels of learning for all students. Rather than waiting to discover which students failed a summative assessment and then sending them off to someone else for Tier 2 interventions, the collaborative team accepts collective responsibility for each student's success by working together in partnership with students to proactively prevent learning difficulties.

Here's How

Putting the team
teaching-assessing
cycle into practice is
what teachers
do best.

Putting the team teaching-assessing cycle into practice is what teachers do best: teach! With the clarity each teacher gains through collaboratively identifying essential standards and creating an essential standards unit plan, the teacher begins instruction by sharing the unit's destination with students (student-friendly learning targets). The teacher posts, displays, and includes targets in unit documents with such consistency that students cannot possibly miss "seeing" and understanding them. Informal conversations with students during instruction quickly shed light on whether they know where they are headed.

Depending on the complexity of the essential standards identified for the current unit, the cycle may take several weeks or more to complete. As the unit progresses, teachers should regularly check for understanding and frequently give feedback to individual students as to how they are progressing toward the targets, allowing students to modify and make adjustments as needed. Due to the fact that different students move through the learning sequence at different rates, it is not necessary for every teacher on a team to be in exactly the same place on the same day. It is essential, however, for each teacher to instructionally prepare his or her students and administer the common formative assessment (or assessments) when the team agrees to.

Decisions made about when to give common formative assessments are primarily based on student need. Which targets are most challenging to students? When might they benefit most from teachers working together to adjust instruction? It is also important to keep teacher schedules in mind. In other words, teachers should administer common formative assessments as close to a scheduled team meeting as possible, on the same day or no more than a day before or after.

Agreeing to give a common formative assessment means that teachers on the team have also agreed to the targets being assessed, the assessment tool or task being used, and the format for sharing the results. In order for the team to analyze progress student by student and target by target, the data must be student specific and target specific. It must also be displayed across all classrooms. This allows individual teachers to reflect on how well their students are progressing as compared to students in other classrooms. Critically important, teachers must collect these data and have them ready for review at the beginning of the team meeting. The advent of support technology makes this more than doable.

Once teachers administer the common formative assessment, and the team meeting begins, we suggest that teams follow a standardized protocol to maximize productivity, including a brief discussion about the assessment tool or task; a set of consistent, straightforward questions for data analysis; and a problem-solving format for reaching consensus on a collective response to assessment results. As teams work through the protocol, their dialogue should also include inquiry into where and why one teacher's results on a particular target are stronger than the rest of the team. This helps the team discover the most effective strategies and materials for helping students master each target. Teachers should share strategies and materials freely as the team works toward consensus on how best to respond to these data.

As noted, teams need to schedule instructional time for responding to CFA results before they begin unit instruction. Instead of plowing ahead to address the next targets, teachers can use the day following their team meeting to deliver mid-unit interventions and extensions for the targets already assessed. These mid-unit interventions might also be called *preventions* because they help students close learning gaps prior to the end-of-unit summative assessment.

Another way of thinking about this comes from a mission statement in the waiting room of a primary care physician, "The mission of this practice is to prevent illness, not just to treat it." These preventative instructional actions are the very remedy that stops academic illness and helps all students experience success.

Depending on the number and complexity of targets, as well as time available for team meetings, the CFA cycle should be repeated as many times as necessary or doable. Once students receive instruction on all the essential learning targets and have opportunities to self-assess and adjust their understanding, teachers administer a common summative assessment. We offer recommendations for administering and responding to common summative assessments in the following section.

Helpful Tools

The following tools will help you accomplish the work for this essential action.

- **Chapter 6 of *Learning by Doing* (DuFour et al., 2016), "Creating Team-Developed Common Formative Assessments":** This chapter provides foundational content knowledge as well as tools that can help schools accomplish the action steps outlined in this section.

- **"Sample Common Formative Assessment for Persuasive Writing" (page 110):** This reproducible shows a sample common formative assessment, demonstrating that this kind of assessment is often short, easy to administer, and linked closely to instruction.

- **"Team Protocol for Common Formative Assessment" (page 112):** Teams can use this form to establish a consistent protocol for engaging in collaborative analysis and determining a collective response to common formative assessment results.

- **"Sample Data for Persuasive Writing" (page 113):** This chart provides an example of how teams might choose to collect and represent formative assessment data.

- **"Team Response for Common Formative Assessment" (page 114):** This template helps teams agree on their collective response to CFA results— Which students need additional support on which targets, and how will you provide that instruction?

Coaching Tips

As is almost always the case, moving from theory (framework) to action (implementation) is very challenging. It is one thing to understand the needed changes in practice and something else entirely to actually implement them. It is at this point that the knowing-doing gap rears its head.

To maximize success, leadership team members must put on their coaching hats and work right alongside their teams. As David B. Peterson and Mary Dee Hicks (1996) remind us in *Leader as Coach*:

Approach your coaching like a gardener who does not try to motivate the plants to grow, but who seeks the right combination of sunlight, nourishment, and water to release the plant's natural growth. A gardener provides an environment conducive to growth, much as a coach creates the conditions in which personal motivation to develop will flourish. (p. 55)

Equally important to successful implementation is a shared understanding between teachers and leadership team members of the coach's role (Peterson & Hicks, 1996). All parties must challenge themselves to interact in a nonevaluative, learning-focused manner, with the center of all conversations focused on student learning, never teacher evaluation.

Coaching, ultimately, is all about promoting reflective thinking. To do so, coaches utilize strategies and language that support teams' or teachers' planning and decision-making skills, ability to reflect on practice, and development as self-directed learners. Table 3.1 highlights several key strategies and language good coaches use.

TABLE 3.1: Key Strategies and Language Good Coaches Use

Coaching Strategies	Coaching Language
Maintaining a nonjudgmental stance	• Let me see if I understand . . . • In other words . . .
Listening	• Tell me what you mean when you say . . . • Let's review the key points so far . . .
Inquiring and probing for specificity rather than telling	• To what extent . . . • What might be another way . . . • What do you see as your next steps . . .

Finally, as busy as leadership team members will be in supporting teams and teachers with implementing the team teaching-assessing cycle, it is critically important for the leadership team to continue to meet regularly. These meetings provide a forum for sharing challenges, problem-solving solutions, and celebrating successes. Coaching is hard work!

Tom Landry (n.d.) says it best, "A coach is someone who tells you what you don't want to hear, who has you see what you don't want to see, so you can be who you have always known you could be." This type of sharing and transparency is crucial to building an environment in which both teachers and leaders can truly thrive and grow.

Coaching is hard work!

Sample Common Formative Assessment for Persuasive Writing

Learning targets:

- I can make a claim and support it with evidence.

- I can organize and explain my ideas through writing.

- I can use correct spelling, punctuation, and grammar in my writing.

Task

You are attending a new high school scheduled to open next school year. As a student, you have been asked to provide input on the selection of a school mascot. The choices are:

 Wolverine—strong animal

 Falcon—bird of prey, trained for hunt

 Monarch—independent ruler

Choose one mascot and write a few sentences explaining why it would be the best choice for your school.

_____

_____

_____

_____

_____

_____

_____

_____

_____

Scoring Criteria

Learning Target	3	2	1
I can make a claim and support it with evidence.	• The claim is clear. • Evidence supports the claim.	• The claim is somewhat clear. • Evidence somewhat supports the claim.	• The claim is unclear or not stated. • Evidence doesn't exist or doesn't support the claim.
I can organize and explain my ideas through writing.	• Introductory and concluding sentences grab the reader's attention and frame the writing. • Supporting sentences are in a clear sequence, and they explain how evidence supports the claim.	• Introductory and concluding sentences are in place but do not grab the reader's attention. • Supporting sentences are in an unclear sequence or somewhat explain how evidence supports the claim.	• Introductory or concluding sentence, or both, is missing. • Supporting sentences are in random order or do not explain how evidence supports the claim.
I can use correct spelling, punctuation, and grammar in my writing.	• There are very few or no spelling, punctuation, or grammatical errors.	• There are some spelling, punctuation, or grammatical errors present, but they don't get in the way of the message.	• There are so many spelling, punctuation, or grammatical errors that it is difficult to grasp the message.

Taking Action © 2018 Solution Tree Press • SolutionTree.com
Visit **go.SolutionTree.com/RTIatWork** to download this free reproducible.

Team Protocol for Common Formative Assessment

Use the following for collaborative analysis and collective response.

1. Consider the assessment task:

    - What worked well?

    - What did not work well?

    - How might you revise the assessment to make it more effective?

2. Analyze these data, and identify areas for targeted response.

    - As a team, which learning targets require more attention?

    - As a team, which students did not master which targets?

    - As a team, which classroom or classrooms require additional support?

    - As an individual teacher, which area was my lowest, and how can I improve?

3. Create a team plan of action to address the needs these data identify, including assessment modifications, curricular modifications, and instructional response.

Sample Data for Persuasive Writing

The following chart is an example of how teams can collect CFA data in a way that shows individual student results and collective classroom results based on specific learning targets. Students need to score a 2 or 3 to demonstrate proficiency.

Student	Making a Claim					Organization and Explanation					Conventions				
	Class 1	Class 2	Class 3	Class 4	Total	Class 1	Class 2	Class 3	Class 4	Total	Class 1	Class 2	Class 3	Class 4	Total
1	3	3	2	3		3	3	1	3		3	3	3	3	
2	3	3	3	3		2	2	3	2		2	3	3	2	
3	3	3	2	3		2	2	1	2		2	3	3	3	
4	3	3	1	3		3	1	1	3		2	2	3	3	
5	3	2	3	2		3	1	2	3		3	3	3	2	
6	3	3	3	3		3	3	3	3		2	3	3	2	
7	3	3	3	3		3	3	3	3		2	3	3	2	
8	3	3	3	3		3	2	3	3		1	1	3	3	
9	3	3	3	3		3	2	3	2		3	2	3	2	
10	3	3	3	3		2	3	2	2		1	2	3	2	
11	3	3	1	3		2	3	1	2		3	3	2	1	
12	3	3	2	2		2	3	1	3		3	1	1	2	
13	2	2	3	3		1	1	2	3		1	2	2	2	
14	3	1	3	3		3	1	2	2		1	1	3	1	
15	3	2	3	3		3	1	2	2		1	2	3	1	
16	3	3	2	3		3	3	1	3		3	3	3	2	
17	3	3	2	2		2	3	1	3		2	3	3	2	
18	3	3	3	2		2	3	2	1		1	3	3	1	
19	3	3	3	3		2	3	2	2		3	2	3	3	
20	3	3	3	3		3	2	2	2		3	3	1	2	
21	3	3	3	3		3	2	3	2		3	2	1	2	
22	3	3	3	3		3	2	2	3		3	1	1	3	
23	3		3	3		3		2	3		2		2	3	
24	3		1			3		1			2		2		
25	3					2					3				
Percent Proficient	100	96	87	100	96	96	77	66	96	84	76	82	83	83	81

Team Response for Common Formative Assessment

After implementing and analyzing a common formative assessment, the team identifies students who need additional time and support, students who are on target (demonstrate minimal mastery), and students who need extension (demonstrate strong mastery and beyond). Agree on an instructional activity for each group. Share lesson-plan outlines and materials with all team members.

Essential standard:		
Need Additional Time and Support	**On Target**	**Need Extension**
Students:	Students:	Students:
Instructional Plan:	Instructional Plan:	Instructional Plan:

Action 4

Give Common End-of-Unit Assessment for Essential Standards

> To begin with the end in mind means to start with a clear understanding of your destination. It means to know where you're going so that you better understand where you are now and so that the steps you take are always in the right direction.
>
> **—Stephen R. Covey**

Once instruction for a unit of study is complete, the team gives the common end-of-unit assessment previously identified on its essential standards chart. As Covey points out in the epigraph, the common end-of-unit assessment clearly defines the "end in mind" and provides the benchmark against which formative assessment data help teachers and students ensure they are moving in the right direction throughout the unit.

In addition, teachers may also occasionally choose to use summative assessments, often referred to as assessments *of* learning, to summarize and verify achievement at a specific moment in time. These summative assessments indicate what students have learned from the instruction provided. In learning-focused classrooms, teachers use all types of assessments to support learning. They provide students with ongoing and consistent formative opportunities to reflect on their learning and decide how best to move forward. They also have multiple summative opportunities to demonstrate proficiency. In turn, teachers are able to continually gather and use data to determine instruction's effectiveness and to identify students who need additional time and support to master the essentials. Since teachers make such important decisions based on assessment data, it is critical that the assessments themselves adhere to professional standards of quality all team members agree to. These include:

- ▶ Clarity of purpose

- ▶ Clarity of learning targets

- ▶ Effective assessment design

- ▶ Calibration of the level of rigor we expect students to demonstrate

Finally, scheduled time and an established process for collaboratively analyzing the assessment results are inherent in the definition of a *common* end-of-unit assessment. Team members share their results to determine the effectiveness of their instruction and to identify students who have not yet achieved mastery of the essential learning outcomes. These students need to participate in Tier 2 interventions to receive additional time and support.

> Scheduled time and established process for collaboratively analyzing the assessment results are inherent in the definition of a *common* end-of-unit assessment.

Here's Why

Simply stated, common end-of-unit assessments are fundamental to the PLC at Work process and to a school's entire system of interventions. They provide the information that identifies the students who need to participate in Tier 2 interventions, as well as the content needed within those interventions. Equally important, these data from common end-of-unit assessments provide a window into the effectiveness of Tier 1 instruction, for both individual teachers and for the team as a whole. Too often, schools fall into the trap of implementing interventions not explicitly linked to classroom instruction. Using data from team-based common end-of-unit assessments ensures interventions and classroom instruction align and, in turn, establishes a firm foundation of support for students who need it most.

Given the importance of common end-of-unit assessments, it is easy to understand why they need to meet standards of high quality. These include the following.

- **Clarity of purpose:** Understanding the purpose and uses for end-of-unit assessments helps both teachers and students understand what is expected when instruction concludes in order to maximize success.

- **Clarity of learning targets:** It is the student-friendly learning targets that delineate the end in mind for the unit and also determine appropriate assessment methods for the end-of-unit assessment.

- **Effective assessment design:** In order for teachers to gather valid and reliable evidence of learning from a common end-of-unit assessment, the assessment design must closely align to the learning targets being assessed and to the instruction these teachers provide, and it must include enough assessment items for each target to certify mastery. The assessment items also must be clearly written and easy for both teachers and students to understand. The goal is to accurately assess what students have learned, not to create a guessing game of expectations.

- **Calibration of the level of rigor we expect students to demonstrate:** Deciding together the level of rigor expected before beginning the unit equips team members to provide instruction that maximizes student success on the end-of-unit assessment. Additionally, when they share data at the conclusion of the unit, teachers can be confident they are comparing apples to apples rather than apples to oranges. Equally important, students feel that the assessment is fair because performance expectations are the same in all classrooms.

In conclusion, teachers actually determine the *what* and *why* of giving a common end-of-unit assessment when they collaboratively select or develop the assessment to include on their essential standards chart. The decisions they make at that time are the ones that determine how effective the assessment is and the quality of data it provides.

Here's How

Fundamental to successfully using common end-of-unit assessments is standardizing the administration process. All teachers on the team must give the assessment within the same time frame and administer it with agreed-on levels of direction, timing, and student support. If they make accommodations for English learners or other students with special needs, those accommodations must be exactly the same in every classroom.

Following assessment administration, the next step is to collect these data in a timely and efficient manner. Data must be formatted in such a way that they show individual student results, specific standard and learning target results—item by item, as well as classroom results. Teachers can easily score, aggregate, and display selected-response items using technology tools. They also need to score open-ended questions using agreed-on scoring guidelines that student work examples support. Lastly, the team must schedule a meeting for analyzing results as soon as possible after teachers administer the assessment. This maximizes the time and opportunity that teachers and students have to act on the results.

At this time, the team is ready to meet. Just as the process for giving a common end-of-unit assessment must be standardized to ensure equity for students, it is also essential to standardize the process teachers use for discussing, analyzing, and responding to the results. Consistently following a standardized protocol helps teams learn to adhere to team norms, maximize use of time, and ensure that all necessary steps to evaluate the assessment, analyze data, and create effective interventions take place.

To that end, any protocol must facilitate identifying individual students needing additional time and support, determining effective instructional practices, discussing strengths and needed revisions of the assessment itself, and preparing for appropriate interventions and extensions.

As with the use of any protocol, utilizing designated roles, such as timekeeper, facilitator, and recorder, can help the team maximize its productivity. Team norms must be established and followed. Careful attention to a standardized protocol and use of effective collaboration strategies result in well-thought-out plans for collectively supporting high levels of learning for all students.

Helpful Tool

The following tool will help you accomplish the work for this essential action.

▶ **"Common Assessment Team Protocol" (page 119):** This protocol is designed to help teacher teams review and discuss common formative or end-of-unit assessment results and how best to support student learning moving forward.

Coaching Tips

Supporting teachers with giving and analyzing common end-of-unit assessments is all about working next to them as they take ownership of the process. The types of actions that teachers often find most useful include helping to proctor classes during the administration of the assessment, assisting with data collection and formatting, providing facilitation support during team meetings, and advocating for team decisions with the leadership team as a whole. Needless to say, the best way to find out what your teams need is to ask them!

Keep in mind that learning to collaborate, share assessment results, and take collective responsibility for student learning challenges is a process. It takes time! Initial efforts don't always go smoothly and require lots of listening and patience on the part of leadership team members. Just as some students require additional time and support to be successful, some teams require additional time and support to become effective. It is the leadership team's role to ensure that teacher teams share a vision for their work's outcomes, to guide and coach teams to that vision, and to celebrate successes, both big and small, along the way.

> Learning to collaborate, share assessment results, and take collective responsibility for student learning challenges is a process.

Common Assessment Team Protocol

This protocol is designed to help teacher teams quickly and efficiently discuss a common assessment. If each teacher reviews his or her own assessment data prior to the team meeting, then the team should be able to collectively complete this activity within a typical team meeting of forty-five to sixty minutes.

1. Which specific students did not demonstrate mastery on which specific standards? (Respond by the student, by the standard, by the target)
2. Which instructional practices proved to be most effective?
3. What patterns can we identify from the student mistakes?
4. How can we improve this assessment?
5. What interventions are needed to provide failed students additional time and support?
6. How will we extend learning for students who have mastered the standard or standards?

Source: Buffum, A., Mattos, M., & Weber, C. (2012). Simplifying response to intervention: Four essential guiding principles. Bloomington, IN: Solution Tree Press.

Action 5

Identify Students for Tier 2 Support by Student, Standard, and Learning Target

I suppose it is tempting, if the only tool you have is a hammer, to treat everything as if it were a nail.

—Abraham H. Maslow

Some students require additional time and support based on the results from the team's common end-of-unit assessment. These additional supports represent Tier 2 interventions—a little more time to master essential standards. The team uses these results to provide Tier 2 interventions organized by student, standard, and learning target in a chart like that in the reproducible "Essential Standards Student Tracking Chart: By the Student, By the Standard, By the Target" (page 123). (Visit **go.SolutionTree.com /RTIatWork** to download all the free reproducibles in this book.)

It is imperative that Tier 2 support is directly related to Tier 1 essential standards. Because teams utilize the team teaching-assessing cycle to provide mid-unit interventions (preventions) at Tier 1, the number of students requiring Tier 2 interventions should be relatively small, hopefully less than 15 percent of the overall students they assess.

The team teaching-assessing cycle is especially effective when dealing with academic content standards that might include learning targets related to knowledge, reasoning, performance, and creating products. In kindergarten as well as in grades 1 and 2, students often acquire discrete skills such as letter-sound recognition, counting and ordering of numbers, and so on. Instruction for these sequential skills may extend over longer periods of time, even entire school years. Since acquiring these skills is ongoing, teachers may use curriculum-based measures (such as oral reading fluency) to identify students in primary grades for Tier 2 help. Tier 2 interventions give students additional time and support with Tier 1 essential standards that teacher teams prioritized.

Here's Why

Essential standards represent the knowledge, skills, and dispositions all students must master to be successful in the current school year, subsequent school years, and in life. Something is essential when the whole cannot exist without that part. While arms are very useful, your heart is truly essential!

While arms are very useful, your heart is truly essential!

Because these prioritized standards are essential and represent the heart of what students must know and be able to do, we must never allow students to flounder short of mastery while the class moves on to the next unit of instruction. Tier 2 interventions provide these students with a little more time and targeted, scaffolded supports that help them to attain proficiency in the essentials.

Here's How

Regardless of the differences in identification processes between ongoing sequential skill development (primary grades) and the mastery of academic content standards (upper grades and secondary), teachers should identify students for Tier 2 support every three weeks at most. Students who are struggling to attain essential standards or skills should not have to wait longer than this for help to arrive. If we wait longer, students sink deeper and deeper into a learning "hole" from which it becomes increasingly difficult to extract them. It is faulty thinking on our part to wait for the benchmark assessment or end-of-quarter grades to find out which students need help. In ten weeks, they can fall so far behind that they never catch up!

All team members must work together to identify students for Tier 2 at grade level or for a particular course. If teams have developed a true sense of collective responsibility, then every member is involved in seeing that all students learn at high levels, not just the ones they teach in homerooms. In many schools, teachers use the teaching-assessing cycle so students in a course or grade level may receive mid-unit preventions from teachers other than their own because they have been regrouped across the grade level for targeted needs. In this scenario, two or three teachers may have worked with a student during the teaching-assessing cycle, and they all discuss how best to meet students' individual needs. In order to take a more holistic, 360-degree view of students, schools also include personnel, such as a counselor, dean, psychologist, or social worker, in the discussion.

Finally, schools should develop a streamlined process for teachers to identify students needing a little more time and support that does not rely on extensive paperwork. We have worked in some schools where teachers admit their reluctance to identify students for Tier 2 help because the paperwork involved is overly time-consuming. Increasingly, we find schools utilizing some kind of technology to streamline the process. Google Docs (www.google.com/docs) offers one of many approaches that allow teachers to quickly and easily identify and schedule students for Tier 2 support. While it is important to record the interventions that students receive, as well as progress-monitoring data indicating how students actually respond to the intervention, it is the school and district leadership's responsibility to be sure this process is not overly time-consuming for teachers. We want teachers to focus on teaching, not completing paperwork.

Helpful Tool

The following tool will help you accomplish the work for this essential action.

▸ **"Essential Standards Student Tracking Chart" (page 123):** Teacher teams can use this chart to record steps toward the mastery of essential standards by tracking progress student by student, standard by standard, and target by target.

Coaching Tips

One of the most important actions the leadership team takes to support teacher teams with identifying students in need of Tier 2 interventions is to ensure that the process is student and teacher friendly, not overly reliant on filling out forms.

One helpful strategy is for leadership team members to role-play a teacher team in the process of identifying students in need of Tier 2 intervention support. They can do this during a schoolwide faculty meeting. To focus everyone's attention on key aspects of the process, it may also be helpful to provide essential questions for follow-up discussion. Sample questions may include:

▶ What data and tools do you see the team using?

▶ How does the team maximize the use of its collaborative time?

▶ How do we inform students about and involve them in Tier 2 participation?

Once teachers have the opportunity to collectively observe and discuss the process, they are ready to begin identifying students on their own. It is important to remember that mastering the process takes time, and leaders should regularly collect feedback from the teams. Continued coaching and facilitation support, as well as regular opportunities to have a voice in streamlining the process, assists teams as they progress toward efficiently and productively identifying students who need Tier 2 help.

This chapter may indeed be the most important part of this book and the RTI process. We should also think of RTI as response to instruction, or RTI² (response to instruction and intervention). Rather than waiting until students fail the summative test and then sending them to Tier 2 intervention, what about finding out which students need additional time and support *before* they fail? What about looking at the classroom as a rehearsal hall in which students receive daily feedback and time to practice that help them to succeed at the final performance, the end-of-unit summative assessment?

> What about finding out which students need additional time and support before they fail?

You may have noticed we haven't mentioned *screen for prior skills* on the team teaching-assessing cycle (see figure 3.5, page 105). While we believe this to be a powerful part of the process, we are concerned that all the details associated with it may overwhelm teams. Therefore, we usually introduce this concept last, as if it were the cherry on top of the cake.

These prior skills are already identified on the reproducible "Essential Standards Chart," in the column Prerequisite Skills. As teams become more familiar with the team teaching-assessing cycle, we envision them creating small pretests to determine which students have the necessary academic vocabulary and prerequisite skills needed for the new unit of instruction. Using the information from these pretests, teachers can introduce vocabulary and prerequisite skills as sponge activities at the beginning of class instruction to provide scaffolding into the new learning several weeks before the actual unit begins. Again, the best intervention is prevention!

Essential Standards Student Tracking Chart
By the Student, By the Standard, By the Target

Student Name	Essential Standards									
	Standard or Outcome	Target 1	Target 2	Target 3	Target 4	Standard or Outcome	Target 1	Target 2	Target 3	Target 4

Conclusion

While reading this chapter, you may have been thinking, "I've heard all this before—this is nothing new." If so, we would remind you of the handwashing analogy at the beginning of this chapter. While you may have heard similar ideas, is every grade-level or course-alike team in your school doing them systematically? We believe that the team teaching-assessing cycle is the absolute bedrock principle that all RTI rests on, not just something we do when our teams want to create essemtial standards unit maps.

In the next chapter, we discuss the essential actions we must coordinate across the entire school rather than via each collaborative team, independently of one another.

CHAPTER 4

Tier 1 Schoolwide Essential Actions

> Leadership and learning are indispensable to each other.
>
> **—John F. Kennedy**

In this chapter, we focus on the top-left portion of the RTI at Work pyramid (see figure 4.1, page 126).

- ▶ This section of the pyramid is part of Tier 1, which represents what *all* students receive as part of their core instruction. Any action or outcome placed in this box is going to be part of the core instructional program for every student.

- ▶ Because it's on the left side, it represents outcomes that educators must coordinate across the entire school. Neither grade levels nor departments should make these decisions in isolation, nor should the administration dictate these decisions. At most schools, the school leadership team—as described in chapter 2 (page 33)—takes lead responsibility for these essential outcomes. At a smaller school, these school staff can work on these decisions collectively.

We must successfully address three essential actions in this portion of the pyramid.

1. Ensure universal access to essential grade-level curriculum.

2. Identify and teach essential academic and social behaviors.

3. Provide preventions to proactively support student success.

In this chapter, we examine each of these critical actions in depth.

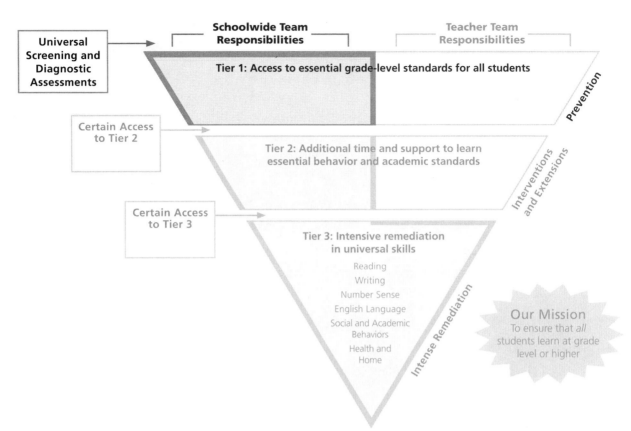

FIGURE 4.1: Focus on Tier 1 schoolwide essential actions.

Action 1

Ensure Access to Essential Grade-Level Curriculum

> No longer do students planning to work after high school need a different and less rigorous curriculum than those planning to go to college.
>
> **—American Diploma Project**

In order for all students to learn at high levels, educators must teach at high levels. In chapter 2, we defined high levels of learning as *high school plus*, meaning every student graduates from high school with the skills and knowledge required to continue learning. Students must master essential grade-level curriculum each year to achieve this outcome. While students might not master every standard introduced in the curriculum, *all* students must learn the academic standards and behaviors deemed essential for success in the next grade or course.

In chapter 3, we outlined a process in which teacher teams work collaboratively at Tier 1 to identify essential academic outcomes. Once they determine these critical standards, the school must guarantee that teachers teach them to students as part of their core instruction. Students can't learn new essential curriculum if their Tier 1 core instruction consists of below-grade-level remedial coursework, or if they are pulled

All students must learn the academic standards and behaviors deemed essential for success in the next grade or course.

from instruction on these standards to receive interventions. Schools must provide interventions *in addition* to Tier 1 essential grade-level instruction, not in place of it.

To achieve this outcome, schools must purposefully and strategically create a master schedule that ensures all students have access to essential grade-level curriculum, while also providing targeted students with supplemental and intensive interventions when necessary. Because a school's master schedule impacts every grade level, department, and program in the school, creating such a schedule requires a schoolwide collaborative effort. Schools must consider coordination between classroom teachers, specialist staff, special education services, and classified support services (such as lunch and transportation schedules). This is why a school's leadership team, which comprises representation across the school, is in the best position to take lead responsibility for this ongoing task.

> Schools must provide interventions in addition to Tier 1 essential grade-level instruction, not in place of it.

Here's Why

When we work with educators, we often ask this question: "If you take a student out of grade-level curriculum and place him or her in a remedial class so the student is taught below grade level all day, where will this student end up at the close of the school year?"

The resounding answer we receive is: "Below grade level!" Research, evidence, and common sense would confirm this reality. We then ask if all the students in their school currently have access to essential grade-level curriculum. More often than not, the answer is "no."

This honest assessment is not a surprise, as most schools perpetuate a traditional 19th century master schedule—designed for only a select few to reach postsecondary education. The purpose of secondary schooling in the United States was first debated and determined in the late 1800s. Reflecting on its purpose, Harvard president Charles Eliot, chair of a national commission on the topic, reported to Congress in 1893:

> Their main function is to prepare for the duties of life that small proportion of all the children in the country—a proportion small in number, but very important to the welfare of the nation—who show themselves able to *profit* by an education prolonged to the eighteenth year, and whose parents are able to support them while they remain in school so long. (as cited in Dorn, 1996, p. 36)

In such a system, educators sort students into tracks based primarily on perceived student ability and prior academic success. They place students deemed to have greater academic potential in higher tracks that prepare them for college, and place students in lower tracks to prepare them for immediate entry into a vocational trade. If a student struggled in a higher track, the solution was not to provide additional time and support but instead, to lower the student's academic expectations and demote him or her to a lower track. While this master schedule design denied most students access to postsecondary opportunities, the economic reality at that time was undeniably different. Most Americans either farmed or worked in factories throughout the 20th century—careers that did not require a high school diploma nor a college degree, so ensuring high levels of learning for all students was not necessary or desirable.

While the economic demands in the United States have changed dramatically since the 1800s, the practice of tracking students in school has not. As Jeannie Oakes (2005) finds in her landmark study *Keeping Track: How Schools Structure Inequality, Second Edition*:

> The deep structure of tracking remains uncannily robust. Most middle and high schools still sort students into classes at different levels based on judgments of student "ability." This sorting continues to disadvantage those in lower track classes. Such students have less access to high-status knowledge, fewer opportunities to engage in stimulating learning activities, and classroom relationships less likely to foster engagement with teachers, peers, and learning. (p. 4)

Unfortunately, many schools continue to "intervene" when students struggle by merely lowering these students' academic expectations. Students are not succeeding in their grade-level algebra 1 class? Place them in a two-year algebra class. Some students are still struggling? Remove them from algebra altogether and place them in a remedial mathematics class. A few students are still struggling? Perhaps they have dropped far enough behind to qualify for special education. At the elementary level, educators demonstrate these same practices when they identify a student's ability as too low to succeed and beg the administration to get the student out of the classroom during certain times to work "at his or her level."

Research proves that ability grouping is an ineffective instructional practice.

When we ask educators why they continue the practice of tracking students, they often claim that they are differentiating for individual student needs. Yet research proves that ability grouping is an ineffective instructional practice. Hattie's (2009) meta-analysis on ability grouping finds that the practice of tracking has minimal effects on student learning—producing just a 0.12 standard deviation—and can have *profoundly* negative effects on equity, as the students that educators perceive to have the lowest ability are most often minorities, English learners, and students from poverty (Hattie, 2009). Unless a school discontinues remedial tracks of core instruction and instead, purposefully designs a master schedule that ensures all students access to rigorous curriculum, there is no level of supplemental or intensive interventions that can compensate for what these students are missing at Tier 1.

Here's How

There is no universal, one-size-fits-all master schedule that ensures all students access to essential grade-level curriculum.

There is no universal, one-size-fits-all master schedule that ensures all students access to essential grade-level curriculum. The basic structures of an elementary and secondary master schedule have significant differences. Additional factors that impact a school's scheduling needs include the school's size, demographics, available resources, and state or province and district requirements. So while we can't offer a specific model schedule to implement, we can provide the following five-step process to assist the leadership team's efforts.

1. Identify essential standards.

2. Dedicate specific times in the master schedule for teaching essential standards.

3. Eliminate below-grade-level learning tracks.

4. Guarantee all students receive essential grade-level curriculum as part of their Tier 1 core instruction.

5. Identify and provide preventions for students needing Tier 1 support in grade-level curriculum.

Identify Essential Standards

If the goal is to ensure that all students have access to essential curriculum as part of their core instruction, then a school must have absolute clarity on the skills, knowledge, and behaviors students must master in each grade and course and agree that every teacher is committed to teaching these standards aligned to the teacher's teaching assignment. While teacher teams take lead responsibility in determining the specific essential standards for their grade or course, the leadership team has important responsibilities too. These include:

▸ Provide each teacher team with the time and resources necessary to successfully complete this task

▸ Monitor each team's progress to ensure it completes this outcome

▸ Determine a process for vertical articulation to ensure that the essential learning outcomes from one grade or course provide students with the prerequisite skills, knowledge, and behaviors needed to succeed in the next grade or course

▸ Coordinate with specialist staff, including special education and English-development staff, to ensure that they clearly understand the essential grade-level standards for each grade or course for which they support students

▸ Plan for revisions (As discussed in chapter 3, identifying essential standards is not a singular act but a continuous process. Because state or provincial and district curriculum guides, textbook adoptions, student needs, and site staffing undoubtedly change over time, teams should review their essential standards annually and revise them as needed.)

Dedicate Specific Times in the Master Schedule for Teaching Essential Standards

Once a school creates a guaranteed and viable curriculum, it must dedicate enough time in the school's master schedule to teach that curriculum effectively. At the elementary level, this requires the leadership team to designate specific times every day or week to teach essential curriculum at each grade level. Educators should consider these blocks of time sacred, in which they keep classroom interruptions to an absolute minimum and don't pull students for interventions. Because essential standards do not represent all core curriculum to be taught, the times educators dedicate for teaching essential standards do not represent all the time allocated for Tier 1 instruction in the school's master schedule.

At the secondary level, multiple pathways of learning usually lead to postsecondary education, such as advanced placement (AP) classes, the International Baccalaureate (IB) program, vocational programs, and career pathway academies. Secondary educators frequently ask us if ensuring high levels of learning means all students must be on the highest collegiate track that the school offers. Or can a student meet this outcome taking vocational coursework? We recommend that all students successfully complete at least the minimum sequence of coursework required for a realistic opportunity to apply to a four-year university.

> **We recommend that all students successfully complete at least the minimum sequence of coursework required for a realistic opportunity to apply to a four-year university.**

For example, the state of California has minimum requirements to apply to a state college. In mathematics, a student must successfully complete the equivalent of algebra 2 to apply to a state college—achieving less would disqualify him or her from even applying to a state-sponsored four-year university. In this case, we recommend that a high school offer no track or sequence of mathematics classes that restricts a student's ability to successfully pass algebra 2 by the time he or she graduates. Anything less would not meet the goal of ensuring all students access to high levels of learning.

Obviously, high schools should continue to offer pathways that go beyond this minimal expectation, such as mathematics tracks that exceed algebra 2, and use their Tier 2 supports to assist students in these classes. Offering vocational pathways is equally acceptable. By ensuring that all students have access to the minimum sequence of classes required to apply to a university, the school gives every student the option of deciding his or her own path—university, community college, trade school, or an internship process. We find that many schools currently remove students for college-prep coursework and place them into vocational tracks, because they deem the student incapable of succeeding on a college-prep track. Vocational pathways can be an outstanding pathway to postsecondary education, but students should leave high school with the academic skills and behaviors necessary to succeed in university and vocational settings.

> **Students should leave high school with the academic skills and behaviors necessary to succeed in university and vocational settings.**

Once the leadership team determines, at each grade level, the required minimum coursework necessary for students to be at grade level on a college-prep learning track, it should then allocate the classes (course sections) necessary to ensure all students can take these or higher-level courses.

Eliminate Below-Grade-Level Learning Tracks

Most schools have what we refer to as *phantom tracks*. It is a learning track that the school knows is below grade level but doesn't call it that; nor does the school usually tell students on this track (or their parents) that they are being taught below grade level and do not have a realistic chance of reaching grade level. For example, we have seen high schools place most of their ninth-grade students in a grade-level algebra 1 course, but then place their lowest mathematics students in an alternative class with a modified name, like *algebra basic*. This course has *algebra* in the name, giving the impression that these students are in an algebra class. But in reality, the curriculum for the course is below grade-level remedial mathematics. From the first day students are in the class, the school knows they will not end the year prepared for the next grade-level mathematics class.

Sadly, the most prevalent and pervasive example of replacing grade-level expectations with remedial core instruction is the way many schools and districts implement traditional special education. While a vast majority of special education students will be independent adults someday—and thus must reach *high school plus*—often their IEP goals and core instructional program focus on remedial outcomes. This is especially the case for students placed in self-contained special day classes. Educators often claim that the school is legally bound to the student's IEP, which requires the student receive these services, to justify these practices. But it is the school and the education experts in the building who primarily write the IEP, so they have both the authority and obligation to recommend revisions to the plan when a special education student is not achieving.

The school's leadership team must honestly examine every class and track provided as part of its core instructional program, and revise or eliminate those that deny access to essential grade-level curriculum. We are not suggesting that some students won't need intensive remediation or special education services built into their daily schedule, but educators must provide this support in addition to their essential grade-level curriculum, not in place of it.

Guarantee All Students Receive Essential Grade-Level Curriculum as Part of Their Tier 1 Core Instruction

Creating a school's master schedule is like being asked to plan a month-long vacation in a weekend's worth of time—you want to do lots of things, but you don't have nearly enough time and resources to fit it all in. When creating a school's master schedule, the leadership team's first priority must be to ensure that every student has access to essential grade-level curriculum. When we say *have access*, we are not suggesting that students are merely given the *opportunity* to take college-prep classes or that the school *hopes* educators are teaching students essential grade-level curriculum. Instead, the leadership team creates processes to assign all students to Tier 1 classes and coursework that meets or exceeds essential grade-level standards and monitors that educators are actually following through. Achieving this goal takes vigilance and accountability. The school staff that schedule students into their core classes must be involved in this process and committed to ensuring this outcome for every student.

It's important to point out that while all students must have access to essential grade-level curriculum, this access does not necessarily have to be provided in a general education classroom. The goal should always be to serve students in the least restrictive environment, but it is likely that some students may have unique learning needs that might require a more specialized classroom setting. When this is the case, these students must still master the same essential curriculum. This is why it is critical that regular education teachers, special education staff, and other specialist staff collaborate together when identifying, teaching, and assessing essential standards. Building shared knowledge on what students must learn and taking collective responsibility for student success are foundational requirements for an effective multitiered system of supports.

Finally, we define the phrase *all students* as those who can or might be independent adults someday. For the very small percentage of students with profound cognitive disabilities, the school should work with highly trained professional experts and the family to determine how to best maximize the student's abilities and teach the skills necessary for the student to live as independent an adult life as possible. But these individualized outcomes will most likely fall short of our definition of high levels of learning, so these students might not require access to all the essential grade-level curriculum as part of their core instructional program.

Identify and Provide Interventions for Students Needing Tier 1 Support in Grade-Level Curriculum

Most schools remove students from grade-level coursework because they believe these students lack the prerequisite skills needed to succeed. This concern is valid. There will undoubtedly be students who are significantly below grade level in foundational skills, including reading, writing, number sense, or proficiency in the school's native language. While tracking these students in remedial classes is not the answer, throwing them into grade-level curriculum to either "sink or swim" is almost as detrimental.

A critical practice in the RTI process is universal screening. Its primary purpose is to proactively identify students who need intensive interventions so educators can begin these supports immediately. A student should not have to fail Tier 1 and Tier 2 to qualify for Tier 3 support, when the school can realistically predict that some students need this level of support due to dramatic gaps in their foundational knowledge, skills, or behavior. (We go deeper into the specifics of how to conduct universal screening in chapter 7 on page 227.)

While universal screening has traditionally focused on identifying students for Tier 3 interventions, we should also use it to provide these students additional time and support in their Tier 1 core instruction. The school leadership team should assume that the students identified for Tier 3 interventions also need additional support at Tier 1 when learning essential grade-level curriculum. Examples of the proactive, preventive core support can be, but are not limited to the following.

> The leadership team should ensure that the most at-risk students have access to the best-trained teachers in their area of need.

- ▸ **Strategic teacher assignments:** Douglas Reeves's (2009b) research concludes that one of a school's most effective learning strategies is to have highly trained teachers work with students most at risk. Unfortunately, many schools do the exact opposite. According to the National Partnership for Teaching in At-Risk Schools, "Not only do the teachers of low-income students tend to be more poorly trained in the subject they teach, they also are far more likely to have significantly less teaching experience" (Mayer, Mullens, & Moore, 2000, p. 3). Part of creating a master schedule is determining teacher assignments—what classes, subjects, and students educators teach. The leadership team should ensure that the most at-risk students have access to the best-trained teachers in their area of need.

- ▸ **Designed classroom accommodations:** Accommodations are targeted supports that help students access information and demonstrate what they know. For example, we can assume that a student reading multiple years below grade level might struggle with reading grade-level textbooks independently. Providing this student with alternative ways to access this content, such as an audio textbook, can be a reasonable way to provide the student access to essential grade-level content. Or if a student's writing ability is significantly below grade level, and a grade-level assessment requires the student to write an essay to demonstrate subject content knowledge, it could be appropriate to allow the student to demonstrate his or her knowledge through an oral presentation.

When providing these supports, it is critical that educators offer students accommodations, not modifications. Accommodations are supports that help students access and learn essential grade-level curriculum, while modifications alter the actual learning goal, usually lowering the bar to make it easier for students to succeed. Because essential standards represent the minimum a student must learn for future success, lowering the rigor on these standards would not meet the definition of *high levels of learning*.

> **Sheltered classes:** Offering sheltered classes is an effective practice for supporting students with foundational gaps, especially in English language. For example, if a targeted student group has significant gaps in English-language development—including a lack of academic vocabulary and basic reading and writing structures—it could be beneficial to group these students together sometimes for targeted Tier 1 core instruction.
>
> A highly trained teacher in the students' area of need can proactively plan lessons that take into account the English-skills gaps and compensate for them through lesson design. Again, it is important to stress that if students are placed in an alternative Tier 1 core setting, the essential standards are the same as in the regular classroom. What is different is how educators teach and support students, but the essential learning targets are the same.
>
> **"Push-in" supports:** A common practice to support students in Tier 1 core instruction is to "push in" specialized staff to support targeted students in their regular education classrooms. When done effectively, this service can provide embedded Tier 1 support for students who need intensive help in learning essential grade-level standards.

The leadership team is probably not the best group to make decisions determining the specific Tier 1 supports for each identified student. Instead, the school intervention team would be best qualified to take the lead. (We discuss the school intervention team in depth in chapter 7.) The process should also be a joint effort between regular education and special education staff. Special education teachers often have training and expertise in designing accommodations for students, while regular education teachers have a deeper knowledge of subject-specific content. Schools need both areas of expertise to plan effective Tier 1 preventions.

The leadership team's responsibility is to take support recommendations from the intervention team and allocate the resources and scheduling necessary to achieve these outcomes. It then regularly evaluates if these resource allocations are actually working.

> When providing these supports, it is critical that educators offer students accommodations, not modifications.

Helpful Tools

The following tools will help you accomplish the work for this essential action.

- **"Ensuring Access to Essential Grade-Level Curriculum" (page 137):** This activity provides a template to help teams identify and discuss their responsibilities regarding access, assessing the current reality, and gathering and presenting recommendations.

- *It's About Time: Planning Interventions and Extensions in Elementary School* **(Buffum & Mattos, 2015):** This book features model elementary schools that offer explanations on how they make their schedules work. While there is no universal master schedule that can achieve the outcomes previously outlined, many schools successfully achieve these outcomes without lengthening their school day, receiving additional funding, or hiring additional staff.

- *It's About Time: Planning Interventions and Extensions in Secondary School* **(Mattos & Buffum, 2015):** This book offers chapters from model secondary schools outlining how these schools make their schedules work.

- **AllThingsPLC (www.allthingsplc.info):** This website offers dozens of examples of model schools that successfully created master schedules, giving all students access to essential grade-level standards and intervention. The resources include a description of each school and contact information. (Visit **go.SolutionTree.com/RTIatWork** to access live links to the websites mentioned in this book.)

Coaching Tips

> School leadership team members should be the school's lead learners.

School leadership team members should be the school's lead learners. A guiding principle we repeatedly emphasize in this book is that achieving these essential actions is an ongoing process, and not singular acts to accomplish. The steps are difficult to achieve, as they represent dramatic shifts in how schools have operated for decades. A school does not get there overnight, nor is it likely that all its initial actions work perfectly.

Cycles of collective inquiry and action research capture the essence of PLC at Work. Professionals first learn together about their current reality and better practices to improve student learning. Then they apply what they have learned. Finally, they collect evidence to determine if these changes have achieved the goal—more students learning at higher levels. They validate actions that are working and discontinue practices and policies that are not improving learning. Then the cycle begins again.

As site practitioners, we can honestly admit that we never developed the perfect master schedule, but we did come closer and closer to this goal over time. Keeping in mind the guiding principle previously described, the leadership team begins its work, reviewing the process for ensuring access to essential grade-level curriculum for all students. In doing so, it quickly becomes clear that every step in the process directly impacts the day-to-day lives of teachers and support staff. It is critical, therefore, to remember that gaining people's commitment to achieving schoolwide goals requires their involvement in decisions that affect their daily work experiences.

How, then, should the leadership team proceed? To begin, it needs to realize that increasing involvement in decisions also means sharing information, authority, and responsibility. The key to effectively facilitating involvement in decisions is to determine the maximum level of involvement *appropriate* to the situation. Types of involvement to consider include the following.

- **None:** In these situations, the leadership team makes the decision and announces it.

- **Recommendations from individuals:** In these situations, the leadership team randomly solicits input from a variety of individual stakeholders and then makes the decision.

- **Recommendations from teams:** In these situations, the leadership team seeks input from all stakeholders via their participation in team meetings. Each team forwards its recommendations, and then the leadership team makes the final decision.

- **Consensus:** In these situations, the leadership team facilitates opportunities for all stakeholders to personally participate in the decision-making process. Once they achieve a shared understanding of the situation, and all voices are heard, the leadership team facilitates a public process for stakeholders to show their level of support. When the whole group's view is apparent to all, they have reached consensus. At this point, all stakeholders must support the decision.

There is no single right way to make decisions. The leadership team needs to carefully consider the following questions to determine how best to make decisions.

- How much do stakeholders need to be involved in order to support the decision?

- How much time is available to make the decision?

- How important is the decision to the stakeholders?

- Who has information or expertise to maximize the quality of the decision?

- How capable (currently) are stakeholders in participating as decision makers?

- What is the potential for using this decision-making opportunity to strengthen the school culture of collaboration and shared leadership?

Clearly, there are benefits and risks to each level of involvement. Therefore, it is imperative that the leadership team carefully considers all aspects of each step in the process for ensuring access to essential grade-level curriculum. Once team members determine the maximum appropriate level of involvement for each step, including a designated lead from the leadership team and expectations and desired outcomes, then they can determine the time line and deadline for completing the work. If committees are formed, committee members must be informed of their role (level of involvement) in the decision-making process.

The process and steps this section outlined provide an excellent vehicle for building the capacity of all stakeholders to participate effectively in the decision-making process. Teachers and support staff members gain understanding of schoolwide challenges, broaden their perspectives beyond individual classroom walls, and learn to accept collective responsibility for all students. In turn, shared leadership becomes the school norm and allows the leadership team to effectively tap stakeholders' expertise throughout RTI implementation.

Ensuring Access to Essential Grade-Level Curriculum

Review all leadership team responsibilities. Designate a team member (or two) to form and lead a committee of stakeholders for discussing each responsibility, assessing the current reality, and gathering and presenting recommendations. Designate a time frame and deadline for each committee. Reach consensus on decisions and action steps, with the understanding that all decisions and actions must be revisited and re-evaluated for effectiveness over time.

Leadership Team Responsibilities	Leadership Team Lead	Current Reality	Committee Input	Time Frame for Committee Work	Decisions and Action Steps
1. Identify essential standards.					
2. Dedicate specific times in the master schedule for teaching essential standards.					
3. Eliminate below-grade-level learning tracks.					
4. Guarantee all students receive essential grade-level curriculum as part of their Tier 1 core instruction.					
5. Identify and provide interventions for students needing Tier 1 support in grade-level curriculum.					

Action 2

Identify and Teach Essential Academic and Social Behaviors

> We are what we repeatedly do. Excellence, then is not an act but a habit.
>
> **—Will Durant**

The second essential action for the leadership team at Tier 1 is to identify schoolwide academic and social behaviors. Just as a school must identify the academic standards all students have to learn for future success, it is equally important that the school identifies and teaches the critical behaviors and dispositions students must demonstrate for future success. Instead of leaving this task up to each teacher or teacher team to determine, the entire school should coordinate this process, and every grade, class, and area of campus should demonstrate these behaviors.

We often share the following story to illustrate the need for schoolwide coordination of essential behaviors. During Mike Mattos's first month as principal in 2004, he surveyed the staff on ways that the administration could better support student learning. The staff's number-one concern was that too many students were tardy to class. As a first step in addressing the problem, Mike called into his office the ten students who had been late to class the most the previous year and asked them what seemed to be a simple question: "Why are you late to class so much?"

The first student responded, "Which teacher?" This response surprised Mike, as the school had a clearly delineated tardy policy that spelled out exactly what the staff response would be each time a student was tardy. So Mike asked the student to explain what he meant by "Which teacher?" The student continued:

> In Mrs. Smith's class, her rule is you must be in your seat, with your materials out of your backpack and on your desk, quiet and ready to learn by the time the tardy bell starts to ring. I can be quiet and in my seat when the bell rings, but if my materials are not out, she will mark [me] tardy. I had most of my tardy marks in her class last year. Now in Mr. Jones's class, he says we have to be in the room by the time the bell is done ringing. I can be jumping through the doorframe of his room as the bell stops ringing, and I'm considered on time. I was only tardy a few times to his class last year. And Mr. Mattos, I should not tell you this . . . but Mr. Anderson does not take roll, so he never catches if we are tardy. Look . . . I had no tardy marks in his class last year.

The other nine students told similar stories. In reality, the school did not have a schoolwide tardy policy—it had fifty-seven teachers with fifty-seven slightly different policies, including at least one teacher who did not seem to value or enforce the expectation of timeliness. This lack of staff agreement on what constitutes a student being on time not only confused the students but made it virtually impossible to effectively teach this behavior schoolwide or intervene collectively when students failed to meet this expectation.

We are not suggesting that all teachers onsite must have the exact same classroom rules and expectations. Undoubtedly, students' developmental needs and abilities are going to be different for kindergarteners than for fifth graders. Also, classroom structures and activities vary greatly between a secondary physical education class compared to a regular mathematics class. For these reasons, allowing teachers to have some personalized classroom expectations is necessary. But some behaviors and dispositions are universal; that is, they are not grade level or course specific. Instead, they are essential for success everywhere on campus and beyond. These behaviors can be categorized into two categories: (1) academic behaviors and (2) social behaviors.

1. **Academic behaviors:** In addition to academic skills and knowledge, some academic behaviors are critical to developing a successful learner.

   - *Metacognition*—Knowledge and beliefs about thinking

   - *Self-concept*—A student's belief in his or her abilities

   - *Self-monitoring*—The ability to plan and prepare for learning

   - *Motivation*—The ability to initiate and maintain interest in tasks

   - *Strategy*—Techniques for organizing and memorizing knowledge

   - *Volition*—The efforts and techniques needed to stay motivated and engaged in learning. Many educators refer to this as demonstrating *grit*.

2. **Social behaviors:** Success in a school and work environment requires the ability to consistently demonstrate socially appropriate behaviors, including a student's ability to self-monitor—

   - Responsible verbal and physical interactions with peers and adults

   - Appropriate language

   - Respect for property and materials

   - Independently staying on a required task

   - Regular attendance

> Success in a school and work environment requires the ability to consistently demonstrate socially appropriate behaviors.

For many students, parents first teach and reinforce these behaviors at home. Many parents expect their children to respect their elders and siblings, keep their hands and bodies to themselves, share with others, take turns, solve disagreements with their words instead of their fists, and not abuse their toys or family belongings in order to teach social behaviors. The home often expects children to complete assigned chores or memorize their home address and telephone number to develop academic behaviors like motivation and responsibility. And in many cases, parents teach specific scholarly behaviors needed to succeed in school. They take their children to purchase school supplies before school starts, help them organize these materials, check daily for homework, set up the best home conditions to study, and require their children to demonstrate the effort needed to succeed.

Equally true, some students come from home environments where parents don't teach these behaviors and, in some cases, model behaviors counterproductive to success in school. For a child who watches a parent physically abuse a family member over a disagreement, it would make sense for that student to model the same behavior over a disagreement on the playground. Likewise, students who grow up in an unsafe neighborhood might have parents who teach them that walking away from a disagreement is a sign of weakness that only promotes future bullying. In regard to academic behaviors, many parents of at-risk students did not excel in school, so it is difficult to teach scholarly behaviors that they never mastered. Finally, some parents would love to check their children's homework every night, but working a second job to pay the rent is a more important need for the family.

In spite of these realities, many schools either consider teaching academic and social behaviors primarily the parents' responsibility or fall into the trap of exclusively applying negative consequences to students who misbehave without teaching the desired behaviors in the first place. This approach is akin to having a school zero-tolerance policy on illiteracy and devising an increasingly negative set of consequences for students who lack the ability to read, all the while never actually teaching struggling readers how to read. If educators want their students to demonstrate the social and academic behaviors needed to succeed in school, then they must first identify these behaviors, systematically teach them, and be prepared to give some students additional time and support until they master them.

Here's Why

Effective educators know that a successful classroom begins with effective classroom management. Decades of research back this universal truth. The Effective Schools research, from Larry Lezotte, Wilbur Brookover, George Weber, and Ronald Edmonds, finds that a common characteristic and an essential correlate of highly effective schools is a safe and orderly environment conducive to teaching and learning (Effective Schools, n.d.).

Research also confirms that mastering academic and social behaviors is not only required in school but is also critical for success in the 21st century workplace. Due to an ever-increasing competitive global economy, successful businesses have moved from a hierarchical leadership structure with layers of management to a more "flattened" organizational structure in which employees work in teams that take a project from concept to completion. Due to this flattening out of the organizational structure, employees are expected to take greater responsibility for their work (Jerald, 2009). This means employees must be able to organize and self-monitor their work, hold themselves accountable to complete tasks and meet deadlines, and collaborate with others.

Luckily, our profession also has a tremendous base of research on how to systematically ensure students master essential behaviors. Schoolwide Positive Behavior Supports (SWPBS; Simonsen, Sugai, & Negron, 2008) is a proactive, systematic approach for

> Effective educators know that a successful classroom begins with effective classroom management.

establishing the school culture and individualized behavior supports needed for schools to be effective learning environments for all students. Specifically, SWPBS advocates that schools identify clear and measurable behavior outcomes, collect and use data to guide their decisions, implement evidence-based practices, and develop systems to ensure that practices are implemented across the school and sustained over time.

Like response to intervention, SWPBS is often represented in the shape of a pyramid (figure 4.2).

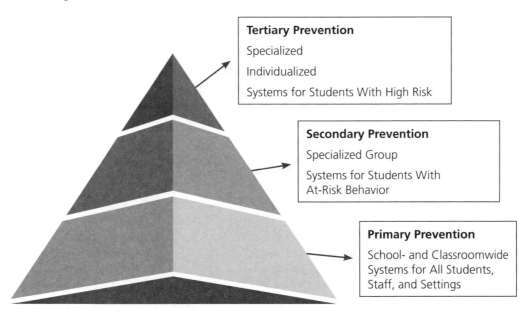

FIGURE 4.2: SWPBS pyramid.

The base of the pyramid represents primary preventions—schoolwide efforts to teach and positively reinforce the academic and social behaviors students need to succeed in school. As students demonstrate at-risk behavior, teachers tier support to provide targeted, supplemental help at the Tier 2 secondary level and highly individualized, intensive behavior interventions at the Tier 3 tertiary level.

Like PLC and RTI, SWPBS is not a program but a process. It does not endorse or dictate a specific behavior curriculum, assessment product, or intervention program, but instead creates processes that empower site educators to make critical decisions based on students' specific learning needs.

We believe that PLCs, RTI, and SWPBS are perfectly complementary processes. PLCs focus on creating a learning-centered school culture and the collaborative structures necessary to achieve the goal of improved student learning. RTI at Work focuses on how to create a tiered process of academic interventions, which would prove most helpful to schools functioning as a PLC in their efforts to answer the question, "How will we respond when students don't learn?"

We believe that PLCs, RTI, and SWPBS are perfectly complementary processes.

However, RTI has not traditionally addressed exactly how to teach academic and social behaviors or how to intervene when students need additional behavioral support. Luckily, this is the focus of SWPBS. Finally, RTI and SWPBS require a learning-centered school culture and collaborative structures to be effective. While RTI and SWPBS do not describe exactly how to do this, PLCs do. So a PLC school should not view RTI and SWPBS as two programs to be implemented but instead, as complementary tools for achieving the same outcome—ensuring high levels of learning for every student.

Here's How

As mentioned in the previous section, the SWPBS research does not endorse or dictate a specific behavior curriculum, assessment product, or intervention program but instead recommends schoolwide processes to identify, teach, and support students in learning essential behaviors. Based on this research and our experience as practitioners, we recommend the following seven steps. Visit **go.SolutionTree.com /RTIatWork** for a free reproducible version of this information.

1. Assign a team, committee, or task force to lead the school's focus on academic and social behaviors.

2. Learn together.

3. Identify a limited number of essential academic and social behaviors.

4. Determine how students will demonstrate mastery of each essential behavior.

5. Design a process to systematically teach essential behaviors across the school.

6. Design targeted privileges and recognitions to promote positive behavior.

7. Monitor essential social and academic behaviors.

Assign a Team, Committee, or Task Force to Lead the School's Focus on Academic and Social Behaviors

If teaching essential behaviors should be a schoolwide effort, then a group made up of schoolwide representatives should lead the process. Because the school's leadership team is purposefully made up of representatives from every grade level or department, this team could then take the lead responsibility in organizing the school's focus on behavior.

Because the school leadership team already has so many responsibilities, some schools find that forming a behavior committee is a more effective way to study, design, promote, and monitor the school's behavior efforts. In the PLC process, a committee is typically a standing body with responsibility for a particular aspect of the school—for example, the behavior committee, the technology committee, and so on. Committees typically continue to function from year to year (Mattos et al., 2016).

Still other schools form a behavior task force to study the topic and report back to the stakeholders with recommendations regarding how to proceed. A task force is typically a temporary group that focuses on a single issue or task. Leaders charge members to investigate options and build shared knowledge on the issue in question, develop recommendations, and help build consensus for their proposals (Mattos et al., 2016). Finally, for smaller faculties it might make the most sense to use faculty meeting time to identify schoolwide behaviors.

Regardless of the format, the ultimate responsibility to ensure a school identifies and teaches essential academic and social behaviors rests with the school's leadership team. They can directly lead the process or delegate the process to another group. But if the leadership team determines that a committee or task force is desirable, it is still responsible for:

> Ensuring that this behavior subcommittee is clear on the desired outcomes

> Providing the time and resources needed to achieve these goals

> Monitoring that goals are being achieved

> Making revisions to the process as needed

> The ultimate responsibility to ensure a school identifies and teaches essential academic and social behaviors rests with the school's leadership team.

Learn Together

Staff opinions should not be the basis for identifying a school's essential behaviors and coming up with a "these are a few of our favorite things" list of outcomes. Professionals base their decisions on research and evidence. In other words, a school should make decisions based on research that demonstrates that a practice has a high likelihood of working or provides evidence that demonstrates the practice is actually working. Therefore, to determine schoolwide essential behaviors, a school could:

> Study relevant educational research on the essential behaviors required for future academic success

> Review research on the behaviors required to succeed in the 21st century workplace

> Research the stages of developmental readiness for specific adolescent behaviors

> Contact and visit model SWPBS schools

> Learn about the cultural norms of the school community

> Access the reproducible "A Data Picture of Our School" in *Learning by Doing* (DuFour, et al., 2016). The leadership team can use this powerful tool to identify strengths and concerns regarding student success across the school.

> Create a behavior "current reality" picture of your school (What do your school's disciplinary data say about your students' behavior needs?)

Identify a Limited Number of Essential Academic and Social Behaviors

Based on what educators learn in the previous step, the school should identify the specific social and academic behaviors all students must learn and consistently demonstrate. The leadership team, behavior committee, or task force could create a draft proposal and then bring it to the entire faculty for input and to build consensus. Alternately, they could dedicate staff meeting time to creating a proposal together.

These essential behaviors should be stated in the positive, meaning the essential behaviors are the actions the school wants its students to demonstrate. Traditionally, schools often write school behavior rules in the negative.

▶ Don't be late to class.

▶ Don't bully others.

▶ Don't steal.

▶ Don't interrupt class instruction.

It is better to teach the positive.

▶ Be on time to class.

▶ Treat others with respect.

▶ Honor the property of others.

▶ Stay on task in class.

For an example of what this might look like in action, let us reflect back to the "tardy story" from when Mike Mattos served as principal at Pioneer Middle School. The school decided to create a task force to study schoolwide behavior expectations and report back to the staff. This task force presented what it learned at a subsequent faculty meeting and proposed four overarching schoolwide behavior expectations.

1. **Respect:** All *Wildcats* (the term the school uses to represent all members of the school community, named after the school's mascot) will show respect to themselves, each other, and school property.

2. **Explore:** All Wildcats will get involved in an extracurricular activity.

3. **Achieve:** All Wildcats will learn the essential academic standards for each of their assigned classes.

4. **Lead:** All Wildcats will take responsibility for making the school a better place. You may achieve this by committing to the service of others.

These expectations became known as the school's REAL Wildcat expectations, or doing things the Wildcat Way. All other school rules, awards, and disciplinary supports flow from these four guiding principles. These behaviors became the staff's

Exclusive Videos from **Your Favorite RTI at Work™ and PLC at Work® Experts**

With videos from Mike Mattos, Austin Buffum, and other industry leaders, this playlist is an excellent companion to the best-selling book. Discover how the RTI at Work process can support continuous improvement and academic success for your school.

INTRODUCTION

What Our Schools Were Designed For
– *Austin Buffum*
▶ 1:34

Education—What Schools Need to Focus On
– *Mike Mattos*
▶ 3:21

Other videos available online

CHAPTER 1: *The RTI at Work Pyramid*

An Overview of the Inverted Pyramid
– *Mike Mattos*
▶ 4:11

Creating Great Schools: Schoolwide Intervention
– *Robert Eaker*
▶ 2:01

Other videos available online

CHAPTER 2: *A Culture of Collective Responsibility*

Creating a Data Picture of Your School with Your Leadership Team
– *Anthony Muhammad*
▶ 7:53

What Is a Team?
– *Rebecca DuFour, Richard DuFour*
▶ 7:47

Other videos available online

CHAPTER 3: *Tier 1 Teacher Team Essential Actions*

Getting Insanely Clear About What Students Have to Learn
– *Mike Mattos*
▶ 12:55

Assessment Practices That Have a Real Impact on Student Learning
– *Luis F. Cruz, Mike Mattos, Sarah Schuhl*
▶ 3:14

Other videos available online

CHAPTER 4: *Tier 1 Schoolwide Essential Actions*

Responsibilities of Teacher-Skill-Intervention-Teams vs. Schoolwide-Will-Intervention-Teams in Tier 2 Interventions
– *Mike Mattos*
10:51

Every Aspect of Your School Sends a Message About Your Mission
– *Tim Brown*
2:35

CHAPTER 5: *Tier 2 Teacher Team Essential Actions*

Behind the Scenes: Elementary Interventions
– *Various*
5:55

Determining Interventions by Classifying Student Errors
– *Cassandra Erkens*
4:47

CHAPTER 6: *Tier 2 Schoolwide Essential Actions*

One School's Plan for Scheduling Intervention and Enrichment
– *Rebecca DuFour*
10:56

A Staff Recommendation Process for Behavior and Attendance Issues
– *Mike Mattos*
3:53   *Other videos available online*

CHAPTER 7: *Tier 3 Schoolwide Essential Actions*

Finding Time for Tier 3 Interventions
– *Mike Mattos*
5:27

School Intervention and School Leadership Team's Role in Tier 3 Intervention
– *Austin Buffum*
8:51

CHAPTER 8: *Tier 3 Intervention Team Essential Actions*

Avoiding IEPs
– *Austin Buffum*
6:15

Tier 3 Intervention Intensity
– *Austin Buffum*
3:02

CLAIM YOUR FREE TRIAL
SolutionTree.com/GlobalPD

 Solution Tree

collective responsibility to teach, model, and intervene for both the adults and students in the school.

Determine How Students Will Demonstrate Mastery of Each Essential Behavior

When teacher teams identify an essential academic standard—such as persuasive writing—it is equally important that the team determines how students demonstrate that they have learned this outcome. To achieve this, teachers can develop a grading rubric and create an assessment process to measure student learning in comparison to the rubric. Essential behaviors are no different. Once a school determines its essential academic and social behaviors, the staff must agree on how students demonstrate these behaviors, considering differences in student ages and learning environments.

For example, if a school determines that demonstrating respect is an essential social behavior, how should students demonstrate this behavior in the classroom during whole-group instruction? During cooperative learning time? On the playground? In the cafeteria? During a pep rally? Also, a student's ability to self-monitor this behavior varies between kindergarten students and fifth graders. Teachers must discuss these considerations before they can explicitly teach, monitor, and intervene on these behaviors. Teachers can capture demonstrated behaviors in a rubric they then teach to students and clearly post strategically around campus to help remind them of these schoolwide expectations.

Design a Process to Systematically Teach Essential Behaviors Across the School

It is unfair to hold students accountable for behaviors that teachers did not effectively teach them. Merely posting classroom rules or providing them in a student-parent handbook is insufficient. Schools should develop a process to systematically and explicitly teach their essential social and academic behaviors. This process should undoubtedly begin at the start of the school year. Moreover, in the same way effective teachers regularly remind and prompt students of classroom procedures, so too should the school plan to revisit their expectations throughout the year. Because some students move in after the start of school, there should also be a process to teach these behaviors to new students.

While many schools already teach social behaviors to start the year, systematically teaching academic behaviors is not common practice. As an example of how to do this, let's go back to the scenario at Mike's school. The staff identified six essential academic behaviors they wanted all students to master, including the ability to:

1. Take notes

2. Research, including determining the validity of a source and citing appropriate references

3. Maintain a calendar of responsibilities, assignments, and due dates

4. Keep work organized and come to class prepared

5. Memorize information

6. Set goals and reflect on progress

At first, staff members decided that incoming sixth graders would take a one-quarter study skills class as part of their elective courses. This class would teach and reinforce these behaviors. Over time, the school realized that not all students took this class, while some students did take it but not until second semester, meaning many students struggled with these skills for half the year until they learned these skills.

Ultimately, the school decided that teachers in every subject would teach one of the essential academic skills during the first month of school. For example, the English language arts team taught Cornell note taking during the first month of school. This ensured that every student in language arts at every grade level learned the skill. The mathematics department taught students how to use a calendar to keep track of assignments and then reinforced the skill during the first month of school. The science department taught Internet research skills and how to cite information.

This process took a limited amount of classroom instructional time but collectively guaranteed that every student knew how to demonstrate these expectations. After the first month of school, if a student was not writing down his or her homework assignments in a daily planner, it was not a skill problem but rather, a *will* problem, as the student chose not to do it. At that point, it is more than fair and reasonable to hold the student accountable for his or her choices.

Design Targeted Privileges and Recognitions to Promote Positive Behavior

There should be more positive reasons for students to demonstrate the right behaviors than threats and punishments to deter negative behaviors. To this end, we recommend that schools develop some standards-based privileges or recognitions that reward all students who demonstrate specific essential behaviors. We call them *standards-based* because many schools have award processes that recognize a very limited number of winners: student of the month, athlete of the year, or valedictorian, to name a few.

Many good students know it is unlikely they will ever win these awards, so they assume a "why try?" attitude. A standards-based behavior privilege sets an expectation and defines the privilege, award, or recognition students earn for meeting this outcome. If ten students meet the expectation, then ten students earn the privilege. If two hundred students achieve the outcome, then two hundred students earn the recognition. Not all positive behavior awards need to be standards based, but the school's goal is to make many winners.

Monitor Essential Social and Academic Behaviors

The leadership team should determine processes to monitor if students are learning and consistently demonstrating essential behaviors. Regularly reviewing information on who is earning positive behavior recognitions, and where behavior infractions are

There should be more positive reasons for students to demonstrate the right behaviors than threats and punishments to deter negative behaviors.

most occurring, can be valuable information to help the school review their schoolwide efforts to teach essential behaviors and target resources to intervene when some students fail to consistently demonstrate them.

What we are advocating for regarding behavior expectations is nothing less than what the adults in the building would want for themselves. A teacher would expect those who evaluate them to be clear regarding the school's staff expectations to ensure they have clarity on exactly how to demonstrate them, positive reinforcement when they do demonstrate them, and frequent monitoring and support if they do not. Our students deserve nothing less.

Helpful Tools

The following tools will help you accomplish the work for this essential action. These practical checklists provide a quick and efficient way for teams to establish common expectations, target instruction, and reinforce positive behavior.

- ▶ **"How Do We Establish Common Expectations?" (page 149):** This activity will help the site leadership team plan for the implementation of schoolwide behavior expectations.

- ▶ **"How Do We Target Instruction?" (page 150):** This activity will help the leadership team plan for the teaching of schoolwide behavior expectations.

- ▶ **"How Do We Reinforce Positive Behavior?" (page 151):** This activity will help the leadership team plan for the reinforcement of schoolwide behavior expectations.

Coaching Tips

The steps outlined in chapter 2 action 2's Here's How section on creating consensus for school culture are the same ones needed for the task of identifying schoolwide behavior expectations. Those three steps include:

1. Provide a compelling case for identifying expectations.

2. Create a doable plan for sharing, monitoring, and rewarding expectations.

3. Build consensus to ensure shared commitment to and responsibility for implementation of the plan.

Do *not* overlook the importance of the first step. Without understanding why this task is necessary, the potential for success with steps two and three dramatically decreases. A compelling case for identifying schoolwide expectations requires sharing experiences both as students and educators, learning from and visiting other schools, and exploring current research on this topic. It is important to assess staff understanding of and readiness to support a possible plan before actually creating a plan.

A doable plan includes multiple attributes, such as:

- ▶ Clearly defined behavior expectations

▶ Strategies and resources for recognizing and rewarding positive behaviors

▶ Strategies and resources for intervening to address misbehaviors

▶ Leadership communication and instruction on the plan to all stakeholders

▶ Systems for monitoring, evaluating, and adjusting the plan

The good news about creating multiple pieces of a doable plan is that there are opportunities for stakeholders to be involved. Inviting staff, students, and parents to actively participate in developing the plan means the plan will be stronger and potentially reach greater consensus in support of it. As you develop and share each part of the plan, you have the opportunity to check the level of understanding and support. You can use the formative feedback gathered along the way to address any misunderstandings and adjust the plan, thus facilitating greater commitment to and ultimate shared responsibility for its implementation.

How Do We Establish Common Expectations?

Goal	Long-Term Vision	First Steps
Achieve collective responsibility.	Staff view the success of all students as part of their professional practices.	❑ Share successes across the grade levels. ❑ Analyze case studies as a staff. ❑ Vertically collaborate. ❑ Horizontally collaborate.
Craft a behavior matrix.	Staff reach consensus on those behaviors that are most significant to student and school success.	❑ Review data. ❑ Collect and validate anecdotal evidence. ❑ Identify three to five behavioral attributes concisely and appropriately. ❑ Define age-appropriate expectations for students and staff. ❑ Identify settings (environments) across the campus for which it is most important to articulate appropriate behaviors.
State positive expectations.	Craft statements that positively state the way in which students will appropriately behave in settings across the campus.	❑ Identify behaviors that *disrupt* learning. ❑ Articulate the optimally desired behaviors that will *support* learning. ❑ Write three to five specific, observable behavioral characteristics for each broad behavioral attribute in each identified setting.
Model the behavioral expectations.	Staff explicitly and intentionally model the behaviors that they expect students to exhibit.	❑ Identify specific ways in which staff can model the behaviors they expect to see from students. ❑ Identify specific times and settings during which staff can model the behaviors they expect to see from students. ❑ Develop a respectful way in which staff can hold one another accountable to effectively and positively model behaviors.

Source: Hierck, T., Coleman, C., & Weber, C. (2011). Pyramid of behavior interventions: Seven keys to a positive learning environment. *Bloomington, IN: Solution Tree Press.*

How Do We Target Instruction?

Goal	Long-Term Vision	First Steps
Effectively manage classrooms with well-communicated and reinforced structures, routines, and procedures.	Staff collaborate about their techniques for establishing structured, predictable learning environments.	❏ Devote time before the school year to reviewing ways in which classrooms will be managed and organized. ❏ During the first few weeks of school, check in with colleagues on the success of their efforts to establish efficient learning environments. ❏ During the first few weeks of school, check with students on their understanding of the rules and routines of a positive learning environment.
Consistently model, reinforce, and monitor.	Staff, at all times, talk the talk and walk the walk, faithfully reinforcing and tracking both positive and negative behaviors.	❏ Follow the same behavioral expectations as students and be open to friendly reminders from colleagues. ❏ Utilize the same method for reinforcing and recognizing positive behavior. ❏ Led by the administration, the staff understand and follow the way in which instances of both positive and negative behavior will be documented and monitored.
Explicitly teach schoolwide behavioral expectations.	Staff regularly and explicitly teach and reteach the behaviors that all students are expected to exhibit.	❏ The school sets aside time during which all students and staff receive explicit instruction on behavioral expectations. ❏ The school communicates the matrix and expectations to all stakeholders (parents, office staff, custodial staff) and shares the plan with the central office. ❏ The behavioral team anticipates times of the year during which behavioral expectations will need to be reviewed.

Source: Hierck, T., Coleman, C., & Weber, C. (2011). Pyramid of behavior interventions: Seven keys to a positive learning environment. Bloomington, IN: Solution Tree Press.

How Do We Reinforce Positive Behavior?

Goal	Long-Term Vision	First Steps
Catch students being good.	Staff consistently and specifically reinforce at least four times as many positive behaviors as negative behaviors.	❑ Ensure focus on and recognition of behaviors, not personalities. ❑ Specifically describe the reasons why positive behaviors are receiving recognition. ❑ Agree to use the same methods to reinforce or to recognize, or both, positive behaviors. ❑ Formally or informally monitor individual and collective efforts to ensure we are recognizing four positive behaviors for every one negative behavior.
Build relationships.	Staff systemically ensure that every student has a positive connection with at least one adult on campus.	❑ School administration identifies students who are involved in any form of extracurricular activities. ❑ Study and implement strategies for building positive communities of learning within every classroom. ❑ Students in the yellow and red zones are assigned (formally or informally) mentors with whom they have established a connection and with whom they will check in regularly.
Provide schoolwide celebrations.	Formally and informally, the school regularly celebrates and recognizes positive behaviors.	❑ Consider a drawing or other systemwide method to further recognize students whose positive behavior has been recognized. ❑ Brainstorm rewards that are low cost or no cost, preferably academic in nature, that will appeal to students and will serve as an incentive. ❑ Ensure that external means of motivating students are balanced by internal means. Over time, the goal is to move to more intrinsic and less extrinsic reinforcement, when students make good decisions for the satisfaction it instills instead of the reward it brings.

Source: Hierck, T., Coleman, C., & Weber, C. (2011). Pyramid of behavior interventions: Seven keys to a positive learning environment. *Bloomington, IN: Solution Tree Press.*

Action 3

Provide Preventions to Proactively Support Student Success

> An ounce of prevention is worth a pound of cure.
>
> **—Benjamin Franklin**

One of the most important guiding principles of an effective system of interventions is this: *The best intervention is prevention.* In *Uniting Academic and Behavior Interventions*, our colleague Chris Weber says it this way, "If it is predictable, it is preventable. It is always better to proactively support student success, than to wait for students to fail to receive additional support" (Buffum, Mattos, Weber, & Hierck, 2015, p. 66).

In the first chapter, we defined *preventions* as interventions that occur during Tier 1 core instruction to help close learning gaps. This captures the thinking in the principle *The best intervention is prevention.* We don't want to wait until the summative assessment to find out which students need more help. Instead, we are constantly assessing which students can benefit from a quick clarification or reteaching.

If there is one grade that best understands the power of prevention it is kindergarten. Teachers of this grade expect many of their students to start the year lacking many of the skills and behaviors needed to function in a classroom setting. The simplest tasks, like lining up or sitting on the floor for instruction, are a foreign concept to some children. So while kindergarten teachers feel the urgency to begin teaching the required curriculum, they know that taking the time to proactively teach these behaviors ultimately saves time. They have their students repeatedly practice getting in and out of a line, walking in a line, and keeping hands and body to oneself while in the line, and they praise students for forming "the best line they have ever seen"!

This is an example of planning for proactive support. If we can predict what might challenge students, and proactively remove these obstacles, then more students feel immediate success and fewer need additional help. This approach saves site resources and provides the best opportunity for students to achieve success.

> We don't want to wait until the summative assessment to find out which students need more help.

> If we can predict what might challenge students, and proactively remove these obstacles, then more students feel immediate success and fewer need additional help.

Here's Why

The most prevalent example of the negative effect of requiring failure before receiving additional help is special education. Special education has traditionally been a "wait to fail" model, meaning that a student has to demonstrate a deep level of failure—that a defined achievement gap measures—before the school provides systematic support. As proven in the first chapter, special education services can be disastrous for students with special needs, primarily because students have fallen so far behind it is almost impossible to catch up when help finally arrives. While special education usually requires long-term failure, even a short delay in providing additional time and support can have potentially severe consequences for students.

For example, between 70 and 80 percent of students who fail in the first year of high school do not graduate (Wyner, Bridgeland, & Diiulio, 2007). So, a ninth grader who fails a required class the first semester of his or her freshman year is significantly more likely to later drop out of school, in comparison to a student who successfully transitions from middle school to high school. Yet how do many high schools identify freshmen who need additional help? Failure. When students earn failing marks after the first grading period, the school might then begin to offer these students additional help. Often a student's grades are so low in a particular course that there is not enough time to catch the student up before permanent marks are recorded at the end of the term, ensuring failure. As Joe Doyle, an administrator at Bloomington High School South, says, "If you wait for kids to fail, they will" (Mattos, 2015).

Here's How

We often ask educators, "Can you predict the students who are going to struggle *before* you begin new instruction?" The answer we receive is often, "Yes!" While we can't proactively predict every student who might need interventions, we can use reliable criteria to catch many students before they fail. These criteria include the following.

▸ **Gaps in prerequisite skills:** There are usually immediate prerequisite skills, knowledge, and behaviors required to learn new essential grade-level curriculum. If a student lacks a specific prerequisite skill, he or she will likely struggle with mastering the next essential standard in that learning progression. (We go deeper into how to provide these preventions in the next chapter.)

▸ **Predictable developmental needs:** Children develop physically and cognitively in certain stages. With these stages come both the acquisition of certain abilities and challenges that can disrupt a student's success in school. For example, we know that the human brain develops the ability to think abstractly during adolescence or puberty. So if a middle school essential academic standard requires abstract thinking, we should be able to predict that some students will struggle with learning this skill if we present information through abstract representations. It is not that these students can't learn an abstract-thinking standard, but we must represent it in a concrete way, like with the use of a physical model or visual representation.

▸ **Transitional needs:** A middle school that serves seventh and eighth graders can predict its incoming seventh graders' needs. These students have probably been assigned to a single teacher every year since kindergarten. Now they are expected to rotate to multiple teachers every day, managing each class's materials and expectations. Every year, some new students struggle with the transition from elementary to secondary school—it is predictable.

▸ **Previous struggles:** If a particular student ended his or her previous school year with clearly identified concerns, shouldn't the educators who serve this student the following year expect to provide additional help? How many at-risk students go home for summer break and come back the following fall all caught up and ready to succeed?

A school leadership team can use these predictable criteria to identify potential obstacles for school success and plan preventions to address these areas of need. For an example of what this might look like, consider the schoolwide transitional preventions at Pioneer Middle School in Tustin, California. Over a five-year period, the school developed the following Tier 1 preventions to address predictable concerns when new students enrolled.

> ▶ **Fifth-grade orientation:** Five district elementary schools sent students to Pioneer Middle School. Pioneer's administrative team worked with these schools in designing an orientation process that begins in March to prepare next year's incoming sixth graders. The orientation process includes three site visits to Pioneer, a fifth-grade parent night, and a sixth-grade registration day before the first day of school.

> ▶ **Sixth-grade mentors:** Through sixth-grade English classes, the school placed each sixth grader in a small group of about seven to ten fellow students. Then it assigned each group an upper-grade mentor. Upper-grade students applied to be mentors, and mentors were selected based on their ability to model and teach the school's essential academic and social behaviors. Mentors met with their group every week throughout the year. The counseling staff designed the topics of discussion each week, and they helped students learn the Wildcat Way.

> ▶ **New student buddies:** The school assigned students who were new to Pioneer as upperclassmen a new student buddy. These buddies, which the counseling staff arrange, helped new students transition into the school.

We don't necessarily offer these examples as specific preventions to copy, but instead, as examples of a process. The school leadership team reviewed its school data—both disciplinary and academic—and noted that at the beginning of the school year new students had the most failure marks and minor disciplinary infractions (for example, tardy to class, missing assignments). Instead of only offering help after students demonstrated these behaviors, the leadership team considered ways to proactively provide extra support at Tier 1 to eliminate these infractions.

Helpful Tool

The following tool will help you accomplish the work for this essential action.

> ▶ **"Preventions to Proactively Support Student Success" (page 156):** This reproducible can help teams brainstorm ways to identify students' need for preventive support and strategies for identifying students requiring that support.

Coaching Tips

Who better to proactively plan preventive strategies to support student success than the teachers who will be working with those students on a daily basis? No one! That said, the leadership team should take the lead and designate time for staff to build a shared understanding of the need for preventions and to brainstorm possible solutions.

This discussion needs to take place annually—before the beginning of the school year and once teachers have received their class lists. While still together as a staff, we recommend having teams spend thirty to forty minutes to begin their work. This allows for cross-team sharing and vertical articulation before heading off to plan on their own.

As noted in previous sections, the basic process for facilitating the development of a schoolwide culture of collective responsibility and for building schoolwide systems in support of all students learning at high levels is the same. Consider these five steps (visit **go.SolutionTree.com/RTIatWork** for a free reproducible version of this information).

1. Dialogue and learn together to build shared understanding.

2. Ensure opportunities for teachers to brainstorm ideas and provide input.

3. Facilitate sharing of information across teams.

4. Establish and communicate clear implementation expectations for all staff and teams, and articulate how you will hold teachers and teams accountable.

5. Revisit action plans to celebrate successes and modify plans as needed.

Keep in mind that none of these steps produces results unless all leadership team members hold themselves and others accountable for following through. Jonathon Saphier (2005), founder and president of Research for Better Teaching, writes:

> Day after day in schools across America, change initiatives, instructional improvement, and better results for children are blocked, sabotaged, or killed through silence and inaction . . . this lack of follow-through results from the avoidance or inability to face conflict openly and make it a creative source of energy among educators. (p. 37)

To summarize, without commitment to and accountability for decisions made regarding schoolwide changes, the result may be inaction. A significant part of the leadership team's role is to collectively agree on strategies for addressing resistance or sabotage.

Preventions to Proactively Support Student Success

As a team, brainstorm typical skills and needs for preventive support and strategies or tools for identifying students requiring that support. Review information on incoming students, assess as necessary, and identify those who require proactive preventions. Create a team plan of action, and forward recommendations to the leadership team for additional schoolwide support. Revisit prevention planning quarterly to ensure no student slips through the cracks.

Team: _____

Reliable Criteria	Strategy or Tool for Identifying Students and Their Needs	Students Needing Support	Skills or Needs Requiring Support	Team Actions	Recommendations to Leadership Team
Previous Struggles					
Gaps in Prerequisite Skills					
Predictable Developmental Needs					
Transitional Needs					

Conclusion

While writing this chapter on Tier 1 schoolwide essential actions, we debated if we should address grading practices. Traditional grading practices that rank student achievement, punish students for initial failure, deny students opportunities to fix mistakes, value promptness over learning, and demotivate struggling students undermine many school intervention programs. Grades should represent what a student learns, not if he or she learned it first, fastest, or in the most-behaved way. Any school committed to a mission of ensuring all students learn at high levels can no longer justify and perpetuate these practices. As defenders of the school's mission, the leadership team should build shared knowledge on grading practices that promote and support a student's opportunity to learn from his or her mistakes, try again, and ultimately demonstrate what he or she has learned.

Having led this process onsite, we have learned that discussing and changing teachers' grading practices can be a volatile process. How a teacher determines grades often represents what he or she values, and values are often deeply personal. We have seen faculty meetings, collaborative teams, and RTI processes disintegrate because grading discussions turned into personal attacks, creating mistrust and deep staff divisions. So we must address this elephant in the room—grading—at some point. But it might not be the place to start one's RTI journey. Instead, it is a mountain that might need to wait until the school builds the learning processes and trust needed to scale this peak.

In conclusion, applying the essential actions chapters 2, 3, and 4 outlined, a school should have in place the critical pieces needed to develop an effective Tier 1 core instructional program. When implemented well, most students should be succeeding in learning essential grade-level curriculum and consistently demonstrating essential behaviors. But no matter how well a school implements these essential actions, some students will need additional time and support. In the next two chapters, we discuss the essential actions needed at Tier 2 to ensure all students master the essential grade-level standards for future success.

PART TWO

TIER 2 ESSENTIAL ACTIONS

CHAPTER 5

Tier 2 Teacher Team Essential Actions

After forty years of intensive research on school learning in the United States as well as abroad, my major conclusion is: What any person in the world can learn, almost all persons can learn if provided with appropriate prior and current conditions of learning.

—Benjamin Bloom

In this chapter, we focus on the middle-right portion of the RTI at Work pyramid (see figure 5.1, page 162). Let us reconsider what this portion of the pyramid visually represents.

▶ This box is part of Tier 2, which represents how a school provides targeted students with the additional time and support needed to master the standards deemed absolutely essential to success in the next grade or course.

▶ This box is on the right side of the pyramid, which represents outcomes the school's collaborative teacher teams lead. The essential actions in this chapter directly relate Tier 2 interventions to the essential academic standards for each grade level or course offered in a school. Therefore, the teachers who identified these standards and teach these classes are best trained and positioned to take lead responsibility for these interventions.

Tier 2 is the primary reason we divided our RTI at Work pyramid into two sections—teacher team responsibilities and schoolwide team responsibilities. There are two primary reasons why students struggle in school—(1) skill interventions and (2) will interventions. *Skill* interventions target students who have not mastered *how* to do specific academic essentials. For example, an essential academic standard in a student's mathematics class is the ability to solve and graph a linear equation. At the end of the unit on this standard, the student still has not mastered the mathematical skills needed to demonstrate proficiency on this standard.

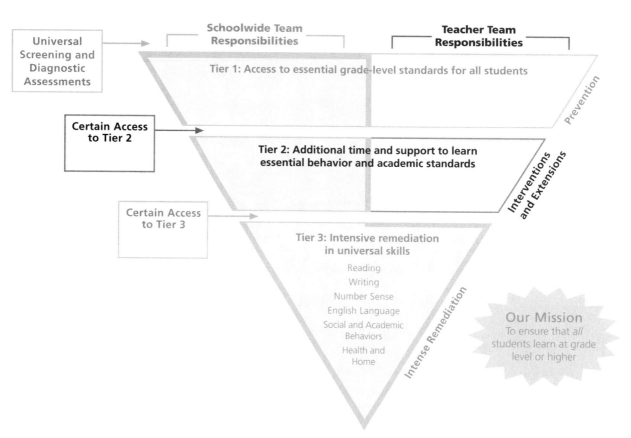

FIGURE 5.1: Focus on Tier 2 teacher team essential actions.

Will interventions target students who have or could have mastered the essential academic standard but lack the essential behaviors—the *will*—to master it. Simplified, it is the difference between "I don't know *how* to do it" and "I don't *want* to do it."

We often ask educators, "How many of you have *skill* and *will* needs in the same intervention?" Usually most of the educators raise their hands. Combining skill and will needs is like having gasoline and a match in the same room. Students with *skill* needs require help with a specific academic skill, while students facing challenges with *will* need support with an essential behavior—two very different targets.

When placed in the same room for their interventions, *will* students often get off task while the teacher reteaches the academic standard for *skill* students. This requires the teacher to stop instruction and redirect the will students' needs. But it makes sense why these students would get off task—they are sitting through instruction on an academic standard that they often already know how to do. These students need behavior supports. Obviously, a student can have both skill and will needs—"I don't know how to do it" *and* "I don't want to learn it." But these are still two different interventions.

Target the cause of the problem, not the symptom.

One of the most important guiding principles of effective interventions is this: *Target the cause of the problem, not the symptom.* Students can fail the same test, but it does not mean they struggled for the same reason. Some students fail due to lacking the skill, while others for deficits in will. Target the right cause, and the intervention is much more likely to be effective.

In this chapter, we discuss the actions collaborative teacher teams (not just individual teachers) can take when students have not mastered essential academic outcomes as part of Tier 1 instruction. Teachers must move on to the next unit of instruction or next set of skills, even when some students have not demonstrated that they have learned what the team identifies as essential. Rather than let these students languish, the school can provide a system of supplemental interventions through which these students receive the additional time and support needed to master these essentials without missing initial instruction in the new set of essentials.

The essential actions that teacher teams must lead at Tier 2 include:

1. Design and lead supplemental interventions for academic essential standards

2. Consider screening in immediate prerequisite skills

3. Monitor the progress of students receiving supplemental supports

4. Extend student learning

Let us consider the specifics of each essential action.

Action 1

Design and Lead Supplemental Interventions for Academic Essential Standards

The price of greatness is responsibility.

—Winston Churchill

In chapter 3, we demonstrated the importance of a teacher team identifying essential standards, unwrapping them into learning targets, and developing an essential standards unit plan, which includes a common end-of-unit assessment. At this point, teachers have given assessments and analyzed the results, and some students are still not able to demonstrate mastery on the end-of-unit summative assessment. These students now receive Tier 2 interventions to supplement all the good instruction and proactive prevention that were part of the team's Tier 1 instruction—the team teaching-assessing cycle.

Collaborative teams design supplemental interventions based on results from common formative and end-of-unit assessments. They direct these interventions at the learning target level, not at fixing the entire essential standard. Which parts of the standard are causing students to struggle? We call this focusing on causes (targets), not symptoms (they didn't demonstrate mastery of the entire standard—they flunked).

As we pointed out in chapter 3, some essential standards at the primary level are very discrete and don't have a number of learning targets. For example, students will count and order numbers 1 through 10. However, beginning in grade 2 and beyond, most academic content standards are composed of many different targets—some represent knowledge, some represent reasoning skills, and others ask students to deliver a performance or create a product. In order to help struggling students master essential standards, we need to know which part or parts are problematic for each student.

The collaborative teacher team's discussion around the common assessment results (both formative and end of unit) includes a comparison, teacher to teacher, as to which teacher or teachers on the team seem to have greater success with certain learning targets. This leads to a discussion of which strategies and materials might have the greatest impact on student achievement, not on who the best teacher is. This information is important in two ways. First, the team might assign students struggling with certain learning targets to the teacher who had the strongest results on those same targets. Second, the team records this discussion so that next year when it is teaching this same essential standard, the entire team can utilize the most powerful strategies as part of its Tier 1 instruction.

Once teacher teams meet to both identify which students need a little more time and support to master essential standards, and discuss which teacher might work best with each group based on assessment results, the school leadership team must establish a schedule through which students can receive this help without missing instruction in new essential standards. This is commonly referred to as *flexible time* built into the school timetable. We recommend that this flexible time be scheduled at least two days per week, for about thirty minutes. Approximately every three weeks, teachers should be able to schedule interventions for students not mastering essential standards during this flexible time. While three weeks is an approximate time line, we can say with certainty that schools should not wait eight to ten weeks for the end of the grading period before helping students.

> Schools should not wait eight to ten weeks for the end of the grading period before helping students.

Teachers must have a streamlined way of scheduling students into flexible time that does not involve laborious paperwork. Many schools are increasingly utilizing technology, such as Google Docs, in order to reduce the paperwork load in scheduling Tier 2 interventions, yet still provide documentation of the school's efforts and the student's response to the interventions. During flexible time, students who demonstrate mastery are able to extend and enrich their learning, thereby answering PLC critical question four (DuFour et al., 2016): What will we do when we discover some students have already learned it? For examples and detailed information on how a variety of schools have created flexible time for Tier 2 interventions and extensions, please see *It's About Time: Planning Interventions and Extensions in Elementary School* (Buffum & Mattos, 2015) and *It's About Time: Planning Interventions and Extensions in Secondary School* (Mattos & Buffum, 2015).

Here's Why

Teacher teams take the lead in designing supplemental Tier 2 interventions because they are the same educators who:

- ▸ Are credentialed and trained in particular grade levels and disciplines

- ▸ Help prioritize the essential standards for their course or grade level

- ▸ Unwrap the essential standards into learning targets

> ▸ Build, administer, and score the common formative assessments and common end-of-unit assessments at the target level

> ▸ Teach the students each day

Who else would take the lead in this important work?

Here's How

We recommend the following six-step process for designing supplemental Tier 2 interventions.

1. **Identify concerns:** The teacher team uses the common end-of-unit assessment data to discuss team members' concerns regarding some of the students who were not successful. The team looks for common patterns affecting groups of students and digs down to discover what may be impacting individual students. It also discusses concerns about the assessment itself, and whether it is constructed in such a way to yield valid and reliable information about the students.

2. **Determine cause:** The teacher team should consider the various streams of formative assessment information it gathers during Tier 1 instruction, as well as the end-of-unit assessment results, in order to diagnose more specifically the causes leading to some students not mastering essential standards. Typically, this discussion results in forming three to five different intervention groupings at a grade level or within a particular course. Each grouping reflects the different causes leading to students' struggles.

3. **Target desired outcome:** The teacher team now discusses exactly what desired outcome each grouping of students must achieve as a result of the supplemental Tier 2 interventions. Rather than discussing what students have not been able to do, the team states exactly what it *wants* them to be able to do. For example, a second-grade mathematics intervention group might desire that students will be able to find the unknown number (variable) in a multiplication equation.

4. **Design intervention steps:** Next, the teacher team brainstorms potential intervention strategies for each targeted group and shares any resources available with the staff assigned to a particular group. Many times, these strategies emerge as the teacher team members compare their scores one with another. When one teacher records results that are significantly better than those of teammates, the teachers collectively inquire about how that teacher produced those results. What strategies, materials, and techniques did he or she use?

   In primary grades, especially in the area of reading, these strategies might be part of a scientific, research-based intervention program. Many excellent programs exist to help primary teachers with students needing assistance with phonological awareness, decoding, fluency, and comprehension. However, beginning in third grade, Tier 2 interventions more often deal with academic content standards in which knowledge and reasoning must be applied to demonstrate mastery of a standard. Prepackaged Tier 2 intervention programs are rarely available for students requiring additional time and support with academic content standards. For example, we do not know of a program one can purchase that is designed to help students struggling with mitosis and meiosis.

Once students move beyond the primary grades, support with foundational reading skills should be part of a school's Tier 3 program. Students struggling with mitosis and meiosis, for example, need targeted instructional strategies at Tier 2 to help them master these important concepts, and some also require ongoing Tier 3 interventions to remediate skills (reading comprehension) and knowledge they should have mastered in prior grades. We call that *core (Tier 1); core (Tier 1) and more (Tier 2); and core (Tier 1) and more (Tier 2) and more (Tier 3)*. Some students require all three.

5. **Monitor progress:** The team now decides what tools to use to monitor the progress of students receiving the supplemental Tier 2 interventions. Again, unless we are dealing with primary students struggling with reading skills, the common end-of-unit assessment questions provide much, if not all, of what we need to know about whether a student has achieved mastery of a learning target or targets underpinning an essential standard.

6. **Assign lead responsibility:** The teacher team next discusses which staff members are most highly qualified to help which students. This important step should consider—

   - Which staff have special training in a particular area (for example, phonemic awareness)

   - Which staff record stronger results on particular targets from the end-of-unit assessment when compared to other teachers on the team

   - Which additional staff (administrators, counselors, instructional aides) might be trained and able to assist certain groups of students

   - How additional staff providing interventions will gain understanding of the essential standards assessed, the learning targets supporting the standards, and the exact causes impacting student achievement

We capture this six-step process in the reproducible "RTI at Work Pro-Solve Intervention Targeting Process: Tier 1 and Tier 2" (page 169), which separates academic skills from behavioral issues. The collaborative teacher team focuses its attention on academic issues first because it has the lead responsibility for this part of the split pyramid supporting students' academic learning. Team members must consider:

▶ Their concerns with each student's performance

▶ Potential causes of these concerns

▶ The actual desired results from the student

▶ What interventions the team should utilize

▶ How they should best monitor the student's progress

▶ Who on the team is best equipped to help this student

Ideally, the schoolwide team informs the collaborative teacher team about any behavioral issues. The schoolwide team takes the lead on this effort because it comprises staff with special training, such as a counselor, school psychologist, behavior specialist, dean of students, and so on. This does not mean teachers have nothing to do with the student's behavior. It simply means that the schoolwide team leads the identification and targeting of a student's behavior because of its members' specialized training and experience. (We discuss the role of the schoolwide team in planning and delivery of Tier 2 intervention the next chapter.)

With all the pressures from the various accountability programs at the district and state or provincial levels, it is imperative that teams have a focused approach to supplemental Tier 2 interventions. These interventions should represent a little more help with the essential standards the teacher teams prioritized, not help with everything on the state or province test. Schools that try to intervene on everything in the curriculum quickly become exhausted and frustrated.

It's important to note that supplemental Tier 2 help should not be reduced to a purchased program. Unless the essential standards relate directly to a specific skill on the reading spectrum, supplemental Tier 2 interventions probably won't come from a purchased program. Because we want these interventions to go beyond "more of what didn't work the first time—louder and slower," teams use professional protocols, like the one previously described, to determine which teacher or teachers are best equipped to help a particular group of students.

Nor should students be referred to as *Tier 2 kids*. Supplemental Tier 2 interventions should be fluid and flexible. Students should be released as soon as they demonstrate mastery and should never be "trapped" in a Tier 2 intervention for a predetermined amount of time. It is ridiculous to assume that all students in a school or district require precisely the same amount of additional time and support to master essential standards.

Helpful Tools

The following tools will help you accomplish the work for this essential action.

▶ **Chapter 7 of *Learning by Doing* (DuFour et al., 2016), "Responding When Some Students Don't Learn":** This chapter provides foundational content knowledge as well as tools that can help schools accomplish the action steps outlined in this section.

▶ **"RTI at Work Pro-Solve Intervention Targeting Process: Tier 1 and Tier 2" (page 169):** Teams can use this form to separate academic skills from behavioral issues and target each student's particular needs for intervention.

▶ **"KASAB Chart" (for the leadership team; page 170):** Teams can use this chart to define the knowledge, attitudes, skills, aspirations, and behaviors needed for intended learning and changes to positively impact student success.

Coaching Tips

Implementing new ways of doing business is much more about relationships and learning than it is about completing tasks and to-do lists. With that in mind, the most important work leadership team members do, as coaches, is to inspire and support those they coach to become model learners. And what does it mean to be a model learner? A *model learner*, we propose, is an educator who engages in study and constant practice, with a commitment to continuous improvement and improved results. This is the work of leading change!

In support of teacher teams as they design and implement Tier 2 interventions, it is incumbent on the leadership team to model, check for understanding, clarify, and celebrate progress teams make for each of the six steps. A helpful tool for coaches is a KASAB chart (Killion, 2008), which can help them define the essential knowledge, attitudes, skills, aspirations, and behaviors needed for the intended learning and changes to positively impact student success. As coaches work side by side with teachers and teams, a KASAB chart helps clarify what to look for, listen for, and provide feedback on. Figure 5.2 shows a completed KASAB chart that identifies teacher changes needed for designing and implementing Tier 2 interventions. This chart may also be helpful as an assessment tool to determine current levels of implementation, and, in turn, what type of coaching support is needed.

Types of Change	Teachers
Knowledge: Conceptual understanding of information, theories, principles, and research	Teachers understand the academic content of essential standards they have identified and the rationale for prioritizing their collaborative work on them.
Attitudes: Beliefs about the value of particular information or strategies	Teachers believe in the importance of mastery rather than coverage and in the efficacy of collaboration to ensure high levels of learning for all students.
Skills: Strategies or processes to apply knowledge	Teachers share and use evidence-based instructional strategies to assist all students in demonstrating mastery of essential standards.
Aspirations: Desire and internal motivation to engage in a certain practice	Teachers demonstrate a sincere desire for all to learn at high levels, and they take ownership for making it happen.
Behaviors: Consistent application of knowledge and skills	Teachers consistently use common formative and summative assessments to inform their instruction and to collaboratively design and implement Tier 2 interventions.

FIGURE 5.2: KASAB chart example.

Simply stated, pay attention to adult learners! They need and deserve differentiated levels of time and support just as much as the students they serve.

RTI at Work Pro-Solve Intervention Targeting Process: Tier 1 and Tier 2

Student: _____

Participant: _____　　　　Meeting date: _____

Targeted Outcomes		1. Concern	2. Cause	3. Desired Outcomes	4. Intervention Steps	5. Who Takes Responsibility
Led by Teacher Teams	Essential standards					
	Immediate prerequisite skills					
	English language					
Led by Schoolwide Teams	Academic behaviors					
	Social behaviors					
	Health and home					

Next meeting date: _____

Source: Buffum, A., Mattos, M., Weber, C., & Hierck, T. (2015). Uniting academic and behavior interventions: Solving the skill or will dilemma. Bloomington, IN: Solution Tree Press.

KASAB Chart

Use the following chart to define the knowledge, attitudes, skills, aspirations, and behaviors needed for the intended learning and changes adults must embrace to positively impact student success.

Types of Change	Teachers
Knowledge:	
Attitudes:	
Skills:	
Aspirations:	
Behaviors:	

Action 2

Consider Screening in Immediate Prerequisite Skills

A stitch in time saves nine.

—Thomas Fuller

Immediate prerequisite skills differ from foundational prerequisite skills in an important way. Immediate prerequisite skills and vocabulary often precede instruction by a few units of instruction, a few weeks, or at most, months. In contrast, foundational prerequisite skills come from instruction delivered in prior years, not in prior months or in prior units from the current year.

For example, in second grade we might expect students to add and subtract multidigit numbers with regrouping. A foundational prerequisite skill might be the ability to add and subtract single-digit numbers, an essential first-grade standard. Students struggling with these kinds of gaps in their learning receive intensive Tier 3 interventions (which we discuss in chapter 7). Other students might struggle with this grade 2 essential standard, not because they are unable to add and subtract single-digit numbers but because they are unable to recognize when regrouping is necessary with two-digit numbers. The teacher introduced this skill earlier in the year, a couple of months prior. While some students demonstrate mastery of this skill when taught, it is now clear that they need reinforcement of this essential immediate prerequisite skill in order to demonstrate mastery in adding and subtracting multidigit numbers. This reinforcement might occur as part of supplemental Tier 2 interventions or as part of the team teaching-assessing cycle in Tier 1.

The third column of the essential standards chart asks teacher teams to identify and discuss what immediate prerequisite skills and vocabulary students need to master a particular essential standard. Teams should utilize the information from the essential standards chart, analyzing the causes of student struggles as the team considers how to design Tier 2 interventions. Some students don't just need more time to practice, but instead, they need reinforcement of immediate prerequisite skills required to master the current essential standard.

If a team wants to improve its results, it should consider screening for prerequisite skills as part of the Tier 1 team teaching-assessing cycle, as shown in the top right portion of figure 5.3 (page 172).

This kind of screening is brief, done unit by unit, essential standard by essential standard, as opposed to universal screening, done at the beginning of the year and broadly applied across an entire domain of learning for a school year or course. Collaborative teacher teams, as part of their essential standards unit plan, consider how and when to screen around a particular unit of instruction. For example, a team might decide to administer a brief screening tool about two weeks before instruction begins on a new unit or essential standard. The information from this screening might tell team members that many of their students have some gaps in immediate prerequisite

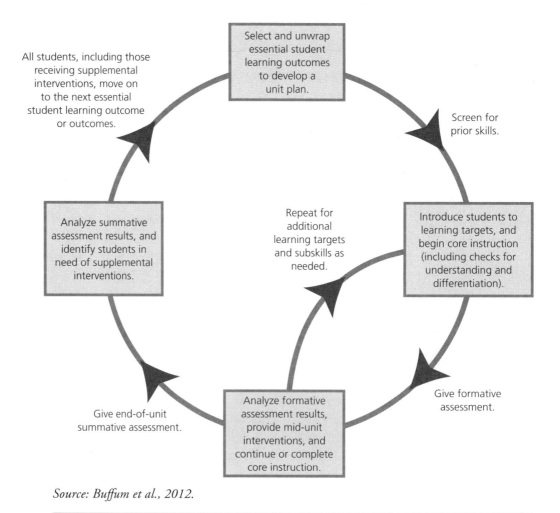

Source: Buffum et al., 2012.

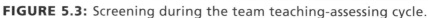

FIGURE 5.3: Screening during the team teaching-assessing cycle.

skills and vocabulary, leading the teachers, during the two weeks prior to introducing the new unit or standard, to start each lesson with a sponge activity directly related to these gaps in prerequisite skills. This Tier 1 application of screening for prerequisite skills truly represents our proclamation that *the best intervention is prevention.*

Here's Why

Supplemental Tier 2 interventions need to target the causes of student struggles. It is important to ask the following kinds of questions about why a student was unable to demonstrate mastery of an essential standard. Was it because the student:

- ▸ Needs more time to master the standard?

- ▸ Isn't motivated to work on the standard?

- ▸ Doesn't understand the way in which the standard was taught?

- ▸ Doesn't have the foundational prerequisite skills from prior years related to mastery of the standard?

- ▸ Doesn't have the immediate prerequisite skills to master the standard?

If, for example, the team's short screening process indicates a direct link between the student's inability to demonstrate mastery and the lack of immediate prerequisite skills, then supplemental Tier 2 interventions would focus first on strengthening these skills as the primary cause of the student's struggles. This is especially true of knowledge that is procedural in nature. Procedural knowledge involves knowing how to do something, and it is often a step-by-step process, as opposed to declarative knowledge, which involves knowing that something is true (for example, George Washington was the first president of the United States).

Students struggling with declarative knowledge simply might need a little more time to master knowing something, while students struggling with essential standards that involve procedural knowledge need to strengthen the immediate prerequisite skills leading up to knowing how to do what is required in the standard. Understanding this difference demonstrates why screening for immediate prerequisite skills is so important in designing interventions for students struggling with essential standards about procedural knowledge.

We started this chapter with a quote from Benjamin Bloom that helps communicate why it is important to screen for immediate prerequisite skills. Bloom claims:

> After forty years of intensive research on school learning in the United States as well as abroad, my major conclusion is: What any person in the world can learn, almost all persons can learn if provided with appropriate *prior* and current conditions of learning. (as cited in Zimmerman & Schunk, 2003, p. 382)

Here's How

Collaborative teacher teams use the information from the third column of the essential standards chart to build brief screeners to give to an entire class in a matter of minutes. For example, figure 5.4 (page 174) shows an essential standards chart for students in grade 2 mathematics.

The collaborative teacher team then quickly constructs a very brief, seven-to-ten-question quiz to give a week or two before teaching this standard to find out how many and which students do not know the place value of digits to 1,000 or how many and which students do not know the meaning of key words such as *greater than* and *less than*. Team members then use this information to help plan their Tier 1 instruction for the unit as well as discuss how they might review this information with students before instruction on the essential standard of *comparing whole numbers to 1,000 by using the symbols* >, <, or =. They can use this same information to inform the conversation around designing supplemental Tier 2 interventions after the common summative assessment reveals that some students have not mastered the essential standards. To what extent is this the result of lacking immediate prerequisite skills?

Standard Description	Example of Rigor	Prerequisite Skills	When Taught?	Common End-of-Unit Assessment	Extension Skills
What is the essential standard students need to learn? Describe in student-friendly vocabulary.	What does proficient student work look like? Provide an example or a description.	What prior knowledge, skills, or vocabulary do students need to master this standard?	When will we teach this standard?	What assessment or assessments will we use to measure student mastery?	What will we do when students have already learned this standard?
I can compare whole numbers to 1,000 by using symbols <, =, or >.	Example: What goes in the box to make this problem correct? 62 ☐ 21 + 31 < > = +	I know the place value of digits from 1 to 1,000. I understand key words: *greater than, less than, fewer, least,* and *most*.	September	Administer the second-grade team-designed CFAs halfway through and at unit's completion.	I can compare money written in decimal form.

FIGURE 5.4: Second-grade mathematics sample essential standards chart.

It is highly likely that teams already have examples of the actual prompts they would need to use to assemble a screener for prerequisite skills. They could pull many of these items from other existing assessments and assemble them into a quick screener. Assembling these brief screening tools helps guarantee a good match between what we are assessing and what we want all students to master. It also helps teams design better supplemental Tier 2 interventions because they helped select or construct the actual items used on the screener.

Helpful Tool

The following tool will help you accomplish the work for this essential action.

▶ **"Essential Standards Chart" (see chapter 3, page 88):** This powerful tool will assist teacher teams in identifying and creating a common understanding of the team's essential standards.

Coaching Tips

The operative word in the title of this section, Consider Screening in Immediate Prerequisite Skills, is *consider*. In other words, this is a recommendation for improving results, rather than an essential step in the process of building student success. As a coach, it's important to bring the concept of screening for immediate prerequisite skills to the teams' attention as they explore avenues of improvement. For teams who are still in the process of learning, practicing, and gaining confidence in the basics of the team teaching-assessing cycle, introducing screening as a mandate may overwhelm, frustrate, or cause resistance from them. We recommend screening as a way to improve results rather than an essential step in the process of building student success.

We recommend screening as a way to improve results rather than an essential step in the process of building student success.

Once teams are ready to consider prescreening, it becomes a perfect opportunity for practicing shared decision making. They need to gather research, consider all the pros and cons, explore screening tools, advocate for their positions, and, hopefully, reach consensus about next steps as a team. Coaches might provide several open-ended questions as a starting point to help facilitate this process. For example:

- ▶ What does research say about the possible advantages of prescreening and formative assessment?

- ▶ How might students use prescreening for self-assessment and goal setting?

- ▶ How can we, as a team, share the work of developing prescreening tools?

- ▶ How can we use the results of prescreening to strengthen our instruction?

As teams work through the potholes on the road to reaching consensus, the challenge for coaches is to stay in a guide-on-the-side role. Providing resources, protocols, and reflective questions supports teams in doing the work for themselves. When teams reach true consensus, they grow more skilled, cohesive, and collaborative—exactly what a coach wants to see happen!

Action 3

Monitor the Progress of Students Receiving Supplemental Supports

> One of the great mistakes is to judge policies and programs by their intentions rather than their results.
>
> **—Milton Friedman**

Imagine that on Tuesday, you take your child to the pediatrician because he or she has a sore throat and fever. The pediatrician prescribes amoxicillin four times daily and asks you to bring your child again on Friday. The doctor wants to monitor your child's progress—to see if he or she is responding to the intervention prescribed. For exactly the same reason, we want to determine if the treatment we prescribe for students receiving supplemental Tier 2 interventions is working. Are the students responding to the intervention? If not, then how should we respond?

Progress monitoring is an essential component of RTI. Without it, there is no R (response) in what we are doing. Without progress monitoring, we simply intervene for a predetermined amount of time and then move on to the next set of essential standards not yet mastered. This is akin to the shift from a focus on teaching to a focus on learning. Here the shift is from a focus on intervening to a focus on asking, "Are the students responding?"

After a team identifies students in need of extra time and support and determines the interventions targeted on the cause of students' struggles, the team monitors how each student responds to the interventions. If an intervention is working, it confirms that the team's diagnosis targeted the right causes. If the student is not responding, it means that the intervention was not targeted properly (incomplete or incorrect diagnosis) or that the diagnosis was correct, but they selected the wrong treatment.

In most cases, teams can use a modified form of the common end-of-unit assessment to progress monitor those students who did not demonstrate mastery of an academic content standard. Unless the underlying cause of the student's struggles with the academic content standard is the result of reading comprehension difficulties, it is logical that a tool that measures mastery of the standard would be used to progress monitor. If students reading at or above grade level are unable to correctly identify the four layers of the earth's crust on the end-of-unit assessment, we ask them to do so again after receiving targeted intervention on another form of the common assessment.

When monitoring the progress of students who struggle with reading, we would most often select a curriculum-based measure (CBM) such as oral reading fluency or words read correctly per minute. Teams can use CBMs to monitor letter-naming fluency, letter-sound fluency, nonsense-word fluency, and phonemic segmenting blending tasks. CBMs offer the added benefits of being standardized across large groups of students and helping to establish growth over time with words read correctly per minute (wrcm; for example, 120 wrcm to 148 wrcm). Accordingly, first-grade and second-grade teachers might be using CBMs to progress monitor their supplemental Tier 2 interventions in reading because they represent skills currently taught and reinforced at their grade level. Students in third grade and beyond would most likely experience progress monitoring using CBMs at Tier 3, since Tier 3 represents the remediation of foundational skills from prior school years.

> We recommend applying some kind of progress-monitoring tool at least every two weeks, if not every week.

Because schools want to understand quickly if students are actually responding to supplemental Tier 2 interventions, we recommend applying some kind of progress-monitoring tool at least every two weeks, if not every week. If and when schools discover that a few students are still not responding, the collaborative teacher team can discuss this at its next meeting and brainstorm possible solutions. It can also potentially discuss these students with the site intervention team (described in chapter 8), which is comprised of staff with different training and perspectives—special education teachers, speech and language pathologists, psychologists, and so on. This discussion may uncover some previously undetermined deficits in foundational skills and knowledge from prior school years that the school's universal screening tools did not detect. In these rare cases, students may then begin to receive intensive Tier 3 interventions in addition to receiving support with ongoing grade-level essential standards.

Here's Why

Progress monitoring provides teachers with information that can help students learn more and faster, and it also helps teachers make better decisions about targeting the type of instruction that works with each student. Simply put, it helps the teachers intervene more effectively and students master material more quickly. In their article, "Progress Monitoring Within a Response-to-Intervention Model," Douglas D. Dexter and Charles Hughes (n.d.) quote the National Center on Student Progress Monitoring's benefits to progress monitoring. Specifically:

> According to the National Center on Student Progress Monitoring, progress monitoring has the following benefits when it is implemented correctly: 1) students learn more quickly because they are receiving more appropriate instruction; 2) teachers make more informed instructional decisions; 3) documentation of student progress is available for accountability

purposes; 4) communication improves between families and professionals about student progress; 5) teachers have higher expectations for their students; and, in many cases, 6) there is a decrease in special education referrals. Overall, progress monitoring is relevant for classroom teachers, special educators, and school psychologists alike because the interpretation of the assessment data is vital when making decisions about the adequacy of student progress and formulating effective instructional programs. (as cited in Fuchs, Compton, Fuchs, Bryant, & Davis, 2008)

When RTI was first implemented across the United States, almost all examples of progress monitoring were through curriculum-based measures, such as oral reading fluency. Teams must determine what measures might be most appropriate to monitor the progress of students based on the nature of essential standards on which students are receiving additional time and support.

Here's How

Collaborative teacher teams meet to discuss and analyze the results from their common end-of-unit assessment. As part of this discussion, they should take the following three steps.

1. Discuss their concerns about specific students and identify underlying causes for student struggles at the learning target level.

2. Decide which teachers will work with which students and why, as described in the section Design and Lead Supplemental Interventions for Academic Essential Standards (page 163).

3. Identify what prompts teachers might use to monitor the progress of students receiving supplemental Tier 2 interventions. (When dealing with academic content standards, teachers should take prompts from the common formative and end-of-unit assessments that comprised the team's essential standards unit plan.)

In about three weeks, the team meets to review the progress-monitoring data in order to make further decisions about individual students. The team releases some students from the interventions because they have demonstrated mastery. Others may require continued time and support. A few may have revealed underlying skill deficits, so teachers might consider them for Tier 3 interventions in addition to ongoing support with the essential standards at Tier 2.

While it is important for the team to capture and record the progress-monitoring data on each student, it is imperative to streamline this documentation process for teachers. Unfortunately, many schools and districts create a paper-documentation trail equivalent to an IEP that places undue burden on teachers. Again, technology use affords schools the opportunity to capture and store these data without placing too great a burden on teachers. We want teachers to focus on teaching and helping students, not on filling out byzantine forms.

> We want teachers to focus on teaching and helping students, not on filling out byzantine forms.

In the book *Simplifying Response to Intervention* (Buffum et al., 2012), we recommend a cyclical process for supplemental Tier 2 interventions similar to the team teaching-assessing cycle used as part of Tier 1 core instruction. Figure 5.5 reinforces that teachers monitor student responses to Tier 2 interventions in a manner similar to that described for the team teaching-assessing cycle at Tier 1.

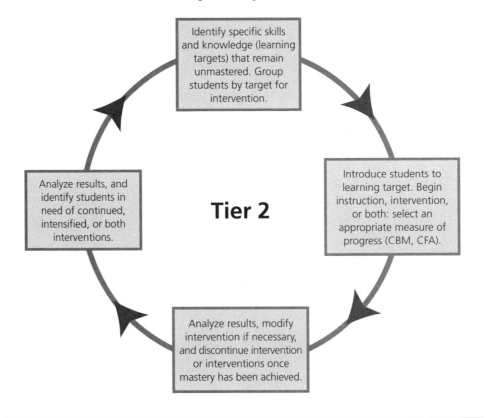

Identify specific skills and knowledge (learning targets) that remain unmastered. Group students by target for intervention.

Introduce students to learning target. Begin instruction, intervention, or both: select an appropriate measure of progress (CBM, CFA).

Tier 2

Analyze results, and identify students in need of continued, intensified, or both interventions.

Analyze results, modify intervention if necessary, and discontinue intervention or interventions once mastery has been achieved.

FIGURE 5.5: Progress monitoring at Tier 2.

Helpful Tools

The following tool will help you accomplish the work for this essential action.

▸ **Chapter 7 of *Learning by Doing* (DuFour et al., 2016), "Responding When Some Students Don't Learn":** This chapter provides foundational content knowledge as well as tools that can help schools accomplish the action steps outlined in this section.

▸ **"RTI at Work Pro-Solve Intervention Monitoring Plan: Tier 1 and Tier 2":** Teams can use this form to separate academic skills from behavioral issues and target each student's particular needs for intervention.

Coaching Tips

The implementation tips we offer at this point are simply reminders of tips we have provided previously. Because teachers are sharing, analyzing, and responding to data, it is important to remember that collective ownership for the process is the goal. Involving and clearly communicating with teachers at every step creates ownership along the way. If it becomes apparent that teacher teams are balking at monitoring progress, it may indicate a need to pause and back up. It may signal a need to clarify expectations, processes, or tools, or teachers have to be more involved in developing the tools and processes they use.

RTI at Work Pro-Solve Intervention Monitoring Plan: Tier 1 and Tier 2

Student: _____

Participant: _____   Meeting date: _____

Targeted Outcomes		Desired Outcomes	Intervention and Action Steps	Who Takes Responsibility	Data Point 1	Data Point 2	Data Point 3	Data Point 4	Data Point 5
Led by Teacher Teams	Essential standards								
	Immediate prerequisite skills								
	English language								
Led by Schoolwide Teams	Academic behaviors								
	Social behaviors								
	Health and home								

Next meeting date: _____

Note that the team completes the first three columns of this chart—Desired Outcomes, Intervention and Action Steps, and Who—as part of the design of the supplemental Tier 2 interventions. In the team's follow-up progress monitoring meeting, team members collect a series of data points in order to document an individual student's progress. Depending on the nature of the essential standard, data points might include results from a curriculum-based measurement (grades 1 and 2), three out of four correct on selected-response items, or a rubric score of four out of five, representing the team's definition of mastery.

Source: Buffum, A., Mattos, M., Weber, C., & Hierck, T. (2015). Uniting academic and behavior interventions: Solving the skill or will dilemma. Bloomington, IN: Solution Tree Press.

Action 4

Extend Student Learning

> Acquire new knowledge whilst thinking over the old, and
> you may become a teacher of others.
>
> **—Confucius**

As teachers gather information about how students are responding to their instruction and intervention, it is inevitable they will discover that some students have already mastered the skills and knowledge that collaborative teacher teams prioritized as essential. The ongoing use of formative assessments, both common and individual, helps reveal those students who have already learned. It is imperative that teachers provide opportunities for these students to extend their learning and not simply mark time, or even worse, be forced to complete meaningless work that is really just more of the same.

Just as teachers must plan to provide supplemental Tier 2 interventions to students who need additional time and support, they also should plan to provide extensions for students who have already mastered the standards. They can achieve this in several ways. Teachers can make the actual content more rigorous; make the process or activities in which the students engage more rigorous; or make the culminating product, which applies what students have learned, more rigorous (Tomlinson, 2000).

Teachers often use extended-learning activities to allow students who have already mastered content to move horizontally through a curriculum. In doing so, they challenge students to look at things from different perspectives, apply skills to new situations or contexts, look for many different ways to solve a problem (not just looking for the correct answer), or use skills learned to create a new outcome or product. This differs from acceleration in that students are not moving ahead vertically with new content as much as digging deeper into current content.

Thomas Guskey (2010), professor of educational policy studies and evaluation at the University of Kentucky, writes:

> Students engaged in extension activities gain valuable learning experiences without necessarily moving ahead in the instructional sequence. This makes it easier for other students who have been doing corrective work (Tier 2 intervention in an RTI model) to resume their place in the instructional sequence when they are done. (p. 56)

The challenge for teachers in designing and implementing extension activities is ensuring that these activities provide students with meaningful learning experiences, rather than saddling them with more work or busywork. Extension "activities must provide students with opportunities to pursue their interests, extend their understanding, and broaden their learning experiences" (Guskey, 2010, p. 56).

Here's Why

RTI should never provide help to struggling students at the expense of our highest-achieving students. Schools should use RTI as a way of optimizing student learning by raising the floor of student achievement while raising the ceiling at the same time. We can best capture this thinking with the saying, "A rising tide lifts all boats." Unfortunately, extension is too often regarded as something extra, something more—a nonessential "nice to have" thing if we can squeeze it in somehow. This viewpoint ignores the importance of student engagement and motivation to learn. Engaging students by letting them make choices related to their own learning enhances their achievement (Reis & Fogarty, 2006; Siegle & McCoach, 2005).

In *Visible Learning and the Science of How We Learn*, John Hattie and Gregory Yates (2014) point out that feedback helps students on their personal journeys, and that the type of feedback required depends on students' achievement outcomes—while students struggling to learn need corrective feedback, highly competent learners require sincere efforts to extend and apply knowledge even further.

Within the context of essential standards and outcomes, each student is on a personal journey. While some students need supplemental Tier 2 supports that include personalized corrective feedback, others need personalized feedback that engages them further in their own journey—extending and enriching their knowledge and ability to apply that knowledge to solve problems in new and challenging ways.

> RTI should never provide help to struggling students at the expense of our highest-achieving students.

Here's How

Collaborative teams must regularly discuss how to differentiate the core content during Tier 1 instruction for students who have already mastered essential standards as well as those who are struggling. Students who need additional time and support receive supplemental Tier 2 interventions during a school's flexible time, while those students who have already mastered essential standards receive extension opportunities. These opportunities should be based on student interest whenever possible.

For example, elementary students who have already mastered essential standards related to spelling or writing might substitute books of interest to them that offer greater depth and complexity. It may also be possible for teachers to use these books to hold whole-class discussions around similar themes.

Other activities to extend elementary student learning might include:

▸ Using technology to access websites of students' favorite authors

▸ Reading challenging material online

▸ Interacting with other advanced readers using literature circle discussion strategies

▸ Working in small groups to compare themes across fiction and nonfiction material

- Conducting independent studies around a particular area of interest

- Completing creative products

- Using technology to create products, stories, and even small books

Many secondary schools have created flexible time in their daily timetables so students needing additional time and support to master essential standards can attend tutorials two or three times per week. While these students are required to attend the mandatory "closed" tutorials, students who have demonstrated mastery of essential standards have the opportunity to select from a listing of "open" tutorials. These open tutorials offer students a wide array of choices based on their interests or current needs. These choices might range from attending a study hall to do homework, to working with their music teacher before the upcoming concert, to making up a missed science lab from last week.

Pioneer Middle School in Tustin, California, has one of the best-known programs of this type. Here, students can elect from a generous list of open tutorials, such as the following.

- Open: Study hall for Maan's spelling lesson-2 makeup (grade 7)

- Open: Core tutorial (grade 6)

- Open: Earth science help (grade 6)

- Open: Core enrichment (grade 8)

- Open: Band or orchestra (grades 6, 7, 8)

- Closed: Mile-run makeup (grades 6, 7, 8)

- Closed: Core homework help (grade 8)

- Open: Study hall (grades 6, 7, 8)

- Open: Grammar review (grade 6)

- Closed: Spanish 1A (grades 7, 8)

Students earn the privilege of selecting an open tutorial around their own areas of interest. This is a great example of how making choices relating to their own learning can more highly engage students, while serving as a motivation to other students who choose not to complete work. If they begin to turn in their work, they can earn the privilege of attending an open tutorial during the next three-week period.

Helpful Tool

The following tool will help you accomplish the work for this essential action.

- **"Essential Standards Chart" (see chapter 3, page 88):** This powerful tool will assist teacher teams in preplanning for extension standards.

Coaching Tips

With all the time demands that teachers face, teachers might view building a bank of resources for extending learning as time consuming and a low priority. Often, teachers simply don't realize how many ideas and resources they already have within their own teams.

To help address this challenge, the leadership team might consider designating an entire faculty meeting, early in the school year, to exploring extension activities. Teams will need to know the faculty meeting's focus ahead of time so they can come with ideas and resources to share. Designating the time, adhering to a singular focus for the meeting, and providing structured facilitation help the leadership team send a clear message that extension is both essential and expected.

Conclusion

In this chapter, we described the critical work of collaborative teacher teams in providing additional time and support to students who, at the end of the unit, have not mastered essential standards the teams prioritized. This additional time focuses like a laser beam on the underlying causes of students' struggles, not on the symptoms such as a letter grade or percentile score. While some students receive this additional time and support to master essential standards, it is equally important for teacher teams to plan and deliver meaningful and engaging extension activities for those students who have demonstrated mastery. All this focuses on academic skills. In the next chapter, we discuss the schoolwide teams' responsibilities in organizing intervention activities for those students who struggle not because they lack skills but because they lack the will to do the work.

CHAPTER 6

Tier 2 Schoolwide Essential Actions

Intelligence plus character—that is the goal of true education.

—Martin Luther King Jr.

In this chapter, we focus on the Tier 2 middle-left portion of the RTI at Work pyramid (see figure 6.1, page 186). Let's consider what this portion of the pyramid visually represents.

- This portion represents how a school provides targeted students with the additional time and support needed to master the knowledge, skills, and behaviors deemed essential to success in the next grade or course.

- The left side of the pyramid represents outcomes that must be coordinated across the school, so the school leadership team takes lead responsibility to ensure it achieves these outcomes. Additionally, the schoolwide support staff primarily guide these interventions.

In the previous chapter, we described why and how teacher teams should take lead responsibility for reteaching essential grade-level academic standards—*skill* interventions—at Tier 2. In this chapter, we describe how the school's leadership team can leverage schoolwide staff to lead *will* interventions for students that still lack the social and academic behaviors to succeed. The leadership team's essential actions at Tier 2 are:

1. Schedule time for supplemental interventions

2. Establish a process for schoolwide student intervention identification

3. Plan and implement supplemental interventions for essential social and academic behaviors

4. Coordinate interventions for students needing skill *and* will supports

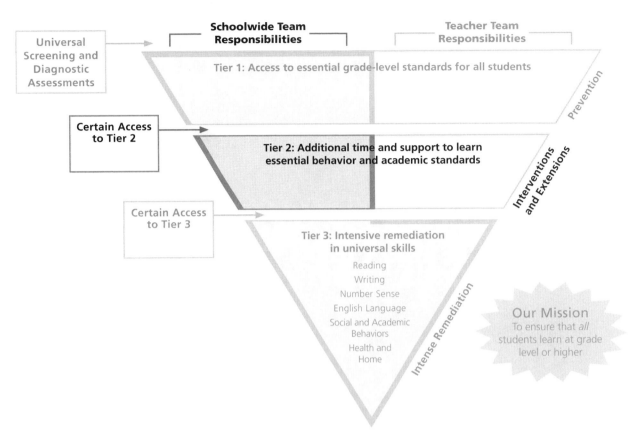

FIGURE 6.1: Focus on Tier 2 schoolwide essential actions.

Let us begin with one of the most important jobs of the school leadership team—scheduling time for Tier 2 interventions.

Action 1

Schedule Time for Supplemental Interventions

The two most powerful warriors are patience and time.

—**Leo Tolstoy**

We have repeatedly stressed that interventions must be provided in addition to new essential grade-level curriculum, not in place of it. So when some students fail to master an essential standard—academic or behavior—by the end of Tier 1, then the school must create a schedule in which these students can continue to work on this standard, while not missing new essential curriculum during core instruction.

Some educators claim that their school doesn't need to create Tier 2 time in their master schedule because each individual teacher provides supplemental interventions in his or her own classroom. As a nation, the United States tried that model for more than two hundred years—it is called a one-room schoolhouse. That model failed to achieve the goal of high levels of learning for all students because it is unrealistic to expect classroom teachers to simultaneously reteach essential grade-level curriculum to some students, while introducing new essential standards to the entire class. There *must* be dedicated time in a school's master schedule to provide Tier 2 interventions, and the staff must take collective responsibility for each student's success.

Creating a master schedule that ensures students access to both Tier 1 essential curriculum *and* Tier 2 interventions requires schoolwide coordination. For this reason, it should not be left to each teacher or teacher team to figure out how to make the schedule work. Instead, the school's leadership team should take primary responsibility for this essential action. The actual schedule will look different from school to school, but the following are some important criteria to consider.

▸ **Frequency:** Teachers should provide Tier 2 intervention time at least twice a week and more often if needed. Due to fiscal, contractual, or transportation needs, it is unlikely a school will be able to lengthen its school day to create Tier 2 time. Instead, this time comes from Tier 1. In other words, some of the time teachers currently use to introduce new curriculum should be repurposed to reteach essential standards. Because this comes at a cost of Tier 1 time, a school should take as much time as necessary to meet the needs of students who require Tier 2 intervention, but no more.

▸ **Duration:** Each session should be about thirty minutes. Consider for a moment how long it takes a teacher to provide direct instruction on a very specific learning target. It rarely requires an hour; in fact, sixty minutes of direct instruction is often too long to keep students highly engaged. Generally speaking, about thirty minutes is a sufficient length of time to provide targeted instruction. Obviously, this block of time could be slightly shorter in the primary grades or might need to be slightly longer to provide transition time for students to get to and from the intervention. This is why we suggest about thirty minutes, give or take.

▸ **Available to all students:** If a school's mission is to ensure all students learn at high levels, then Tier 2 time must be scheduled when all students can attend. This means it must be during the school's instructional day. There are two significant drawbacks to providing interventions before or after school. First, some students will not be able to attend due to transportation or family needs. That means these students will not receive the help they need. Second, teachers are not usually required to work with students during these times. If a school's faculty are the best trained staff to provide skill interventions, but they are not available during a school's Tier 2 time, then the interventions will most likely be much less effective. When teachers carve out Tier 2 time from a school's current instruction day, they ensure that they are contractually available to teach students, and by law the students must be in attendance.

Because we advocate for intervention time to be embedded during the school day, we are often asked if it is acceptable to provide any interventions before school, after school, or during off-track times (like summer school). We are not against utilizing these times, but the school must assume that some students will not be able to attend. So the school should offer the same interventions during the school day too.

▶ **Never introduce *new* essential curriculum:** The faculty must commit to never introducing *new* essential curriculum during Tier 2 time. This time is to reteach essentials, so if new essential standards are introduced at the same time, the students receiving reteaching will fall behind. A school can introduce nonessential curriculum during Tier 2.

We have helped schools all over the world implement RTI, and we can say definitively that we have never visited a school that has an effective system of interventions that does *not* have supplemental intervention time embedded in its weekly schedule.

Here's Why

No research supports that all students learn at the exact same speed, so why should the time allotted to learn specific content be exactly the same for all students? Even so, time-restricting practices are prevalent in many schools. From the use of rigid pacing guides that predetermine how many days a teacher can spend teaching each standard, to the traditional secondary master schedule that provides every student with the same number of instructional minutes for every class each day, these practices were designed to cover material and rank student achievement, instead of ensuring all students succeed.

If we condense what it takes to have all students learn into a simple formula, the equation would look like this (Bloom, 1968; Buffum et al., 2012; Guskey & Pigott, 1988):

$$\text{Targeted Instruction} + \text{Time} = \text{Learning}$$

If a school can make both teaching and time variables in this equation and target them to meet each student's individual learning and developmental needs, the school is more likely to achieve high levels of learning for every student. Applying this formula into practice requires creating flexible blocks of time in a school's master schedule.

Schools often tell us they have transitioned to a block schedule, which provided more time for teachers to differentiate in class. While we are not opposed to block scheduling, we do not consider larger blocks of Tier 1 class time the same as creating flexible time. If a high school has a traditional six-period day, or a block schedule in which students take four classes every other day for a larger block of time, each student is still getting the same number of minutes as compared to other students following the same schedule. The premise of flexible time is that some students need more time to learn the curriculum, while some might require less. So the school must create a flexible block of time in which some students receive more time on an essential standard, while others extend learning because they have already mastered the curriculum.

> No research supports that all students learn at the exact same speed, so why should the time allotted to learn specific content be exactly the same for all students?

Here's How

As previously mentioned, the specific schedule used to create Tier 2 intervention time is likely to look different from school to school. Elementary and secondary master schedules work quite differently. State or province regulations, district policies, contractual agreements, site resources, and student needs all impact the specific design of a school's master schedule. So while we can't provide a universal, generic, all-purpose Tier 2 master schedule, we can recommend the following seven steps for the school leadership team to take to create the right schedule for its school.

1. Learn together.

2. Look beyond the bell schedule.

3. Determine the frequency and duration needed for Tier 2 interventions.

4. Create a draft plan.

5. Solicit staff input and build consensus.

6. Teach students the purpose of the new schedule and the specific steps of how it works.

7. Predetermine how to monitor and revise the process.

Learn Together

Many schools, differing in size and demographics, have successfully embedded intervention time during their existing school day. So to quote the old adage: *Why reinvent the wheel?*, we suggest that the leadership team creates a task force to study how to schedule supplemental intervention time during the school day. We recommend the following potential resources.

▸ See *It's About Time: Planning Interventions and Extensions in Elementary School* (Buffum & Mattos, 2015) and *It's About Time: Planning Interventions and Extensions in Secondary School* (Mattos & Buffum, 2015) to learn how other elementary and secondary schools created intervention time in their school day. We selected the featured schools because they significantly increased student achievement, and because their new schedule was created within their existing conditions—they did not lengthen their school day nor receive additional funding to make the intervention time possible.

▸ Visit AllThingsPLC (www.allthingsplc.info/evidence) to locate and contact the dozens of model schools listed there that have successfully created intervention time during the school day. Each school submitted a written narrative as well as contact information.

▸ Contact your local region, state, or province office of education and inquire about model schools in your area that would be worth visiting. Because these offices support many area schools and districts, they often have a good idea of schools that are further along on the journey.

When choosing the team members to help build intervention time into the schedule, we recommend including teacher leaders and, potentially, teacher union representations. When done well, creating intervention time during the school day should not only help students, but also help teachers. Including teachers in the planning process will best ensure this outcome.

Look Beyond the Bell Schedule

Most schools assume that the biggest obstacle to creating an intervention period is actually manipulating the minutes in the school's master schedule to create the time. Yet, schools revise their bell schedules regularly throughout the year for things like school assemblies, pep rallies, testing schedules, or poor weather. Creating an assembly schedule does not require a task force. The process only requires simple mathematics—subtracting minutes from some periods, adding the minutes up, and inserting an extra period into the daily schedule. Alternative schedules that a school has already created for a school assembly can often be easily modified into a supplemental intervention period bell schedule.

The real obstacles begin when a school considers the logistics of having potentially hundreds of students transitioning to specific interventions. Critical questions arise, such as:

▶ How do we successfully use this time to support student learning?

▶ How do we determine what interventions to offer?

▶ How do we assign staff?

▶ How do we transition students to the right help sessions?

▶ How do we hold students accountable to attend?

▶ How do we efficiently monitor student progress?

▶ What do we do with students who don't need extra help?

▶ What if students need help in multiple academic areas?

▶ How do we keep the process from becoming a paperwork nightmare?

▶ How can we achieve these outcomes within our current resources and without asking teachers to work beyond their contractual obligations?

> More than learning how to schedule the time, it is important to learn how to use the time once it is scheduled.

These are all legitimate and difficult logistical questions that can stall a school's efforts to provide students additional time for learning. When contacting model schools, we recommend that the task force dig deeper than just asking to see the school's bell schedule. More than learning how to schedule the time, it is important to learn how to use the time once it is scheduled.

Determine the Frequency and Duration Needed for Tier 2 Interventions

We mentioned earlier in this section the criteria for creating supplemental intervention time: weekly for about thirty minutes. Within these general guidelines, there is flexibility for schools to tailor the time to fit the needs of their students. When Mike Mattos was principal of Marjorie Veeh Elementary, a school that served mostly at-risk students, the staff dedicated time every day to providing supplemental help, because these students had many academic gaps to fill. Additionally, the primary Tier 2 time each day was slightly shorter because younger students are not developmentally ready for large blocks of direct instruction. Upper-grades students could focus longer, and often their essential learning targets were more complex, requiring a longer block of time to effectively teach.

When Mike later became principal of Pioneer Middle School, the staff dedicated two time slots per week to providing Tier 2 interventions, because most of the students entered the school at grade level. The intervention period was the same for all grades. This was not only because the developmental needs were similar for the middle school grades but also because the structure of a secondary master schedule is very different. At the elementary level, each grade level can run different daily schedules and not disrupt the other grades. At the secondary level, the entire school runs on the same bell schedule.

After studying the topic, the task force should determine the desired frequency and duration of Tier 2 intervention time needed at its school to meet its students' needs.

Create a Draft Plan

After learning about the process and determining specific school needs, the task force is then ready to create a proposal for how the school can provide Tier 2 interventions during the school day. This plan should not only address how to create time within the school day but also the logistics of how to use that time. (See the reproducible "Creating Flexible Time Worksheet: Critical Considerations" on page 195 to assist with this process.) The task force should work closely with the site leadership when creating this draft plan.

Solicit Staff Input and Build Consensus

The draft plan is just that—a draft. It is critical to share this plan with the faculty, along with the reasoning and rationale behind the plan. The leadership team should consider how to solicit staff feedback—concerns and suggestions—on how to improve the plan. Our experience is that some staff members resist *any* changes to the master schedule and will use this opportunity only to point out potential problems. When allowed, these naysayers often dominate the conversation. This is why the leadership team must plan ahead how to solicit feedback from everyone, not just the most vocal staff.

Also, when teachers raise potential concerns, it is important to press for potential solutions. Keeping the current schedule should not be the solution. Remind the faculty that if the current schedule is meeting the mission of all students learning at high levels, then there would have been no need to create a task force to find ways to improve it. While you cannot guarantee that the proposed new schedule will work perfectly, there is no doubt that the current schedule is not.

Teach Students the Purpose of the New Schedule and the Specific Steps of How It Works

When flexible time is well targeted, students transition to different locations, staff members, and activities on any given day. Transitional times in a school day can trigger student misbehaviors, so it is critical to teach students specific actions, processes, and behaviors that they must demonstrate during these times.

Before Mike Mattos and the staff at Pioneer Middle School started their Tier 2 intervention period, they taught students the reasoning behind the schedule change, the goals of their new tutorial period, and the specific steps in the process. They had a dry run in which students just practiced the transition from their last class to their tutorial location. Teachers carefully taught students the routine before they asked them to participate in a flexible period in which 1,500 middle school students were expected to transition to different interventions and extension opportunities across the entire campus. They shared the rationale and design with parents as well.

Predetermine How to Monitor and Revise the Process

Regardless of how well you complete the previous steps, you will not come up with a perfect plan. You will experience unexpected bumps. It is easier for a school's faculty to commit to trying a new schedule if they know that there will be opportunities to tweak the process if it is not working. For example, the leadership at Pioneer Middle School pledged that it would survey the entire staff after three months of trying the new schedule, and it would make revisions as needed. Additionally, every faculty member and student completed a survey at the end of the year.

Having worked with hundreds of schools on how to create supplemental intervention time, let us also share some advice on potential pitfalls to avoid when designing this time.

> **Intervention time should not be "fun and games" for some students:** We have seen schools decide that students who do not need Tier 2 interventions receive privileges, such as—

> > ▸ Extra lunch and social time

> > ▸ The opportunity to leave campus early

> > ▸ Enrichment activities, like learning how to play guitar or participating in the intramural dodgeball tournament

It is easier for a school's faculty to commit to trying a new schedule if they know that there will be opportunities to tweak the process if it is not working.

There are two problems with this approach. First, most schools create their Tier 2 time from existing core instructional time. Yet these schools do not allow students to leave campus early or take extended lunch as part of their core instructional day. When we offer students these options, they lose instructional time. Tier 2 time should not come at the cost of students who master essential standards during core instruction. The second problem is when we offer students these privileges, it makes the students assigned to required reteaching feel punished. Students should not perceive interventions as punitive actions.

> **Tier 2 interventions should not be in place of electives or specials:** As we discussed in chapter 1, there is a difference between extension and enrichment. All students deserve access to enrichment subjects, such as music, drama, computer technology, and art. Most schools offer these through "specials" time (elementary) or elective classes (secondary). Tier 2 reteaching should not be scheduled in place of these opportunities.

> **Student assignments must be flexible and fluid:** We have seen many schools create an intervention period, and then assign a group of students to each teacher for the year. This teacher is expected to counsel, advise, and help his or her assigned students. This model has many drawbacks. First, what if a student needs help in physics, but for advisory the student is assigned to the art teacher? Conversely, what if the student needs help in art but is assigned to a science teacher? The goal should be to have the best-trained educators in a subject to help students receive help in their area. And even if every staff member on campus was an expert in every subject at your school, it is impossible to expect that all the students randomly assigned to a teacher will have the exact same intervention and extension needs. The more diverse the needs in the room, the more impossible it is for a single teacher to address all needs at the same time.

> Another variation of this problem is when schools assign students to the same Tier 2 intervention groups for weeks at a time. When Tier 2 is targeted well—by student, standard, and learning target—students should move fluidly from group to group, based on their individual needs. More often, schools that assign students to the same intervention for weeks at a time do so because of the inconvenience of regrouping students frequently.

> **The intervention period is not a cure-all:** When the Pioneer Middle School faculty was surveyed after the first three months of their Tier 2 tutorial period, its biggest concern was that there were some students who teachers wanted to see more often, but multiple teachers were requesting these students for extra help. When this is the case, these students probably need Tier 3 support too.

Tier 2 time should not come at the cost of students who master essential standards during core instruction.

Helpful Tools

The following tools will help you accomplish the work for this essential action.

▶ **"Creating Flexible Time Worksheet: Critical Considerations":** This form provides teams with a list of questions they can consider when creating effective flexible time in their schedules to provide interventions and enrichment.

▶ **"Using Flexible Time Well" (page 196):** Teams can use these critical questions to help them draft a plan for using flexible time well.

Coaching Tips

To ensure successful implementation of flexible time, the task force must consider and address one additional challenge to changing the schedule: How will the task force involve teachers, students, and parents throughout all steps of the process, including researching, drafting a plan, trying it out, and revising? Following are several suggestions for addressing this challenge.

▶ Each member of the task force takes on the role of a communication liaison for designated groups of stakeholders. For example, the team should assign members to communicate with teachers in specific grade levels or departments, specific student leadership groups, or specific parent groups.

▶ As communication liaison, each task force member is responsible for sharing information, gathering input as necessary, and reporting on task force decisions.

▶ Task force members might also form and coordinate the work of topic-specific committees to research, brainstorm, and propose solutions to critical considerations.

> Rushing the process usually creates lack of clarity, poor follow-through, and, ultimately, resistance.

Beware! In order to keep stakeholders informed and involved, the task force (and leadership team) needs to be patient and allow enough time for all voices to be heard as staff complete the work. Rushing the process usually creates lack of clarity, poor follow-through, and, ultimately, resistance. On the other hand, taking the time needed to bring everyone along on the journey means each team member will understand and support the final plan, thus leading to greater outcomes for student learning.

Creating Flexible Time Worksheet
Critical Considerations

Discuss and address the following considerations.

1. Do we have frequent time, during the school day, to reteach and enrich students?
2. Is it directive? Can you require students to attend?
3. Is it timely (weekly)?
4. How long does it take for students to get help? How long does it take a student to get out once it has worked?
5. Is it targeted? Is the time used to reteach specific essential standards?
6. Is the time used to enrich and extend learning for students who have already mastered essential standards?

Using Flexible Time Well

As you draft your plan for using flexible time well, discuss and address the following critical considerations.

1.	How will you successfully use this time to support and extend student learning?
2.	How will you determine which interventions to offer?
3.	How will you determine which staff member should lead each intervention?
4.	How will students transition to the correct help sessions?
5.	How will the school hold students accountable?
6.	How will the school monitor student progress efficiently?
7.	How will this time serve students who don't need extra help?
8.	How will this time serve students who need help in multiple academic areas?
9.	How will we avoid a process that becomes a paperwork nightmare?
10.	How will we use only current resources and without asking teachers to work beyond their contractual obligations to achieve our desired outcomes?

Action 2

Establish a Process for Schoolwide Student Intervention Identification

Real knowledge is to know the extent of one's ignorance.

—Confucius

As discussed in chapter 1, one defining characteristic of a multitiered system of supports is that a school's interventions are systematic—the school can guarantee that every student in need of help will receive it, regardless of the teachers to whom he or she is assigned. A systematic response is composed of five steps.

1. Identify students who need help.

2. Determine the right intervention to meet students' learning needs.

3. Monitor each student's progress to determine if the intervention is working.

4. Revise if the student is not responding to the intervention.

5. Extend once the student has mastered essential curriculum.

Of these five steps, there is one step a school must do perfectly—*identify the students who need help.* If the school does not initially *determine* the best intervention for those identified students, it will realize this problem as it *monitors* each student's progress. But a school cannot perform any of these steps unless it identifies the student in the first place. A system of intervention is useless for any student who slips through the cracks.

> A system of intervention is useless for any student who slips through the cracks.

How does a school develop a flawless identification process? It must employ three identification processes: (1) universal screening, (2) common assessments, and (3) a staff-recommended process. The first two are assessment-driven processes that were introduced in previous chapters.

1. **Universal screening:** We can use universal screening (see chapter 4 and chapter 7) to identify students who enter the school year significantly below grade level in foundational skills. It is a proactive process, best completed before the school year begins, to identify students who need both preventions at Tier 1 and intensive Tier 3 remediation.

2. **Common assessments:** Team common assessments measure student progress on Tier 1 essential academic standards. Chapter 3 provided specific suggestions on how teacher teams can use common assessment information to identify and target exactly which students have not mastered specific essential academic standards.

However, students are much more than the sum of their test scores. As we state in *Simplifying Response to Intervention* (Buffum et al., 2012):

> Beyond objective assessment data, there is subjective information that best comes from the school professionals who work with the students every day. This observational information is vital to identifying students for additional help and determining why each student is struggling. For this reason, the third way a school should identify students for additional support is to create a systematic and timely process for staff members to recommend students who need help. (p. 163)

Visually, figure 6.2 captures a school's staff recommendation process in the certain access to Tier 2 area of the RTI at Work pyramid.

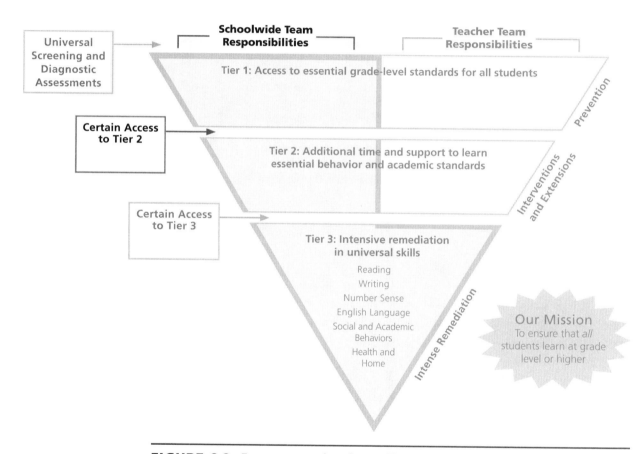

FIGURE 6.2: Focus on a school's staff recommendation process at Tier 2.

Creating a systematic, timely staff recommendation process to identify students who need additional schoolwide supplemental interventions is critical to a highly effective system of interventions.

Here's Why

In the previous chapter, we discussed how teacher teams can use common assessments to identify students for Tier 2 skill interventions. While team-created common assessments that align to essential academic standards are the best way to identify students in need of *skill* interventions, these assessments are not sufficient to identify every student struggling at Tier 1. This is because common assessments measure a student's need for academic support, but not every student struggles at school for academic reasons. For example, if a mathematics team identifies *order of operations* as an essential standard and then administers an assessment on this topic, the information provided would be an outstanding way to identify students in need of additional instruction and practice to master this skill. But this mathematics assessment would be ineffective to identify a student who is:

> Not every student struggles at school for academic reasons.

- ▶ Demonstrating aggressive behavior toward peers

- ▶ Lacking the effort needed to succeed

- ▶ Consistently absent

- ▶ Facing a medical condition that impacts education

- ▶ Having trouble making friends

- ▶ Dealing with a difficult home situation, such as divorcing parents

These problems are a reality in every classroom and can impact a student's academic success. Any school dedicated to ensuring the success of every student must be prepared to support students who need additional help with:

- ▶ Essential social behaviors, such as respectful behavior toward peers or proper attendance

- ▶ Essential academic behaviors, such as demonstrating motivation and effort

- ▶ Proper attendance

- ▶ Health concerns, such as a student who is severely diabetic and needs to learn to self-monitor

- ▶ Home difficulties, such as a student who is depressed at school because his or her parents separated

Teachers do not measure these potential obstacles to student success through universal screening tests or team common assessments; instead, they usually observe them. This is why, in addition to using common assessments to identify students in need of Tier 2 academic skill interventions, a school must also have a schoolwide staff recommendation process to identify students who need *will* interventions.

Practically every school has a process to solicit teacher input on student progress—report cards. Unfortunately, using this information to target Tier 2 interventions has some crippling drawbacks. First, report card processes are rarely timely. Most schools have teachers submit student grades on a quarterly basis. That means one-fourth of the year passes before teachers can use that information to identify students in need of additional help. How far behind can a student get in nine weeks? In many cases, nine weeks is long enough for a student to dig such a deep hole that it becomes the student's educational grave. In addition, grades rarely inform stakeholders of the reasons the student is struggling. What information can a school gain about a student from a letter grade of F, besides the obvious conclusion that he or she is failing?

Finally, at most schools, the process of determining grades varies greatly from teacher to teacher. Some teachers place a greater weight on effort, and others much less. Some teachers let student behavior influence a student's academic marks, and others not. Because of this variance, it is problematic to use traditional report card practices as the primary way teachers share information to identify students for additional support. So just using traditional grade reporting practices is not a sufficient way for staff members to systematically identify students for additional help.

Here's How

Because the goal is to identify students across the entire school for additional help, designing and implementing this process is a leadership team responsibility. While specific identification procedures vary from school to school, we recommend aligning the process to the following criteria.

▸ **Timely:** An effective staff recommendation process must be timely. We recommend soliciting teacher input at least once every three weeks.

▸ **Mandatory:** Participation from all site educators must be mandatory. If we excuse even one teacher from the process, then this teacher's students are much less likely to receive additional time and support. Consequently, a school couldn't tell parents it doesn't matter which teacher their child has— it *would* matter.

▸ **Deliberate:** All staff members should start the year knowing when the identification process takes place, how they will gather the information, and what criteria to use for identifying students in need.

▸ **Efficient:** The process should not require an unreasonable amount of time for teachers to complete.

Many educators assume that this identification process must be designed around official RTI forms and documentation. This is not necessarily the case. Some schools have teachers systematically identify students for extra help through dedicated grade-level meetings. These schools designate at least one grade-level team meeting each month as their student identification meeting. All staff members who work with students from the designated grade level attend the meeting, including administrators, special education teachers, and support staff. Each attending staff member comes to the meeting with a list of students who need additional time and support. The members discuss and recommend students collectively and determine appropriate interventions.

There is a powerful benefit to having in attendance all staff members who work with a particular grade level or student group, as the school can more effectively problem-solve each student's needs. The staff get a 360-degree view of the student's entire school day. See figure 6.3 for an elementary view.

So, for example, if teachers have behavior concerns, the team can determine if these behaviors are being demonstrated all day (class time, recess, specialist time, and so on), or just in particular settings. Also, because all teacher team and schoolwide team members participate, they can coordinate interventions based on whether a student needs support that falls under the lead responsibility of the teacher team or interventions the schoolwide team leads.

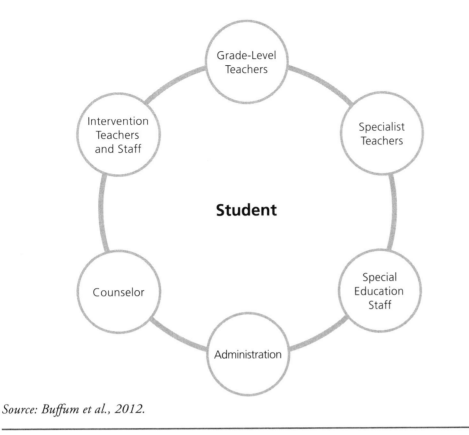

Source: Buffum et al., 2012.

FIGURE 6.3: Elementary 360-degree view.

See figure 6.4 for a secondary view.

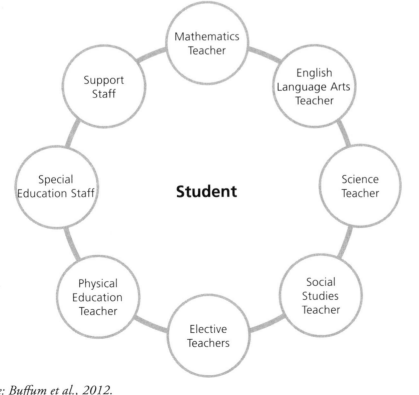

Source: Buffum et al., 2012.

FIGURE 6.4: Secondary 360-degree view.

Using a set meeting time to identify students for additional help might not work well at a larger school, where there are hundreds of students at each grade level. For example, at a large comprehensive high school, it would not be practical to have every staff member who works with freshmen meet and discuss the individual needs of every ninth grader in need of help. The meeting could potentially take hours.

Instead of meeting, a school could solicit staff recommendations through a recommendation process. Approximately every three weeks, larger schools develop a process to have all teachers refer students in need of additional support. These recommendations can be submitted in writing or electronically. A school might use its current progress reporting process, usually done through the school's student data-management software, to collect this information from each teacher.

It is important that teachers provide more than a letter grade for each at-risk student, but also use targeted comment codes as to why the student is struggling. For example, a mathematics teacher may refer three students from his or her first-period class who are currently failing. Along with the letter grade, the teacher may add a comment for each student to indicate poor attendance, late or missing work, or low test scores. Administrative or counseling staff can serve as intervention coordinators, using this combined student information to get the 360-degree view of each student's needs, meet with each student, determine if he or she needs schoolwide interventions, and take primary responsibility to ensure that these interventions take place.

As the leadership designs an identification process for its school, it is critical that the process is not too laborious. Because teachers can use RTI to identify students for special education, some districts have created teacher identification and documentation processes that rival IEP paperwork. When this happens, teachers have told us that they resist referring students for schoolwide interventions because it is just not worth filling out the paperwork. We acknowledge that they need some levels of documentation for the few students who, after effectively applying *all three tiers*, have still not responded to the help and should be considered for special education.

But in the initial stages of RTI, most students referred for Tier 2 are not going to ever need Tier 3 supports, let alone special education. So, to ask teachers to complete laborious amounts of documentation to refer students for Tier 2 help is unnecessary and actually detrimental to some students because it discourages teachers from referring them when learning gaps are small.

Contacting and learning from other schools is a great place to start.

Like creating time for supplemental interventions, many schools have figured out effective, efficient ways for engaging their staff in identifying students for extra help. Contacting and learning from other schools is a great place to start.

Helpful Tool

The following tool will help you accomplish the work for this essential action.

▶ **"Establishing a Process for Schoolwide Student Intervention Identification" (page 204):** Using a three-point scale, teams can assess whether their school's intervention identification process is not in place, partially in place, or 100 percent in place.

Coaching Tips

As previously discussed, the leadership team is responsible for designing and implementing an effective process to identify students for intervention support. That said, the process never works effectively unless all stakeholders understand the process and, therefore, actively participate to support that process. The leadership team must communicate, communicate, communicate to build shared understanding.

In his article, "Leading Change: Why Transformation Efforts Fail," John Kotter (2007) points out that a key reason change efforts fail is due to under-communicating the vision by a factor of ten. In other words, leaders too often provide ten times less communication of the vision than is actually needed. Virtually all the criteria we recommend in the previous section are related to effective communication. First, stakeholders must understand *why* their participation in a student intervention identification process is necessary. Once that understanding is in place, there is a much greater likelihood that they will also support all steps in the process.

Leadership team members can use the reproducible "Establishing a Process for Schoolwide Student Intervention Identification" (page 204) to align their work with the recommended criteria. First, they collaboratively self-assess the current reality and then identify challenges or obstacles. They can then identify action steps to overcome each obstacle. Kotter (2007), again, sums up the importance of communication, "Without credible communication, and a lot of it, the hearts and minds of the troops are never captured" (p. 6).

Establishing a Process for Schoolwide Student Intervention Identification

Use a three-point scale to assess your current reality: one point—not in place, two points—partially in place, or three points—100 percent in place.

Critical Criteria to Consider	Current Reality	Challenges or Obstacles	Next Steps to Effectively Meet These Criteria
Timely ☐ Minimum of once every three weeks			
Mandatory ☐ All teachers participate.			
Deliberate: All staff know— ☐ When the identification process takes place ☐ How information is gathered ☐ What criteria to use for identifying students in need			
Efficient ☐ Minimal time needed ☐ Minimal paperwork ☐ No student falls through the cracks.			

Action 3

Plan and Implement Supplemental Interventions for Essential Social and Academic Behaviors

Human behavior flows from three main sources: desire, emotion, and knowledge.

—Plato

In chapter 4, we discussed how a school's leadership team should oversee a process to identify and teach schoolwide essential social and academic behaviors. Just as one would not expect every student to master essential *academic* standards by the end of initial instruction, a school must not assume every student will consistently demonstrate essential behaviors merely because they reviewed them at the beginning of the year. Undoubtedly, some students need additional time and support.

The leadership team is responsible for planning and implementing these supplemental behavior interventions. The interventions should target students who have difficulty with:

- Social behaviors—

  - Staying on task

  - Using appropriate language

  - Keeping their hands and other body parts to themselves

  - Self-monitoring impulsive behaviors

  - Making friends

  - Coming to class and school on time

  - Appropriately responding to conflicts with others

  - Speaking in front of others

- Academic behaviors—

  - Completing assignments

  - Demonstrating sufficient effort

  - Keeping work organized

  - Retrieving materials on demand

- Health and home—

  - Participating in class or school due to health complications

  - Focusing on school due to problems at home

Unless a school offers systematic interventions that effectively address these concerns, some students will struggle academically because they lack these essential behaviors.

Here's Why

While the previous lists do not represent all the behavior needs that can impact a student's success in school, they do capture prevalent concerns that exist in most classrooms. Unfortunately, many schools fail to effectively address these needs because they leave it up to each teacher to intervene when students struggle due to behavior. When a student is demonstrating disruptive classroom behavior, the teacher might meet with the student, contact the parent, temporarily remove the student from class, assign lunchtime or after-school detention, or lower the student's report card marks. Teachers usually contact the administration only when a student's behavior concerns become extreme.

While we are not suggesting that teachers should abdicate responsibility for addressing student classroom behaviors, there are significant pitfalls to this individualistic, "leave it up to each teacher" approach. First, we often find that teacher-preparation programs usually teach classroom-management techniques but rarely train teachers in assessing and targeting systemic behavior concerns. There is a big difference between managing student behavior and using functional behavioral assessment information to target the cause of a student's misbehaviors. A school psychologist or counselor often has this type of training, but it would require schoolwide coordination to systematically include them when providing Tier 2 behavior supports.

Second, making each teacher responsible for classroom behavior creates inconsistency and inequity for students. For example, when a student fails to complete homework, one teacher might require him or her to come in at lunch to make up the assignment; another teacher might call home and expect parents to fix the problem; and another might just give the student an F and be done with it. A systematic intervention process ensures that students receive additional time and support *regardless* of which teacher they are assigned to. This promise must apply to behavior interventions too.

Another drawback to individual teacher responses for behavior interventions is that they restrict the ability to provide coordinated behavior interventions for students. When a student lacks an essential behavior—such as staying on task in class—the student usually demonstrates this behavior in every class. Having each of the student's teachers individually address this behavior can create disjointed and often contradictory expectations for the student. When a student demonstrates misbehaviors across the school day, the best way to respond is with a coordinated, schoolwide intervention plan. This is difficult to achieve when the school has an individualistic approach to Tier 2 interventions.

Finally, even if every teacher is a behavior intervention expert, it is unrealistic to expect him or her to have the time to provide behavior interventions. When students are capable of doing their homework but just lack the motivation and effort to get the work done, then teachers must require students to complete the work—but how? If every teacher is responsible for this, when will he or she provide this help? In class? The teacher is providing instruction to all students. At lunch or after school? Contractual obligations rarely compensate teachers for helping students at these times. Follow the student home and help? Of course not. It might be possible for a school to utilize other schoolwide staff to oversee students who need to complete work, but individual teachers rarely have the authority to allocate and assign these staff members. It takes a schoolwide, systematic effort, which is why the leadership team must coordinate Tier 2 behavior interventions.

Here's How

Tier 2 behavior interventions should directly target the schoolwide essential social and academic behaviors the school identifies at Tier 1. To effectively respond, we recommend the school's leadership team consider the following five steps.

1. Regularly review schoolwide behavior information.

2. Target the cause, not the symptom.

3. Learn together.

4. Allocate time and resources to target specific behavior interventions.

5. Monitor each intervention's effectiveness and revise as needed.

Regularly Review Schoolwide Behavior Information

While supplemental interventions should target the individual needs of each student identified for behavior help, taking an overall view of the school's behavior needs is equally important. On a regular basis, the leadership team should analyze trends in schoolwide behavior data, including behavior referrals to the office, absence and tardy data, and teacher recommendations for interventions.

Reviewing this information means the leadership team might determine that certain behavioral needs are actually still in Tier 1. For example, when teachers at Pioneer Middle School referred students for schoolwide behavior interventions for the first time, staff identified over seven hundred students in need of help with missing assignments—almost 40 percent of the student body. When that many students have the same need, it signals a Tier 1 problem. Obviously, a large portion of the students did not learn the academic behaviors necessary to consistently complete their homework, are lacking the academic skills needed to independently complete the work, or have obstacles at home stopping them from getting the work done. Readdressing these behaviors at Tier 1 would be the most effective way to help this many students.

Additionally, reviewing this big-picture information helps the leadership team prioritize its efforts and resources. We find that some schools have many students with behavior needs, but they begin the RTI process with very few schoolwide behavior interventions. Under the weight of so many needs, the task of providing behavior supports can seem overwhelming. The leadership team looks at the bigger picture to identify the school's most pressing needs and where immediate action steps will be most effective.

Target the Cause, Not the Symptom

We often hear questions such as, "What intervention is best for getting a student to do his or her work?" and "What intervention do you use for a student with attendance problems?" Our answer is, "We don't know." Do all students fail to turn in homework assignments for the same reason? Are all students absent from school for the same reason? Of course not. Missing assignments are a symptom. Absences are a symptom of a problem, not the cause of the problem. To effectively intervene, the school must identify what causes each student's problem. It must ask, "*Why* isn't this student completing homework?" and "*Why* is this student absent from school?" This is why we recommend schools not only target interventions by student, by standard but also by kid, by cause. Eliminate what causes the problem, and you fix the problem.

> To effectively intervene, the school must identify what causes each student's problem.

To prove this point, and to model a process a school-leadership team can use to target supplemental behavior interventions, let's dig deeper into a behavioral need that many schools have—getting students to complete their homework. The leadership team can use the reproducible "Reasons Why Students Might Fail to Complete Homework" (page 214) to help identify causes for missing homework. To begin, the leadership team should brainstorm reasons why a student might fail to complete a homework assignment, recording each answer down the first column. Possible answers might include that the student:

- ▶ Chose not to

- ▶ Might have after-school responsibilities (such as watching younger siblings while parents work) and is unable to get the assignment done

- ▶ Did not know how to do the work

- ▶ Forgot to write down the assignment

- ▶ Lacks the supplies at home to complete the work

- ▶ Did the assignment but left it at home

- ▶ Knows how to do the work, and does not understand why the teacher is requiring him or her to practice (seems like busywork)

After brainstorming likely reasons, the leadership team can then list across each row the current interventions the school provides to address missing assignments. Our experience is that most schools can only list about three interventions. For example, they:

- ▶ Contact the parents and ask them to monitor their child to be sure he or she does the work

- ▶ Assign the student to some form of detention as a punishment

- ▶ Give the student a failing grade, with the expectation that the mark will persuade the student to be more motivated in the future

Now, the leadership team should identify which of these interventions effectively addresses each cause, which would be potentially counterproductive, and which are not addressed by the school's current interventions. For example, contacting the parents may not help the student who is watching younger siblings because his or her parents are at work. And assigning an F grade does not help the student who left class without the ability to do the work. After completing this step, many schools realize one-size-fits-all, punitive consequences are not only insufficient at addressing all needs, but can actually be a deterrent to developing a student's internal desire to apply effort at school.

With this information, the leadership team can now begin to design interventions that target each specific cause.

▶ How can we support a student who is disorganized and fails to bring completed assignments to class?

▶ How can we require students to complete the work when they just don't want to?

The team can use this same process to brainstorm solutions to other behavior interventions, such as attendance or disruptive classroom behavior.

Learn Together

A constant theme in this book is the process of collective inquiry. If a staff wants to get better results, they must learn about better practices. Most schools approach behavior interventions with what we call the *bigger hammer* philosophy. When students demonstrate misbehavior, we implement punitive consequences to make the student more responsible. If the intervention does not work, and the student continues to demonstrate the misbehavior, then we need to apply even more severe consequences—a bigger hammer.

As a profession, there is more definitive research on how to effectively intervene for behavior needs than for academic needs. The research is clear that using punitive consequences is generally ineffective as a behavior modifier (Horner, Sugai, & Lewis, 2015). Instead, effective behavior interventions' characteristics include:

> The research is clear that using punitive consequences is generally ineffective as a behavior modifier.

▶ Building positive relationships with students

▶ Teaching or reteaching specific behaviors needed for success

▶ Targeting specific behaviors on which the student needs to focus

▶ Identifying the cause or trigger for counterproductive behaviors and working to address and eliminate these causes

▶ Providing frequent, short-cycle opportunities for self-assessment and feedback

▶ Awarding targeted, positive recognitions and privileges earned for demonstrating desired behaviors

▶ Coordinating efforts across the student's school day and between school and home

It is difficult to achieve these goals if a hammer is the only tool in the team's behavior intervention toolbox. When all you have is a hammer, every misbehaving student looks like a nail.

Allocate Time and Resources to Target Specific Behavior Interventions

While classroom teachers certainly play a role in providing behavior interventions, schoolwide staff should take lead responsibility. Schoolwide staff include administrators, counselors, the school psychologist, special education staff, health services staff, instructional aides, and other classified staff.

Because the goal is to target the cause of each behavior need, staff should be assigned to lead specific interventions based on their expertise. The goal is to:

▸ Assemble the right team of people to lead each behavior intervention

▸ Schedule frequent, dedicated times for each team to meet

▸ Allocate the resources needed to provide targeted help for each identified student

To provide a concrete example, consider how a school could create a Tier 2 attendance team to lead supplemental interventions in this area. The leadership team should first ask, "Who on our staff has knowledge or expertise that would help identify, diagnose, coordinate, and monitor interventions for students who have emerging attendance problems?" The leadership team might decide that the school's attendance secretary would be valuable to such a team, as this person keeps the daily attendance records and speaks with students and parents regarding each absence.

Because some students are late to school due to factors beyond their control—such as a parent that consistently drives his or her child late—the attendance team should include someone trained with counseling parents and family. A school counselor might be perfect for this task. Finally, some students fully understand the school's attendance and tardy policies and instead, choose to not meet these expectations. In this case, interventions that hold students accountable to meeting this goal could be necessary. A school administrator would be best for this. The leadership team could form a Tier 2 attendance team comprising the attendance secretary, a counselor, and a site administrator.

Next, the leadership team would want to schedule frequent, regular meetings for this team in which members can take these five steps.

1. Review recent school attendance information to identify students that might be in need of attendance support.

2. Discuss each identified student to determine what causes the student's attendance problems.

3. Design a course of action for each student.

4. Determine if other staff members should be included in a student's plan.

5. Monitor if each plan is working and revise as needed.

Notice that this example represents an ongoing, problem-solving process to systematically target and implement Tier 2 attendance interventions. The key is not trying to find a universal, one-size-fits-all, perfect attendance intervention. Instead, it is about identifying the best-trained staff to lead specific interventions and creating dedicated time to problem solve together.

Monitor Each Intervention's Effectiveness and Revise as Needed

Many schools perpetuate interventions that are not very effective. For example, we have worked with schools whose intervention is to suspend students from school who have tardiness problems. Let's think about this—a student is missing valuable class time, so the intervention to get the student to class on time is to prevent him or her from attending class. If a school wants to continue such a practice, the leadership team should monitor the intervention's effectiveness. How many targeted students, after being removed from class as a consequence for missing class, improve their timeliness after the consequence? Did the intervention achieve the goal? If so, then keep the practice in the school's intervention toolbox. But if most students do not improve, why continue a practice with little evidence that it works?

We do *not* intend for the preceding recommendations and examples to suggest that behavior interventions must only be positive experiences for students. Some interventions require students to do things that are not fun or enjoyable. What we are suggesting is the intent of any intervention should not be to punish students for mistakes or misbehavior, but instead, teach students the right actions.

> The intent of any intervention should not be to punish students for mistakes or misbehavior, but instead, teach students the right actions.

To illustrate this point, let's revisit a story we shared in chapter 4. When Mike was principal at Pioneer Middle School, he surveyed the staff about concerns that would help more students succeed in school. The staff's biggest concern was that too many students were late to class. While the school had a clearly defined policy regarding the consequences that students should receive for each tardy to class, Mike interviewed students and found that the staff did not interpret or implement these policies consistently across the school. The staff decided to clearly identify four essential guiding behaviors to teach and reinforce across the campus: **r**espect, **e**xplore, **a**chieve, and **l**ead (REAL).

If a student was sent to an administrator for multiple tardies, the conversation with the student would sound like this before the staff committed to these four guiding behavior expectations: "Your teacher referred you because you have been late to school for the fifth time. According to our school tardy policy, on the fifth tardy, you receive a referral to the office, we contact your parents, and we assign you to an hour of after-school detention. If you continue to be late to class, we might have to place you in in-school suspension and lower your grade. Your detention is assigned for Thursday. If you don't show, the detention time will be doubled. You need to be on time."

This approach assumes that the student's behavior requires a punishment to properly motivate him or her to not make the mistake again. Imagine if the student is late to school because a parent gets drunk each night and fails to get up early enough to get him or her to school on time. This student has to deal with an alcoholic parent *and* get punished at school because of it. That is truly adding insult to injury. Even in cases in which the student's tardy problem is because the student chooses to be late, will punitive consequences alone improve the student's attitude about school?

After the Pioneer Middle School staff identified and taught their four behavior expectations, the student conversation about being tardy sounded much different.

"Your teacher referred you to me because you have been late to school for the fifth time. You know, we design our expectations to help you succeed in this school, in high school, and for the rest of your life. Now, what are our four REAL Wildcat expectations—respect, explore, achieve, and lead? Can you explain to me how coming to class late is showing respect to the teacher, your classmates, and yourself? How will coming late to class help you achieve at learning essential standards in class? How will coming late to class help you be a positive leader for others?

"I am going to assign you to our after-school 'reflection' room for Thursday. At the beginning of the year, you learned about a goal-setting process. I want you to use our school's goal-setting form to create a plan on how we are going to improve your classroom attendance. I want you to think about why you are coming late to school and what specific steps you can take to improve. I will also be contacting your parents to see if we can work together to help support you. We will catch up on Friday and review your plan together. I want to be part of the plan, because there could be factors beyond your control that are stopping you from getting to class on time.

"Consider for a moment what would happen if one of our teachers came late to school all the time. What would happen? That's right, that teacher might be fired. You are a young adult now. Why would I watch you demonstrate a behavior now that could someday hurt you? We care about you and will do whatever it takes to ensure you succeed at Pioneer. I'll see you Friday."

Notice that the consequences are the same in both examples. The student receives a referral to the office, after-school detention, and parental contact. But the intent and the tone are markedly different. In the first example, the consequence's intent is clearly punitive. The assumption is if the student's experience is negative enough, it will deter future violations of school rules. There is no effort to understand *why* the student is tardy or teach the student the behaviors he or she lacks.

The second example stresses the importance of the behavior and then teaches the student how to better meet the expectation. We doubt the student will enjoy meeting with the administrator or attending after-school detention or reflection regardless of the approach. However, the student's attitude about the experience, and hence his or her likelihood of learning from the experience, is very different. In the end, we find that the *adults* in the building respond much better to positive supports from their supervisors instead of punitive, fear-based policies. Why would students be any different?

Helpful Tools

The following tools will help you accomplish the work for this essential action.

- ▶ **"Reasons Why Students Might Fail to Complete Homework" (page 214):** The activity helps teams determine possible reasons why a student might fail to complete a homework assignment and the interventions they could use to be most effective in addressing these concerns. Educators can use this same process to brainstorm and target other types of Tier 2 behavior interventions.

- ▶ **"Supplemental Interventions for Essential Academic and Social Behaviors: Critical Questions" (page 215):** This reproducible provides four critical questions teams must consider when developing an effective supplemental intervention system to help students with essential academic and social behaviors.

Coaching Tips

Interestingly enough, virtually everything a leadership team needs to know to effectively plan and implement supplemental interventions for essential academic and social behaviors is explained in detail in the previous sections. The question leadership team members must ask themselves is, "Do we have the skill and the will to follow through?" Most school staff have the skills needed to develop and implement an effective supplemental intervention process. Together, they can research, collectively work on, and address whatever skills might be missing.

More often, the more challenging question is, *Do we have the will?* Overcoming the history of an education system built to categorize and weed out students who are unsuccessful and dependent on individual teacher autonomy for addressing any needs students might demonstrate is a significant cultural change and an even greater challenge. This is the reason we recommend spending extensive and consistent time and effort on building a culture of collective responsibility for high levels of student learning. Within such a culture, stakeholders readily accept the challenge of learning together to build any needed skills and holding each other accountable for embracing and demonstrating the will needed to make changes for their students.

Reasons Why Students Might Fail to Complete Homework

In the first column, list logical reasons why a student might fail to complete a homework assignment. Across each row, list the current responses and interventions currently applied to the reason you listed for why students fail to complete a homework assignment. Next to each potential cause, place a plus sign for each response and intervention that would likely help the student improve. Place a minus sign for each response and intervention that would *not* likely help the student improve. Finally, circle each logical cause for which your school has no response and intervention to help the student improve.

Logical Reasons Why Students Might Fail to Complete Homework	Current Site Responses and Interventions for Missing Homework							

Supplemental Interventions for Essential Academic and Social Behaviors: Critical Questions

To ensure the development of an effective supplemental intervention system to help students with essential academic and social behaviors, carefully and collaboratively think through the following four questions.

1. How will we regularly review schoolwide behavior information?

   a. How often and when will we meet?

   b. What information do we need to review?

2. How will we target the cause of student misbehaviors, not just the symptoms?

   a. Which behaviors happening across our school need our attention?

   b. Who has expertise in assisting with this challenge?

   c. What are appropriate intervention strategies?

3. What do we need to learn together?

   a. What research do we need?

   b. Who, beyond this team, needs to be involved?

4. How will we allocate time and resources?

   a. What focus team or teams do we need? Who needs to be on each team?

   b. How often and when will these teams meet?

   c. What will be the process for requesting and allocating resources to support the focus team or teams?

Action 4

Coordinate Interventions for Students Needing Skill *and* Will Supports

> Every science consists in the coordination of facts; if the different observations were entirely isolated, there would be no science.
>
> **—Auguste Comte**

When we created our RTI at Work pyramid, we intentionally split Tier 2 into two parts.

1. Teacher-team area on the right side of Tier 2, which focuses on reteaching essential grade-level academic standards—*skill* interventions

2. Schoolwide area on the left side of Tier 2, which focuses on reteaching essential academic and social behaviors—*will* interventions (which the school's leadership team leads)

We know that some students struggle in school for academic reasons—that is, they lack essential academic skills and knowledge needed to succeed in core curriculum. For other students, their struggles are due to an inability to consistently demonstrate the behaviors and motivation necessary for academic success. Dividing lead responsibility for skill and will interventions is the key to making Tier 2 achievable.

Often the students most at risk demonstrate both needs, as there is a strong connection between low academic skills and problem behavior (Fleming, Harachi, Cortes, Abbott, & Catalano, 2004; Morrison, Anthony, Storino, & Dillon, 2001; Nelson, Benner, Lane, & Smith, 2004). To successfully intervene when students demonstrate academic and behavioral difficulties, the school must have a process to coordinate skill and will interventions. Because this requires coordination between classroom teachers and schoolwide support staff, the school's leadership team should lead responsibility for this outcome.

Here's Why

As discussed earlier in this chapter, successful interventions require educators to address the cause of the student's difficulties, not just the symptoms. It can be difficult to determine if a student's behavior is causing the academic struggles or if the academic struggles are prompting the negative behaviors when a student demonstrates academic failure and behavior. Many schools struggle with targeting interventions for these students because they endlessly debate this "chicken or egg" question. As we write in our book *Uniting Academic and Behavior Interventions: Solving the Skill or Will Dilemma* (Buffum et al., 2015):

The reason we struggle with the skill-or-will dilemma is because we are asking the wrong question. It is not a "chicken or egg" question, but rather a "chicken and egg" solution. If you were a farmer, and your goal was to successfully raise a flock of healthy chickens, you would not need chickens or eggs—you would need chickens and eggs. Likewise, if our job as educators is to raise healthy, productive, successful adults, our students will not need either the academic skills or the behaviors and dispositions needed to succeed as an adult, but both the skill and the will. (p. 12)

Creating a systematic, collaborative process to coordinate skill and will interventions for targeted students is the key to achieving this outcome.

Here's How

Traditionally, there have been two RTI models regarding how to target student interventions. The first is a protocol-driven process. In this approach, the school creates a defined process of exactly how the school responds when students struggle. Based on predetermined time lines, assessments, and cut scores, it places students into specific interventions. This design's strength is that it is very systematic; it is very hard for a student to slip through the cracks. The problem is that it can be inflexible to students' individual needs. The second approach is a problem-solving model. When someone refers a student for help, the school does not have predetermined interventions but instead, studies the student's unique needs. Based on the student's individual needs, the school determines interventions. This design is that it is sensitive to each student's needs, but it is far less systematic.

We see many schools and districts approach interventions with either an exclusively protocol-driven process that fails to consider the unique combination of symptoms and causes each student demonstrates, or a problem-solving model that lacks the systematic safeguards necessary to ensure every student who needs additional help gets it. Successfully responding when students need additional support does not require either schoolwide protocols designed to classify student needs into predetermined interventions *or* a problem-solving process designed to dig deeply into each student's individual needs. It takes protocols *and* problem-solving processes—a *pro-solve* process—as protocols create an effective, systematic process to ensure a student's access to schoolwide interventions does not depend on his or her teacher, and problem-solving enables a school to tailor its collective efforts to each student's unique needs (Buffum et al., 2015).

We offer the following four steps and tools to achieve this outcome.

1. Systematically identify students who could potentially benefit from both skill and will interventions.

2. Schedule meeting time to plan and coordinate skill and will interventions.

3. Utilize the pro-solve process.

4. Monitor and revise.

Systematically Identify Students Who Could Potentially Benefit From Both Skill and Will Interventions

As discussed earlier in this chapter, we recommend that a school has a systematic process, approximately every three weeks, in which to identify students who might need Tier 2 support. Because this process is designed to create a 360-degree view of the student's entire school day, it helps identify students who might need both academic and behavior supports.

Schedule Meeting Time to Plan and Coordinate Skill and Will Interventions

Because the goal is to coordinate skill and will interventions, the process must include the teachers responsible for meeting the targeted student's academic needs and the schoolwide staff who lead Tier 2 behavior supports.

Utilize the Pro-Solve Process

Determining the appropriate academic and behavior interventions for an individual student requires a highly effective problem-solving process. This process must identify not only the obstacles hindering a student's success but also what causes these obstacles, the best interventions to address these needs, the desired outcomes, and who will be the lead person or team responsible for carrying out each intervention. These goals are captured in the reproducible "RTI at Work Pro-Solve Intervention Targeting Process: Tier 1 and Tier 2" (page 169) (Buffum et al., 2015).

At the heart of the protocol is a sequence of five critical questions that helps determine the causes and potential solutions for a student in need of academic and behavior interventions.

1. **What is the concern?** Obviously, it is unlikely a student would be referred for interventions unless there is at least one concern regarding the student's current level of achievement. Because students struggle due to both academic and behavioral needs, consider both skill and will concerns.

2. **What is the cause of the concern?** Many struggling students demonstrate the same academic and behavioral concerns, such as low test scores, poor grades, inconsistent attendance, missing assignments, and disruptive behavior. It is critical to remember that these concerns represent similar symptoms, but the underlying causes can vary from student to student. For example, poor attendance can be a concern numerous students demonstrate, but this does not mean the cause of each student's absences is the same. The key is to determine *why* each student is missing school. Eliminate the cause, and solve the problem.

3. **What is the desired outcome?** Many schools fall into the trap of focusing on eliminating the negative concern, instead of targeting the desired positive outcomes. For example, the concern might be that a student inappropriately blurts out answers during whole-group instruction thus demonstrating disruptive behavior. Instead of discussing what steps the school

> Eliminate the cause, and solve the problem.

staff can take to stop the disruptive behavior, a better discussion would be to determine the appropriate academic behaviors the student must learn to successfully participate in whole-group learning opportunities.

4. **What steps should we take to best achieve the desired outcome?** By moving beyond assigning students to interventions based on common symptoms and instead, diagnosing the cause of each student's struggles and then determining the desired positive outcomes, the school is now ready to identify the interventions and action steps necessary to meet each student's specific needs.

5. **Who is going to take lead responsibility to ensure each intervention is implemented?** The best-made plans are useless if they are not effectively implemented. Yet when everyone is responsible for an intervention, no one is responsible. At some point, the buck must stop with someone to ensure an intervention moves from a plan to action.

Notice that we divided the rows of the "RTI at Work Pro-Solve Intervention Targeting Process: Tier 1 and Tier 2" (page 169) tool into broad sections: collaborative teacher-team responsibilities and schoolwide responsibilities. Teacher teams should take lead responsibility for reteaching the following.

▶ **Essential grade-level standards:** These are the academic skills and knowledge the teacher team identifies as essential for every student to master to be adequately prepared for success in the next course or grade level.

▶ **Immediate prerequisite skills:** These are the specific academic skills and knowledge that represent the immediate building blocks to essential grade-level standards. They were most likely taught either in a previous unit, in a previous school year, or in the previous course within a subject-based sequence of coursework.

▶ **English language:** At Tier 2, students who need support in English language have already learned basic conversational English but might still need assistance with subject-specific academic vocabulary and the written structures of English.

Schoolwide resources should take the lead for the following.

▶ **Academic behaviors:** School support staff can help students who need assistance in academic behaviors, such as completing assignments, studying and organizing, staying focused and on task, and participating in classroom activities.

▶ **Social behaviors:** Interventions in social behaviors can include assistance with school attendance, positive peer relationships, sportsmanship in competitive activities, and appropriate school language.

▶ **Health and home:** Sometimes specific health concerns and home factors can negatively affect student achievement in school, such as a student who might miss class time due to a mild bout of asthma caused by a windy day or a student upset at school because his or her parent is being deployed for military duty. The school's health and counseling staff could provide supplemental support, thus helping the student attend and stay focused in class.

Monitor and Revise

While we designed the pro-solve targeting process to determine a student's needs, identify effective interventions, and assign responsibilities for carrying out the intervention plan, it is unlikely that initial results create a perfect intervention plan. Once you develop an intervention plan, team members must monitor student progress to determine if students are achieving the desired outcomes.

Because the pro-solve process forces the team to determine the specific desired outcomes for the targeted student, it should guide what data the team collects to monitor student progress and who will be responsible. Included in the pro-solve activity is a complementary monitoring form (Buffum et al., 2015). We aligned this form to the outcomes determined through asking pro-solve questions and designed it to simplify the paperwork associated with the monitoring process. Because all staff refer students for additional help every three weeks, it seems logical to complete and review this monitoring form about every three weeks. The team can use this information to revise a student's plan, discontinue services as the student achieves goals, and prompt celebration when the student is succeeding.

Helpful Tools

The following tools will help you accomplish the work for this essential action.

▶ **"RTI at Work Pro-Solve Intervention Targeting Process: Tier 1 and Tier 2" (see chapter 5, page 169):** This activity is designed to help identify, diagnose, target, and monitor Tier 2 academic and behavior interventions.

▶ **"RTI at Work Pro-Solve Intervention Monitoring Plan: Tier 1 and Tier 2" (see chapter 5, page 179):** Teams should use this activity in coordination with the "RTI at Work Pro-Solve Intervention Targeting Process: Tier 1 and Tier 2" reproducible. Members can record a student's progress in meeting his or her academic and behavior goals.

Coaching Tips

Communicate, communicate, communicate!

As mentioned previously, you need the same strategy for successful coordination of interventions for students with multiple needs—communicate, communicate, communicate! Within that communication, the leadership team must ensure that all stakeholders:

▶ Understand why a coordinated system is necessary

▶ Have opportunities to provide input

▶ Understand their role in making any decisions needed

- ▸ Can articulate how and when they need to participate

- ▸ Actively support the system once it is in place

Meeting these communication needs requires multiple and ongoing forms of communication—print, technological, verbal, and collaborative. In other words, use every possible channel, especially those used for nonessential information (for example, newsletters, blogs, and faculty meetings).

Perhaps even more important, every leadership team member must walk the talk. For example, requesting staff participation in other activities when they're needed in a pro-solve meeting sends a mixed message. Casual conversations over lunch must consistently communicate the same message that formal forms of communication send. Fundamentally, communication depends on both words and deeds, and often day-to-day conversations and behaviors are the most powerful vehicles for sharing important information.

> Every leadership team member must walk the talk.

Conclusion

The goal of Tier 2 is to approach and solve problems when they are small. When a student first begins to struggle with a new essential academic standard, or fails to demonstrate the behaviors necessary to succeed, the school should be ready to respond quickly and effectively. We don't allow students to fall too far behind when we systematically identify students through common assessments and frequent teacher recommendation procedures. And by assigning lead responsibilities for skill and will interventions across the school, it becomes realistic to respond effectively, even when school resources are limited. Over time, the school should have fewer and fewer students in need of Tier 3 intensive interventions.

But regardless of how well a school implements Tier 1 and Tier 2, there undoubtedly will be students who need more. Some students might have crippling gaps in essential skills that they should have mastered years ago. These foundational skills are not the focus of Tier 1 or Tier 2—this is the purpose of Tier 3. The next two chapters focus on how to provide these intensive interventions.

PART THREE

TIER 3 ESSENTIAL ACTIONS

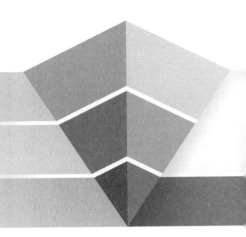

CHAPTER 7

Tier 3 Schoolwide Essential Actions

All students can be successful given the right environment. By supporting them both inside and outside the classroom, we can ensure they gain the skills they need to excel in adulthood.

—Jasper Fox

In this chapter, we focus on Tier 3 of the RTI at Work pyramid (see figure 7.1, page 226). We have previously identified supports that students receive at Tier 2 as *interventions* (a little more help with current essential standards), and at Tier 3 as *remediation* (intensive support with prior skills and knowledge from previous school years). These two tiers have different learning outcomes. For the purpose of readability, chapters 7 and 8 will refer to Tier 3 intensive supports as *interventions*. While all intervention is not remedial, all remediation represents interventions focused on deficits in skills, knowledge, dispositions, and behaviors that are much more intensive than those at Tier 2 and should, therefore, be understood as remediation. In the same sense, we ask you to think of Tier 1 intervention as prevention.

Visually, this portion of the pyramid represents the following.

▸ Tier 3 describes how a school provides remediation to struggling students by offering intensive interventions in universal skills.

▸ Teams must coordinate these interventions across the school, so two school-wide teams take lead responsibility to plan and coordinate this intensive help. The school leadership team takes lead responsibility for allocating and coordinating time and resources to support students in need of intensive help, while the school intervention team takes primary responsibility for problem solving, diagnosing, planning, and monitoring the interventions provided for each student at Tier 3.

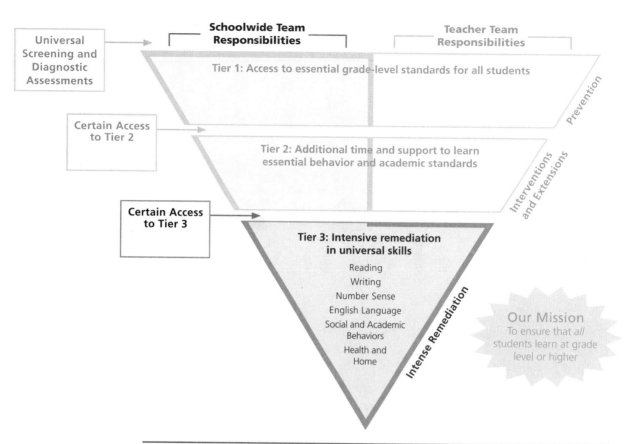

FIGURE 7.1: Focus on Tier 3 schoolwide essential actions.

If a school provides students access to essential grade-level curriculum and effective initial teaching during Tier 1 core instruction, and targeted supplemental academic and behavioral help in meeting these standards at Tier 2, then most students should be succeeding. But there inevitably will be a number of students who still struggle because they lack the critical foundational skills needed to learn—skills that span all subject areas and grade levels. These six universal skills of learning include:

1. Decode and comprehend grade-level text.

2. Write effectively.

3. Apply number sense.

4. Comprehend the English language (or the school's primary language).

5. Consistently demonstrate social and academic behaviors.

6. Overcome complications due to health or home.

These universal skills represent much more than a student needing help in a specific learning standard. Instead, they represent a series of skills that enable a student to comprehend instruction, access information, demonstrate understanding, and behaviorally function in a school setting. If a student is significantly behind in just one of these universal skills, he or she will struggle in virtually every grade level, course, and subject, and usually a school's most at-risk youth are behind in more than one.

Elementary schools do not assume that students entering kindergarten possess basic literacy, numeracy, and self-monitoring skills, so these universal skills comprise most of the essential grade-level standards in the primary grades. Due to this schoolwide focus in the early years of school, most students enter upper grades with at least an adequate level of mastery in these foundational skills.

Beyond the primary grades, schools generally assume that students entering upper elementary, middle, and high school already possess these universal skills, and so does the state or province grade-level curriculum. Students who have not mastered these skills need intensive instruction to catch up, as these skills are no longer part of grade-level core instruction.

Determining the individual needs of a school's most at-risk youth, creating a master schedule that provides multiple tiers of support, and allocating the resources necessary to achieve these outcomes require a schoolwide effort. For this reason, we recommend two schoolwide teams take lead responsibility for Tier 3 interventions: the school leadership team and site intervention team. In this chapter, we discuss the responsibilities of the school leadership team at Tier 3. Its essential actions should include the following.

1. Identify students needing intensive support.

2. Create a dynamic, problem-solving site intervention team.

3. Prioritize resources based on greatest student needs.

4. Create a systematic and timely process to refer students to the site intervention team.

5. Assess intervention effectiveness.

Let's explore each of these essential actions.

Action 1

Identify Students Needing Intensive Support

> Of the five steps that comprise certain access, there is one step that a school must get right every time: Identify.
>
> **—Austin Buffum, Mike Mattos, and Chris Weber**

Because the best intervention is prevention, schools must create a timely process to identify students who are severely challenged academically or behaviorally or both. This process is typically known as *universal screening*. Rather than waiting weeks for students to fail and fail again, schools should strive to identify these students as early as possible and place them into intensive, Tier 3 interventions—no later than the first week of school.

We sometimes observe schools waiting for benchmark assessment results or end-of-semester grades to appear before triggering interventions for failing students. These assessment results often arrive in December or January, measuring standards that were taught as many as ten to twelve weeks prior. Students can't wait that long for help to arrive. Students might dig a hole so deep that they can never get out!

Unless these students are new to the school or school district, we probably already know enough about them to avoid waiting for them to fail yet once again before referring them to our most intensive interventions. This kind of universal screening does not rely on a series of tests but instead, on data and knowledge we have already accumulated relating to our students who are most in need of supports.

Here's Why

Honestly, how many times have you witnessed the following scenario? A student with a reading comprehension level several grades below his or her current grade level, and lacking fluency with key arithmetic operations, goes home for the summer. When school resumes in the fall, this student returns reading at or above his or her current grade level and having reliable fluency with all arithmetic operations. Probably not very often!

Students with extreme deficits in social and academic behaviors seldom, if ever, completely heal over the summer break.

Why would we wait to see if some kind of miracle occurs over summer break? If we are concerned about false positives (students placed into Tier 3 that don't actually need that level of support), frequent progress monitoring would soon reveal that something significant has happened to the student academically (Fuchs & Fuchs, 2007), and we can remove him or her from Tier 3 supports. This thinking should apply to behavioral interventions as well. Students with extreme deficits in social and academic behaviors seldom, if ever, completely heal over the summer break.

Administering nationally normed universal screening instruments can consume many precious days, if not weeks, of instruction time and may do little to inform a school regarding which students need intensive Tier 3 help. They already possess this information. Except for newly enrolled students, schools already know who these students are and should provide them with intensive supports as soon as school begins. This is not to say that schools should not administer diagnostic assessments at the beginning of the year to better target exactly what interventions would best benefit these students who are struggling. This idea is similar to vision screening that many elementary schools do—students come to the nurse's office and read from the Snellen eye chart. The school refers those students who can't accurately read line six, E D F C Z P, to an ophthalmologist to receive a more diagnostic evaluation. This is an example of screening followed by a more diagnostic assessment. Notice that we didn't have an ophthalmologist exam for every student in the school.

Some schools with whom we have worked administer a highly diagnostic screener to every student every year. This may take as much as the first two weeks of the school year to complete. In schools where most students are reading at or above grade level, we ask what these schools are doing with this highly diagnostic information. In most cases, the answer is *not much*. Instead, we recommend that schools administer a highly diagnostic screening tool in reading or mathematics at the beginning of the year to those students who we know from previous years must continue to receive intensive Tier 3 interventions. This information can help target the continuing causes of their struggles, and thus help target the interventions they receive.

This approach allows schools to place their students in greatest need in intensive Tier 3 interventions the very first week of school. Schools then follow up with just these students using a highly diagnostic assessment that helps target the Tier 3 interventions on *causes* rather than symptoms.

Here's How

Schools should use the information they have already gathered to identify students in need of intensive Tier 3 interventions. For academic interventions, this information could include state tests, end-of-course exams, common summative and formative assessments, diagnostic assessments, running records, and informal assessment data. For behavioral interventions, schools should use information such as functional behavioral analyses and other behavior screening scales to initially place students into intensive Tier 3 interventions at the beginning of the school year. For transfer students new to the school, we encourage teacher teams to create their own universal screeners directly tied to the essential standards they have prioritized for all students to master.

For example, the third column of the reproducible "Essential Standards Chart" (see chapter 3, page 88) asks teams to identify prerequisite skills and academic vocabulary that must be in place for students to master the essential standards they prioritized. In these cases, we encourage teams to create a brief, universal screener based on these same prior skills and vocabulary. Other options exist, such as the Northwest Evaluation Association's (NWEA) Measures of Academic Progress. Students new to the school can quickly take this computer-adaptive test so teachers can compare the scale scores of these students to those of existing students to identify those who are far behind the school's expectations.

While some insist that these universal screening tools be nationally normed instruments, it's impossible for such a nationally normed instrument to be as closely aligned to what a particular team, at a particular school, in a particular district, in a particular state prioritizes as essential. Instead, imagine the efficacy of a universal screening tool a staff constructs around the prerequisite skills related directly to those standards they prioritize as essential for all students to master, as we discuss in the next chapter. Based on this logic, we encourage grade-level collaborative teams to create their own universal screening tools to administer during the first week of instruction to students new to their school. Based on results from this kind of screener, they should immediately place some students in intensive Tier 3 interventions.

We do not believe in the trickle-down approach to RTI. In this approach, almost all students begin the school year assigned to new classes with new teachers and receive Tier 1 instruction. After a few weeks, or sometimes months, we discover that certain students need more help with the essential standards the team identifies. These students now begin to receive Tier 2 supplemental interventions. After a few more months, these students continue to struggle and fall further behind, and then eventually trickle down into Tier 3 intensive interventions.

> We do not believe in the trickle-down approach to RTI.

Here's why we don't believe that this approach is appropriate—except in a few, isolated instances. We should already know which students are one or more grade levels behind in prerequisite skills needed to master essential grade-level standards. We know this for two reasons: (1) they went to our school or school district last year, and we have lots of information already that confirms they are far behind, and (2) the school administered universal screening tools to new students (not the entire school) during the very first week that indicated they are far behind grade-level expectations.

In some cases, a student does not show up on our radar at the beginning of the year based on what we already know about the student or with universal screening. Perhaps the student disengages and becomes depressed because some tragic event has befallen the student and his or her family. This is but one example of how a student might draw our concern later in the year. In this instance, the site intervention team becomes involved (discussed in chapter 8).

Systematic, timely, and targeted identification of our students in greatest need is the one area of RTI at Work with which we must be perfect. We must identify with near perfection the students who are failing academically or behaviorally because if we don't, it may be too late to help them.

Helpful Tool

The following tool will help you accomplish the work for this essential action.

▶ **"Universal Screening Planning Guide" (page 232):** This guide helps teams determine which criteria, personnel, and processes to use to screen students needing intervention support in universal skills of reading, writing, number sense, English language, social and academic behaviors, and health and home.

Coaching Tips

> The concept of universal screening needs to apply to every teacher and, as a result, every student.

To accurately and effectively identify students needing intensive support, keep in mind that the concept of universal screening needs to apply to every teacher and, as a result, every student. We must identify students who are failing in art or business education classes as well as those in English language arts and mathematics classes.

That said, once again—communicate, communicate, communicate! In a staff meeting devoted to the singular topic of universal screening, provide all teachers and support staff members with background information to facilitate a shared understanding of *what* universal screening means and *why* it is imperative. To ensure understanding, staff members must see examples of universal screening tools, dialogue with each other, raise questions, and challenge each other's thinking. A short survey can provide an overview of both understanding of the concepts and the level of support for implementation. If the survey shows either is lacking, it is essential to spend additional time strengthening these key outcomes.

Finally, teams must establish a clearly articulated schoolwide expectation for developing and using universal screening tools before moving to implementation. This expectation needs to include all teachers and all subject areas, as well as support staff who focus on student behavior. Include a deadline and accountability for developing screening tools. Additionally, teachers must know the expectations for using their universal screeners, collecting the data, and communicating to the leadership team their results and recommendations for students in need of Tier 3 support.

As with all decisions and actions, once the process for referring students for Tier 3 support is up and running, the leadership team must revisit and reevaluate its effectiveness on a regular basis. Staff input, as well as student learning results, must be a part of the evaluation.

As a final note, it is important to remember that RTI at Work is based on a fundamental commitment to *all* students learning at high levels. Creating a systematic and timely process for referring students to Tier 3 support is critical to making that commitment a reality.

Universal Screening Planning Guide

Use the following guide to screen students needing intervention.

Universal Skill	At-Risk Criteria What criteria will be used to determine whether a student is in need of intensive support?	Screening Process What screening assessment, process, or both will be used to identify students in need of intensive support?	When When will the screening process take place?	Who Who will administer the screening?	Intensive Support Available What intensive intervention or interventions will be used to accelerate student learning and support the identified students?
Reading					
Writing					
Number sense					
English language					
Social and academic behaviors					
Health and home					

Universal Screening Planning Guide Protocol

This activity is designed to assist a leadership team plan for universal screening by creating a process to identify students in need of intensive support *before* they fail. Because the purpose is to provide preventive support, it is best if this activity is completed prior to the start of the school year.

For each universal skill, answer a question for each column.

1. **At-risk criteria:** At each grade level, what criteria will be used to determine whether a student is in need of intensive support? For example, in reading, an elementary school may determine that any student entering first grade without the ability to properly recognize all twenty-six letters (uppercase and lowercase) is extremely at risk in reading and will be considered for immediate, intensive support. At a high school, any student whose reading ability is two or more years below grade level (grade-level equivalent) could be considered for immediate, intensive support.

2. **Screening process:** What screening assessment, process, or both will be used to identify students in need of intensive support? The leadership team should identify the most effective, efficient, and timely process to gather the at-risk criteria data on each student.

3. **When:** When will the screening process take place? Obviously, if the purpose of universal screening is to provide preventive support, then this data should be collected either prior to the start of the school year or as early in the school year as possible. Finally, as new students will enroll in the school throughout the year, it is important to consider how these students can be screened during the enrollment process.

4. **Who:** Who will administer the screening? As the leadership team has representation from every teacher team, as well as responsibility for coordinating school support staff, this team is best positioned to organize the resources necessary.

5. **Intensive support available:** What intensive intervention or interventions will be used to accelerate student learning and support the identified student? There is no point in universal screening if there is no plan to provide these students extra support in their area or areas of need.

One final consideration: for a school new to universal screening, it may be overwhelming to begin universal screening in all six universal skills, at all grade levels, immediately. In this case, we recommend that the leadership team identify the universal skill (reading, writing, number sense, English language, social and academic behaviors, health and home) that is currently the greatest area of need in its school. Start by focusing on this one. As the school builds skill and competence in this area, others can be added.

Source: Adapted from Buffum, A., Mattos, M., & Weber, C. (2012). Simplifying response to intervention: Four essential guiding principles. *Bloomington, IN: Solution Tree Press.*

Action 2

Create a Dynamic, Problem-Solving Site Intervention Team

> The significant problems we face cannot be solved at the same level of thinking we were at when we created them.
>
> **—Albert Einstein**

The site intervention team leads the school's focused microview on specific students in need of Tier 3 intensive support. It coordinates the Tier 3 interventions for students already identified at the beginning of the school year, as well as considers when and how to move a student into Tier 3 interventions who was previously not identified. It is unlikely that an individual teacher or teacher team has the diverse expertise and resources to diagnose the needs of a student requiring Tier 3 interventions. Nor would a teacher or teacher team have the authority to assign schoolwide resources (for example, school psychologist, speech and language pathologist, counselor, or special education teachers) needed to provide these interventions. The site intervention team primarily focuses on the individual needs of the most at-risk students.

> The site intervention team primarily focuses on the individual needs of the most at-risk students.

Here's Why

With vexing, persistent medical problems, doctors often refer us to specialists or even to more than one specialist in order to receive a second or third opinion regarding a course of treatment. In much the same way, education specialists, working with classroom teachers, should address vexing, persistent academic or behavioral problems to best serve individual students. This in no way minimizes the importance of classroom teachers but instead recognizes the overwhelming tasks we expect them to undertake each and every day.

Elementary teachers are responsible for somewhere between twenty to forty students, and we expect them to prepare and deliver instruction in reading, writing, mathematics, science, social studies, and so on. Secondary teachers see literally hundreds of students each day, each one a unique individual with specific learning needs. How can we possibly expect classroom teachers to diagnose and prescribe interventions to solve complex problems without consulting and working with education specialists such as a school psychologist, speech and language pathologist, counselor, content specialists, and special education teachers?

Again, the site intervention team must solve students' complex problems, not merely labeling students or referring them for special education testing, although that may indeed be the best course of action for some. A team of educators with specialized training and perspective, working with the classroom teachers, is best to conduct this lifesaving work.

Here's How

But what is the best team structure to brainstorm solutions to a really tough problem—a team of people who all possess the same expertise, or a team of people with diverse expertise? The logical answer, of course, is diverse expertise. If a student struggles in a specific essential academic skill—like the ability to solve a linear mathematics equation, then the similarly trained algebra team would be a perfectly designed team to identify effective interventions for the singular need. But if a student has significant gaps in foundational reading, number sense, and behavior, the algebra team would not be the most effective problem-solving team for this student. A team composed of expertise in all the student's areas of need would be best. Because the site intervention team should purposely have highly trained educators in the universal skills focused on at Tier 3, this diverse team has the best chance to diagnose, target, prioritize, and monitor the intervention needs of students who face daunting problems.

The reproducible "Building a Site Intervention Team" (page 237) shows how schools can go about assembling this team. (Visit **go.SolutionTree.com/RTIatWork** to download the free reproducibles in this book.) Even if a particular role is unavailable to the school, this form asks schools to find the person best able to perform that function. For example, many classroom teachers have a special education background or reading specialist credential and training. Schools should consider these lifesaving roles during the hiring process.

For example, consider the high school principal who has an opening to fill in social science but also has a vacancy for varsity girls' basketball coach. For years, high school principals have been mindful of the need to look for teachers who might have a background in a cocurricular area. Imagine if one of the three finalists for this social science opening played basketball at the collegiate level, but has not coached recently. Perhaps this would be the teacher selected for the opening.

Similarly, what if one of the three finalists for a third-grade teaching opening had previously taught special education and has a reading specialist certification? What if one of the three finalists majored in behavioral psychology? Remaining mindful of the specific roles needed on a site intervention team should be part of the hiring decisions for K–12 schools.

> Remaining mindful of the specific roles needed on a site intervention team should be part of the hiring decisions for K–12 schools.

Helpful Tools

The following tools will help you accomplish the work for this essential action.

- ▶ **"Building a Site Intervention Team" (page 237):** This template helps the leadership team determine who is most highly trained to fill a particular role, especially when someone with the exact title listed is not available.

- ▶ **"Dimensions of Success" (page 238):** This form helps leadership teams determine their effectiveness across three dimensions: (1) results, (2) process, and (3) relationship.

Coaching Tips

In thinking about the establishment and potential impact of a site intervention team, writer and critic Marcel Proust (1923) claims that the real voyage in discovery consists not in seeking new landscapes, but in having new eyes. How, you might wonder, does this statement apply to a site intervention team?

▶ The site intervention team's power results from not only seeking new intervention strategies but in seeing each student with new eyes. This is why diverse team membership is so important. Each member brings a different expertise and a unique perspective to understanding students and brainstorming ways to best support student success.

▶ A voyage of discovery is one that requires thoughtful reflection. Questions such as the following may help team members think about the students' view of their world and school.

   ▶ How does my school respond when I am struggling?

   ▶ What message do I get from my teachers and peers?

   ▶ What is important to me?

▶ Additionally, the site intervention team must establish a meeting culture of open dialogue and respect for all voices. To accomplish this, it may be helpful to consider the Interaction Associates' RPR (results, process, and relationship) model (Harris, n.d.).

> The site intervention team must establish a meeting culture of open dialogue and respect for all voices.

Interaction Associates (Harris, n.d.) suggests that facilitative leaders attend equally to three dimensions of success—(1) results, (2) process, and (3) relationship—to build strategic, self-aware, and highly collaborative teams.

1. **Results** refer to achieving a goal and accomplishing a task.

2. **Process** refers to how a team does the work, how it designs and manages the work, and how the team measures and evaluates the work.

3. **Relationship** refers to the quality of team members' experiences, their relationships with each other and with the organization as a whole, and to the level of trust and respect team members show each other.

In order to maximize success, facilitative leaders, and in turn, facilitative teams, pay attention to all three dimensions and build and maintain a balanced view of what success really is. Clearly understood goals, tasks, meeting roles, and team norms are essential to this balanced view of success. Equally important, teams must consistently take advantage of facilitative protocols that ensure effective use of time and maximum participation.

Building a Site Intervention Team

Team members: _____

Use the following to build a site intervention team. Remember, when you don't have access to someone with the exact title or role in the first column, ask yourself, "Which staff member is best trained to meet this need?"

Essential Role	Recommended	Staff Members Best Trained to Meet This Need
Administration	Principal	
Reading	Reading specialist	
Writing	English language arts specialist	
Mathematics	Mathematics specialist	
English language	English learner specialist	
Language	Speech and language pathologist	
Teaching differentiation	Special education teacher	
Behavior	Psychologist	
Social-family	Counselor	
Instructional resources	Librarian	
Community resources	Community resource officer, social worker, counselor	

When will this team meet? (Determine a weekly meeting time and location.)

- Time: _____

- Location: _____

What are the team norms?

_____

_____

_____

_____

_____

_____

_____

Source: Adapted from Buffum, A., & Mattos, M. (2014, May). Criteria for selecting essential standards. *Presented at the Simplifying Response to Intervention Workshop, Prince George, British Columbia.*

Dimensions of Success

Effective teams, like effective leaders, balance their focus across three dimensions: (1) results, (2) process, and (3) relationship.

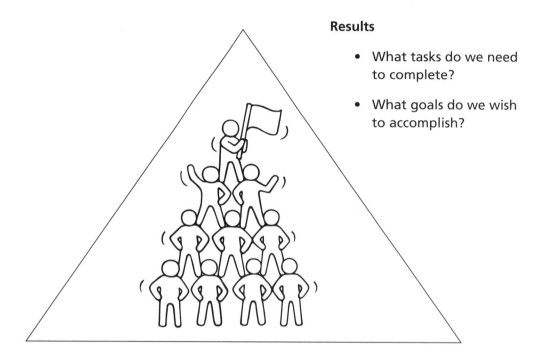

Results

- What tasks do we need to complete?

- What goals do we wish to accomplish?

Process

- How do we do our work?

- How do we design and manage our work?

- How do we monitor and evaluate our work?

Relationship

- How do people experience each other on our team?

- How do we relate to our whole school?

- How do we feel about our involvement and contributions?

Source: Adapted from Interaction Associates (Harris, n.d.).

Action 3

Prioritize Resources Based on Greatest Student Needs

> Nothing is more unequal than the equal treatment of unequal people.
>
> **—Thomas Jefferson**

Students requiring Tier 3 interventions are the most at-risk students in our schools. Schools need to utilize their very best available resources and think outside the box as they prioritize how to best use what they have on hand.

An example of this kind of thinking occurs in a scene from the movie *Apollo 13* (Hallowell & Howard, 1995). Having discovered that the flight crew will die from increasing levels of carbon dioxide, the flight director tells staff at the Johnson Space Center to fit a square peg into a round hole, and quickly. We next see a flight engineer dump a box representing everything available on the lunar and command modules and say to a group of engineers, "We've got to make this fit into the hole for this, using nothing but that [an assortment of every available thing inside the modules]" (Hallowell & Howard, 1995).

This metaphor relates what we ask schools to do: take a system of schooling designed to sift and sort students into a rank order based on their perceived ability, and turn it into a system that ensures high levels of learning for all students. The catch is that we ask most schools to make this fundamental change using only their current resources. In order to perform this lifesaving work, schools need to prioritize using resources in new ways never considered as part of the past paradigm, just as the flight engineers cobbled together what was available to them into an unconventional device that saved the lives of three astronauts.

Here's Why

Students requiring intensive Tier 3 interventions are severely behind academically and often suffer from extreme behavior and attendance issues as well. In medicine, triage is the process of prioritizing patients' treatments based on the severity of their condition. As a result, the patients most in need receive access to the most powerful and effective medical resources on hand in order to save lives.

Education also needs to use triage, specifically with students whose reading comprehension skills are two to four years below grade level, students whose writing skills are so low that they are unable to express in writing what they may know, students who lack a sense of numbers (numeracy) and are unable to respond to the mathematical demands of life, students who lack command of the English language, and students who suffer as a result of extremely poor attendance and behavior. We must prioritize students who suffer from one or more of these maladies to access the best of a school's resources and personnel.

What happens to these students if they don't receive access to the best support and resources? What happens to students who fail in our current education system? The long-term outcomes for these students are highly correlated with poverty, poor health care, a shortened lifespan, and incarceration in prison. On average, school dropouts earn 50 percent less per year than those with a high school diploma. They are less likely to hold a job that offers health insurance or a pension plan, and thus are more likely to experience health problems (Rouse, 2005).

As the Center for Health and Justice (2009) notes:

> According to a report published by the Center for Labor Market Studies (CLMS, 2009) at Northeastern University, almost 1 in 10 males (9%) between the ages of 16 and 24 years who had dropped out of high school [was] in jail, prison, or a juvenile justice institution on any given day in 2006–07. The rate among African Americans in this group, however, was two and a half times (23%) the overall rate. The rates among their racial/ethnic group counterparts were all significantly lower (7% among Asians, 6% among Hispanics, and 7% among Whites). Young African-American male drop-outs also experienced the highest jobless rate (69%) in an average month in 2008, followed by Asians (57%), Whites (54%), and Hispanics (47%). Additionally, male drop-outs from all racial/ethnic groups were 47 times more likely to be incarcerated and more than 4 times as likely to be jobless than their college-graduate peers during these respective time periods.

Students who are not succeeding in school face overwhelming odds in the 21st century.

Perhaps there was a time in the United States in which failing students could reinvent themselves later in life and begin to enjoy a life of health and security. Those days are gone. Students who are not succeeding in school face overwhelming odds in the 21st century, and this is why we must do whatever it takes to turn things around for them before it is too late.

Here's How

The saying that best captures the *how* of prioritizing a school's resources for students with the greatest needs is *all hands on deck*! The key to providing intensive interventions for these students is to utilize the staff most highly trained in the specific area of need. Consider that a family doctor or general practitioner is well-versed in a broad range of maladies that impact his or her patients. He or she is, in fact, a generalist, as the term *general practitioner* describes. Within the medical profession, there are doctors who have highly specialized training in a particular area of medicine and are board certified.

Similarly, in education we have classroom teachers with training and certification around a broad domain of learning, such as mathematics, science, or English language arts. Elementary teachers have even broader training around many domains of learning. In schools, we also have personnel with highly specialized training in a more targeted area of learning—speech and language pathologists, occupational therapists, special education teachers, psychologists, counselors, and behavior specialists, to name a few.

Unfortunately, in too many schools the silo mentality culture that has developed over time isolates these highly specialized educators. The fact that these specialists must comply with a series of laws, regulations, and guidelines that reinforce this feeling of isolation and autonomy partly drives this mentality. All too often we hear statements from a speech and language pathologist at an elementary school like, "I'm too busy serving the students on my caseload. I don't have time to collaborate with classroom teachers, although I probably have a lot of ideas and materials that would help their struggling students."

Another exacerbating factor is that many of these specialists are itinerant employees who move between a number of schools each week. This makes it difficult for them to interact and serve as a resource to classroom teachers. Sometimes the school or school district culture discourages interaction between specialists and classroom teachers. These itinerant employees often report to someone other than the school principal and are evaluated on how well they have complied with the regulations under which they operate and not on how well they have been able to support the efforts of the schools they serve to help all students learn at high levels.

All hands on deck recognizes the fact that classroom teachers (generalists) alone can never be successful in helping *all* students learn at high levels. Better utilizing the specific skills and training of their specialists in consulting with classroom teachers as well as working with their students most in need—much in the same way that general practitioners utilize the skills and specific training of medical specialists when their patients require a more intensive level of support—is the only way we have seen schools become successful in this mission.

> Classroom teachers (generalists) alone can never be successful in helping all students learn at high levels.

Specialists can serve as a resource in one of two main ways. First, specialists can and should be seen as a resource to classroom teachers, much in the same way that a family doctor might consult with a specialist. Regular education teachers should have ongoing access to a school's speech and language pathologist, special education teachers, and occupational therapists so they are better able to provide interventions to struggling students and prevent them from falling so far behind that they eventually end up on the specialist's caseload. School psychologists and counselors should also be readily available to support classroom teachers dealing with extreme behavioral issues.

Second, many schools find creative ways of having specialists actually deliver intensive, Tier 3 interventions to struggling students who are not part of their official caseload. These schools adopt more of the *all hands on deck* philosophy and pry their specialists away from exclusively working with students in their caseloads in order to help non-identified students who need exactly the same interventions as the students they regularly serve. Section 613(a)(4) of the Individuals With Disabilities Education Act (IDEA) and its implementing regulations at 34 CFR §300.208(a)(1) permit using special education–funded personnel.

Melody Musgrove (2013), director of the Office of Special Education Programs for the U.S. Department of Education, writes (as cited in Pierce, 2015):

> Pursuant to 34 CFR §300.208(a), special education teachers fully funded by Part B (non-CEIS) funds may perform duties for children without disabilities if they would already be performing these same duties in order

to provide special education and related services to children with disabilities. For example, a special education teacher is assigned to provide five
hours of reading instruction per week to three students with disabilities
consistent with those students' IEPs. The IEPs provide that the students
need specialized reading instruction that is at grade level but handled at
a slower pace because of auditory processing issues. The school decides
that, although they are not children with disabilities, there are two general education children who would benefit from this instruction. The
special education teacher must prepare lesson plans for each of these
classes regardless of the number of children in the class. She may do so
and conduct the class for all five children because she is only providing
special education and related services for the three children with disabilities and the two children without disabilities are benefiting from
that work. (p. 2)

Another practical strategy in prioritizing resources, beyond the use of specialists,
is to consider which classroom teachers are best prepared and trained to work with
the students most in need. Keeping with the medical analogy, which of our general
practitioners may have some specialized training or experience with a particular area
of medicine? We might ask, "In looking at the results from our common assessment,
which of us seems to have had greatest success with a particular area of learning?"

In many high schools, first-year teachers teach the lowest level, remedial freshman
English and mathematics classes. This is not to say that a first-year teacher might not
be the most effective with these students. However, what usually drives this decision
is that the first-year teacher, hoping to obtain a good evaluation that leads to tenure,
won't complain. In many elementary schools, we see teachers merely rotate the lowest-
achieving students between the team members every four to six weeks, so no one
teacher is "stuck" with these students for too long.

Instead, the leadership team asks the following questions to urge a more thoughtful
approach to prioritizing teacher resources.

> ▶ "Does one of our teachers have specialized training around what these stu-
>   dents need? Is one of our classroom teachers credentialed or experienced in a
>   specialized area?"

> ▶ "Has one or more of our teachers demonstrated greater success on common
>   assessments during our comparison of scores, teacher to teacher?"

> ▶ "Is one of our teachers currently pursuing an advanced degree with a
>   special emphasis on a specific area of need, such as phonemic awareness
>   or decoding?"

> ▶ "Is one of our teachers currently researching a specific area of need as part of
>   his or her thesis or dissertation?"

These are the questions we should ask and answer in completing the fourth column
of the reproducible "RTI at Work Pro-Solve Intervention Targeting Process: Tier 3"
(page 244), Who Takes Responsibility. Remember, this does not mean that others do

not bear some responsibility in delivering Tier 3 intensive interventions—it identifies which staff will take the lead or primary responsibility for designing and delivering this lifesaving help. The school leadership team must ensure that the powerful resources existing at the school are available to students requiring this help. This might mean that we need to adjust schedules and re-examine normal routines and protocols, all of which are within the school leadership team's control.

All hands on deck means precisely what we described. Instead of *my* room, *my* class, and *my* students, successful RTI at Work schools take collective responsibility so that *we*, as an entire school, utilize and prioritize all the resources available to meet our goal of high levels of learning for all students.

Helpful Tool

The following tool will help you accomplish the work for this essential action.

> ▸ **"RTI at Work Pro-Solve Intervention Targeting Process: Tier 3" (page 244):** Teams can use this form to separate academic skills from behavioral issues and target each student's particular needs for intensive intervention.

> Successful RTI at Work schools take collective responsibility so that *we*, as an entire school, utilize and prioritize all the resources available to meet our goal of high levels of learning for all students.

Coaching Tips

Building a deep and shared understanding of what Tier 3 is all about and why it is essential increases the likelihood that teachers will support the steps needed to implement Tier 3, including prioritizing resources.

Each of the steps for prioritizing resources, as well as the rationale for taking them, must be shared and discussed with all staff. To maximize teacher engagement, place real students at the center of the work to personalize the discussion.

A full staff meeting might look like this: teachers sit in assigned mixed groups (cross grade level or cross content). Each group receives a description of a student with Tier 3 needs. The descriptions can be based on real students in the school, but to protect confidentiality, the names should be changed. Each group then determines what the student needs and how and when to provide support for addressing those needs, including who might best provide the needed support. Following at least twenty to thirty minutes for discussion, each group charts and shares its recommendations.

Once each group presents its recommendations, the leadership team clarifies how to use those recommendations, how to make relevant decisions, and when teachers can expect to hear about next steps. Clear communication is key!

To summarize, clear, ongoing communication and appropriate staff involvement in decision making continue to strengthen the cultural norm of taking collective responsibility for *all* students learning at high levels.

RTI at Work Pro-Solve Intervention Targeting Process: Tier 3

Student: _____

Participant: _____   Meeting date: _____

	Targeted Outcomes	Desired Outcomes	Intervention and Action Steps	Who Takes Responsibility	Data Point 1	Data Point 2	Data Point 3	Data Point 4	Data Point 5
Led by Intervention Teams	Foundational reading								
	Foundational writing								
	Foundational number sense								
	Foundational language								
	Academic behaviors								
	Social behaviors								
	Health and home								

Next meeting date: _____

Source: Buffum, A., Mattos, M., Weber, C., & Hierck, T. (2015). Uniting academic and behavior interventions: Solving the skill or will dilemma. Bloomington, IN: Solution Tree Press.

Action 4

Create a Systematic and Timely Process to Refer Students to the Site Intervention Team

As if you could kill time without injuring eternity.

—Henry David Thoreau

While teachers can identify most students proactively for Tier 3 interventions through universal screening practices (see essential action 1 in chapter 7, page 227), some students don't begin the year needing intensive support but develop the need at a later point. This need could develop over time, such as when a student fails to succeed in Tier 1 and Tier 2 supports—or it could happen suddenly, as when a student's parent dies unexpectedly, causing tremendous upheaval in the student's life. When this happens, the school must have a systematic, timely, and targeted process to refer these students to the site intervention team.

Here's Why

If students are "drowning," we can't wait one more day for them to fall even further behind academically or start demonstrating self-destructive behavior. Time is of the essence. We cannot allow a single struggling student to slip through the cracks unnoticed because our process is not systematic. Nor can the student wait weeks for help to arrive—it must be timely.

Here's How

In the days before school begins, the school leadership team uses information from the previous school years to assemble a list of students struggling for academic or behavior reasons during the previous years. Teams should immediately place students in Tier 3 intensive interventions during the first week of school, and teachers should relay their progress-monitoring data during the first few weeks of intervention to the site intervention team. This allows the site intervention team to adjust the interventions and administer new diagnostic assessments to better target the causes of students' struggles. In rare cases, these progress-monitoring data may indicate that a student no longer requires Tier 3 intensive interventions if some kind of miracle or change has occurred over the summer!

Teachers should administer students new to the school a series of brief, universal screeners in reading, writing, and number sense during the first week of school. We recommend closely aligning these screeners to the prerequisite skills the "Essential Standards Chart" (page 88) identifies for that grade level or content area, as well as those prioritized by teams from previous years and prior courses. These screeners might be constructed using many of the prompts or questions collaborative teacher teams already created to formatively assess these prerequisite skills. These teacher-created screeners should not be too long—the goal of screening is to detect deficiencies or gaps, and then target specific causes through the subsequent use of diagnostic assessments.

If you use commercially available universal screening tools, it is imperative to calibrate the results to the specific essential learnings the collaborative teacher teams identify. Everything, including the efficacy of universal screening, revolves around the school's commitment that all students must master these essential grade-level skills.

Sometimes, students who did not previously show up as struggling during universal screening begin to struggle later in the year. For this reason, it is important that the school's site intervention team hold regularly scheduled meetings, at least every three weeks, in which students are referred. Many schools only convene site intervention team meetings as needed, and then all too often, only to consider special education placement. It is imperative that classroom teachers and interventionists have a way to regularly refer students to the site intervention team in a timely fashion for consideration of placement in Tier 3 interventions. Holding site intervention team meetings every three weeks acts as a safeguard against students drifting further behind until problems become critical. We recommend that the site intervention team hold time slots open in its regularly scheduled meetings to discuss students with these emerging needs. Again, we recommend using the reproducible "RTI at Work Pro-Solve Intervention Monitoring Plan: Tier 3" (page 248) to guide conversations around these students.

> Holding site intervention team meetings every three weeks acts as a safeguard against students drifting further behind until problems become critical.

It is not enough for us to develop systems of Tier 3 support for students and then allow them to languish and fail as they wait for a cumbersome process to provide access to that help. If you have ever dealt with a sick child, spouse, parent, or friend, you know how frustrating it can be to know that help exists inside that hospital, but accessing that help might take weeks or even months. We must create a process that is both systematic and timely so students don't wait so long for help that it might be too late to save them.

Helpful Tool

The following tool will help you accomplish the work for this essential action.

▶ **"RTI at Work Pro-Solve Intervention Monitoring Plan: Tier 3" (page 248):** Teams should use this activity in coordination with the "RTI at Work Pro-Solve Intervention Targeting Process: Tier 3" reproducible (page 244). Members can record a student's progress in meeting his or her academic and behavior goals at Tier 3.

Coaching Tips

In order for any process to be systematic and timely, every person on campus must understand the rationale for the system, the logistics of the system, and the role he or she plays in ensuring the system works effectively. The leadership team might create and offer a Tier 3 referral process handbook that explains the rationale for the process and outlines, step by step, how the process works.

Additionally, the leadership team should hold at least one faculty meeting each year to focus on the importance of the referral process. One strategy for engaging staff members in this process might be to role-play an actual site intervention team meeting. The leadership team should assign seats for the meeting to create teams with diverse perspectives, and then give each team several profiles of students (which the site intervention team creates) who require Tier 3 services, including students who have fallen further behind due to attending a school that does not have a systematic and timely referral process.

To conclude the meeting, the leadership team asks staff members to share any insights they have gained as to *why* a systematic and timely referral process is important, *how* the process works, and *what* role they play in its success. Only when every adult on campus clearly understands and supports the referral process will the school have the potential to ensure that no students fall through the cracks.

RTI at Work Pro-Solve Intervention Monitoring Plan: Tier 3

Student: _____

Participant: _____   Meeting date: _____

Targeted Outcomes		Desired Outcomes	Intervention and Action Steps	Who Takes Responsibility	Data Point 1	Data Point 2	Data Point 3	Data Point 4	Data Point 5
Led by Intervention Teams	Foundational reading								
	Foundational writing								
	Foundational number sense								
	Foundational language								
	Academic behaviors								
	Social behaviors								
	Health and home								

Next meeting date: _____

Source: Buffum, A., Mattos, M., Weber, C., & Hierck, T. (2015). Uniting academic and behavior interventions: Solving the skill or will dilemma. Bloomington, IN: Solution Tree Press.

Action 5

Assess Intervention Effectiveness

Follow effective action with quiet reflection. From the
quiet reflection will come even more effective action.

—Peter F. Drucker

A system of interventions is only as effective as each individual intervention of which it is comprised. We have seen schools devote significant time and effort to identify students for additional help and create scheduled time to provide the support, but then place students into ineffective interventions. If a school builds a system of interventions with unproven instructional programs and practices, then all it has done is guarantee students access to support that won't offer much help.

No single intervention works perfectly for every targeted student, but an intervention should achieve its purpose a majority of the time. When this is not the case, either the school is not targeting students well—meaning the intervention works, but the assigned students don't have the specific needs of the intervention—or students are targeted correctly and the intervention is just ineffective at achieving its goal. When the intervention is ineffective not only is it not helping the students but it is also using valuable resources that could be repurposed for better results. Because the school leadership team is responsible for allocating school resources—both fiscal and personnel—it's important that it regularly assesses each intervention's effectiveness.

> A system of interventions is only as effective as each individual intervention of which it is comprised.

Here's Why

Unfortunately, many schools continue to build their interventions with practices that don't work, have never worked, and have no promise of getting better results the following year (Buffum et al., 2012). The numerous examples discussed throughout this book include traditional special education practices, retention, and punitive actions mistakenly intended to motivate better behavior. Let's explore another example—summer school.

Thousands of schools each year offer abbreviated summer classes. While some students use this option to accelerate learning, such as taking a required class to open up their schedule for an additional class during the next school year, most students are required to take summer school due to failure during the school year. The goal is for the student to make up a class or receive remediation over the summer to get them back on track and ready for the next year. While the intention is good, the way most schools provide summer school makes achieving these goals nearly impossible. Consider how summer school is commonly designed.

▸ **Broad indicators:** The school identifies students for summer school using broad indicators, such as the student failed a class or scored well below grade level on end-of-year assessments, or the services are included in a special education student's IEP. Students can fail on these indicators for markedly different reasons. Yet typically, students don't receive deeper diagnostic assessments to identify their wide range of needs, and they are all placed in the same summer school course.

▸ **Shortened time span:** For example, the school assigns a student to summer school because he or she fails a semester of freshman English—a class required for graduation. During the school year, the course met every day for about eighteen weeks. In summer school, the make-up class is typically about six weeks long. To make up for the shortened time span, the student attends class for three hours each day. But how realistic is it to fit an entire semester's worth of reading, discussion, and writing into those compacted weeks? Add to the timing difficulty the certainty that some students are enrolled because they are reluctant readers, have difficulty writing, or lack motivation.

▸ **Teacher assignment:** Mike taught summer school every year he was a classroom teacher, often assigned to teach at a different school than his school-year assignment. In the new classroom, he had limited teaching materials. He did not know anything about the students except that they failed the class during the school year. The summer school term was just about over by the time he began to build a rapport with and understanding of each student.

Looking at these factors, what is the likelihood that students assigned to summer school are going to master the essential skills and knowledge they failed to master during the previous school year and return the following fall ready to succeed? Students might make up credits needed to graduate, but it is highly unlikely that they will actually learn the essential content.

Not surprising, in Hattie's (2009) meta-analysis of the research on summer school effectiveness, he finds the impact rate of 0.23. When asked if going to summer school makes a difference, his answer is, "In general, not much . . ." (Hattie, 2009, p. 77). Yet, in spite of what research and common sense prove is an ineffective intervention, thousands of schools across the United States assign students to summer school every year. This seasonal program is expensive, costing tens of thousands of dollars to extend the school year for some students. And, like every summer, very few of these students enter school the following year significantly better prepared for success (Cooper, Charlton, Valentine, Muhlenbruck, & Borman, 2000).

Here is the critical point: we are not suggesting that summer school is inherently bad. The problem rests in how schools have traditionally implemented summer school—it is not designed to align to the traits of effective interventions. In the next section, we explore how the leadership team can assess the effectiveness of its existing site interventions as well as make these interventions more effective.

Here's How

There are six essential characteristics of an effective intervention.

1. **Targeted:** The more targeted the intervention, the more likely it will work. An effective intervention identifies the specific standard, learning target, or behavior to be retaught. All the students assigned to the intervention should have the same need.

2. **Systematic:** There must be a systematic process to identify every student who needs a specific intervention. Even if the intervention is effective, a student will not benefit from it if the school is ignorant of the student's needs.

3. **Research based:** Research or evidence should support the instructional practice being used so it has a high likelihood of working. This means that the school can reference research that the practice can work or cite evidence that the intervention is working.

4. **Administered by a trained professional:** An intervention is only as effective as the person administering it. If the practice is proven to work, but the staff member implementing it is untrained or incompetent at it, then the intervention is unlikely to work.

5. **Timely:** You should not allow students to fail too long before receiving an intervention. When this happens, they can fall too far behind to fully benefit from the intervention.

6. **Directive:** Intervention must be a directive, meaning students must be required to attend if they have the need. When interventions are optional, often the students who need the help the most don't choose to attend. If the most at-risk students in the school were already actively seeking extra help, they would probably not be at-risk. Even when an intervention is effective, a student does not benefit if he or she does not attend.

> Even when an intervention is effective, a student does not benefit if he or she does not attend.

All six characteristics are essential, meaning for an intervention to be effective, it must align with all six traits.

We created the reproducible tool, "Intervention Evaluation and Alignment Chart" (page 255), to help schools evaluate their current site interventions and align them to the six characteristics. The site intervention team and teacher teams can also use it to plan and assess specific interventions they might lead.

1. **Targeted:** What *exactly* is the intervention's purpose? What specific skill, content, or behavior should students learn by the end of the intervention? If you can't specify this, it's a clear indication that the intervention is not targeted enough. To remedy this problem, make the intervention more focused.

2. **Systematic:** Is there a systematic process to identify every student who needs help in the intervention's targeted area? Once identified, can all the students that need the intervention actually receive the intervention? If the team answers *no* to either of these questions, what steps can you take to make the intervention more systematic?

3. **Research based:** What research or evidence validates that the intervention has a high likelihood of working? If you can't cite any, then discontinue the practice and study better practices to reteach the targeted outcome.

4. **Administered by a trained professional:** Who is currently administering the intervention? Are they properly trained and competent at this task? If not, does the school have staff better trained, or can the school provide the staff member additional training and support to become more effective?

5. **Timely:** How long does it take to identify and place students in the intervention? We suggest it should not take longer than three weeks.

6. **Directive:** Are targeted students required to attend? If not, what steps can you take to ensure students needing help are present for the intervention?

After determining the current reality of the intervention in relation to the six criteria, teachers, the site intervention team, or the school leadership team should identify where the intervention is out of alignment and determine steps to fix it.

Referring back to the summer school example, here is what the six characteristics within the process might look like at a middle school. The leadership team wants to improve the effectiveness of its summer school mathematics offerings, specifically for students who failed seventh-grade prealgebra.

1. **Targeted:** The teachers place students in a summer school mathematics program because they fail prealgebra. Instead of trying to reteach all the prealgebra curriculum, the team decides to have the mathematics department identify the specific skills students must learn to master the essential algebra 1 standards taught during the first semester of the following year.

2. **Systematic:** The seventh-grade prealgebra teachers receive a list of the prerequisite skills to be taught in the summer session. At the end of the year, these teachers identify prealgebra students who could benefit from extra teaching and practice on these specific skills.

3. **Research based:** The prealgebra team discusses instructional practices that proved effective and ineffective while teaching these standards during the regular school year and gives this information to the teachers who are teaching the summer school course.

4. **Administered by a trained professional:** The school identifies the teachers who are best trained to reteach this content and encourages them to apply for this extended-learning opportunity.

5. **Timely:** Traditional summer school is usually offered right after the regular school year ends. This often means that at the end of summer school, students are home for about one month before school starts. Because the targeted mathematics outcomes of this course relate to the first units of study the following fall, the school decides to move summer school closer to the start of school. This new jump-start approach prepares students for immediate success in their new grade-level mathematics class.

6. **Directive:** Teachers notify and highly encourage parents of identified students to have their children attend this targeted summer school class. If a parent is unable or unwilling to have his or her child attend, the school creates an alternative way to intervene. The school assigns students who do not attend this summer school class to a two-period block mathematics class at the start of the school year. This class provides the teacher with the time to both reteach the prealgebra skills needed for success in algebra 1 (the same skills taught during summer school) and also teach the new mathematics curriculum. Because the second option is offered during the regular school year, the school can require the student to receive the help without needing parental consent.

For the leadership team, we recommend that time is allotted so it can evaluate all the school's interventions at least twice a year.

1. **At the midpoint of each year:** At this point in the year, there has been sufficient time for the school's interventions to work.

2. **At the end of the year:** With this information, the school can reconsider revising and reallocating resources for the coming year.

We know that most schools have very limited resources. The beauty of the evaluation and alignment process is that it is designed to help a school get better results with the resources it has, instead of trying to secure more resources to get better results. We used this process at our schools, so we can say with confidence that it works!

Helpful Tools

The following tools will help you accomplish the work for this essential action.

▶ **"Intervention Evaluation and Alignment Chart" (page 255):** Teachers, the site intervention team, or the school leadership team can use this tool to evaluate and improve the effectiveness of a specific intervention.

▶ **"Intervention Evaluation and Alignment Chart Protocol" (page 256):** This protocol guides team discussions as members complete the "Intervention Evaluation and Alignment Chart."

Coaching Tips

Research consistently and continuously points out the value of formative assessment and the positive impact it has on student learning when done well (Chappuis et al., 2012; Hattie, 2009; Wiliam, 2011). Given the fact that assessing interventions for effectiveness is a form of formative assessment, it is not surprising that doing so is essential to the overall success of RTI at Work. When assessing interventions for effectiveness, schools should consider the following underlying formative assessment questions.

▶ How well are our current actions achieving our desired outcomes?

▶ What strategies can we use to increase our effectiveness?

►   What goals for improvement do we need to commit to?

Keeping in mind that teams of teachers are routinely implementing interventions in their classrooms during Tier 1 instruction and collaboratively implementing Tier 2 interventions in response to common formative assessments, it is important to not only recommend but to facilitate opportunities for teachers to experience the process for assessing intervention effectiveness. The same criteria described in the previous sections are equally applicable to Tier 1 and 2 interventions, and the conversations among teams as they consider each criterion are foundational to making improvements.

> **The power of formative assessment lies in its focus on improvement rather than judgment or evaluation.**

Though this may seem like "preaching to the choir," keep in mind that the power of formative assessment lies in its focus on improvement rather than judgment or evaluation. When all participants approach the process of assessing intervention effectiveness with the dual lenses of identifying and celebrating what is working well and identifying and problem-solving what is not working well, the dialogue remains open and productive. If, however, the approach becomes one of judgment or evaluation, the conversations often become stilted and defensive, thus hampering creative thinking and yielding few solutions or improvements.

To ensure that the dialogue taking place during the process of assessing interventions for effectiveness maintains a positive focus, it is important for the leadership team to apply the same formative assessment questions to themselves and their work. Questions to consider might include:

►   How well are our current actions achieving our desired outcomes? What evidence do we have that our school culture is becoming one of collective responsibility for high levels of student learning?

►   To what degree do team meetings and staff meetings utilize norms and protocols to strengthen collaboration and teamwork?

►   What strategies are we, as a leadership team, using that are working well? How do we know?

►   What areas are in need of improvement? How do we know?

►   What goals and time lines do we need to agree on to enhance the development of systematic support for all students?

►   What actions do we need to take to increase our effectiveness as a leadership team? How will we monitor our progress?

In summary, formative assessment in all its forms and uses is critical to moving forward. Robert Garmston says it best: "Anyone too busy to reflect on one's practice is also too busy to improve" (Garmston & Wellman, 2009, p. 144). Reflection is an essential part of formative assessment. By reflecting on our errors and successes, we gain the knowledge and confidence we need to improve.

Intervention Evaluation and Alignment Chart

First, identify the intervention you want to evaluate. Write it in the far-left column. Be as specific as possible. Then, working from left to right, evaluate the intervention against each of the six essential characteristics.

Current Site Interventions	Targeted	Systematic	Research Based	Administered by a Trained Professional	Timely	Directive	Alignment Steps
	+, ✓, ×	+, ✓, ×	+, ✓, ×	+, ✓, ×	+, ✓, ×	+, ✓, ×	

Intervention Evaluation and Alignment Chart Protocol

Use the following protocol to guide team discussions as team members complete the "Intervention Evaluation and Alignment Chart."

This leadership team or site intervention team can use this activity to evaluate schoolwide interventions, or the teacher team can use it to evaluate teacher-led interventions. We recommend completing this activity twice per year—prior to the start of the school year and at the midpoint of each school year.

First, brainstorm your current site interventions in the left column—one intervention per box. For each intervention, ask the following questions.

1. **Targeted:** What exactly is the intervention's purpose? What specific skill, content, or behavior should students learn by the end of the intervention? If you can't specify this, it's a clear indication that the intervention is not targeted enough. To remedy this problem, make the intervention more focused.

2. **Systematic:** Is there a systematic process to identify every student who needs help in the intervention's targeted area? Once identified, can all the students that need the intervention actually receive the intervention? If the team answers no to either of these questions, what steps can you take to make the intervention more systematic?

3. **Research based:** What research or evidence validates that the intervention has a high likelihood of working? If you can't cite any, then discontinue the practice and study better practices to reteach the targeted outcome.

4. **Administered by a trained professional:** Who is currently administering the intervention? Are they properly trained and competent at this task? If not, does the school have staff who are better trained, or can the school provide the staff member additional training and support to become more effective?

5. **Timely:** How long does it take to identify and place students in the intervention? We suggest it should not take longer than three weeks.

6. **Directive:** Are targeted students required to attend? If not, what steps can you take to ensure students needing help are present for the intervention?

7. **Alignment steps:** This is the most important step! Because all the characteristics are essential to an intervention's effectiveness, any X on the chart must be addressed. For example, if a particular intervention has an X under Directive, then the team should discuss and determine how the staff will require students to attend. Fix the X, and the intervention becomes more effective.

Conclusion

Successfully completing the five essential actions in this chapter enables the leadership team to create the time, resources, and collaborative structures necessary to provide intensive interventions. The next step is to make sure each student in need of Tier 3 support receives interventions that target his or her individual needs. The site intervention team will lead this process, which is the focus of the next chapter.

CHAPTER 8

Tier 3 Intervention Team Essential Actions

In this chapter, we once again focus on Tier 3 of the RTI at Work pyramid. However, while chapter 7 focused on the role of the school leadership team in relation to Tier 3, this chapter focuses on the contributions of the site intervention team to the same section of the pyramid—Tier 3.

While the school leadership team is responsible for the macroview of Tier 3, including the scheduling and allocation of resources, the site intervention team is responsible for the microview—determining the specific needs of each student requiring intensive support. See figure 8.1 (page 260).

The site intervention team's essential responsibilities at Tier 3 are:

1. Diagnose, target, prioritize, and monitor Tier 3 interventions

2. Ensure proper intervention intensity

3. Determine if special education is needed and justifiable

Of these three outcomes, the first is paramount to providing effective Tier 3 interventions.

Action 1

Diagnose, Target, Prioritize, and Monitor Tier 3 Interventions

> No problem can withstand the assault of sustained thinking.
>
> **—Voltaire**

Consider for a moment the characteristics that define students who need intensive interventions. These students are multiple years below grade level in the foundational skills that are absolutely indispensable to success in school, including the following five.

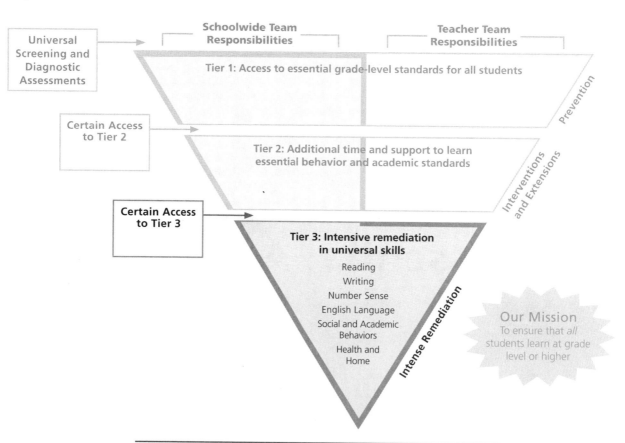

FIGURE 8.1: Focus on Tier 3 intervention team essential actions.

1. The ability to decode and comprehend text

2. An understanding of numbers, sequencing, and basic mathematical functions

3. The skills to convey ideas through the written word

4. The ability to comprehend and speak the native tongue of the school

5. A demonstration of basic social and academic behaviors

Students with these characteristics often come from home environments that cannot provide academic support, and in some cases, actually contribute to the student's struggles in school. Some of these students have identified learning disabilities, but most do not (Brooks-Gunn & Duncan, 1997; O'Connor & Fernandez, 2006).

Targeting each student's specific needs is critical to responding effectively.

While these students often need intensive interventions in the same foundational skills, they do not all struggle for the same reasons. Some students could be below grade level in reading because they can't decode text, while others have decoding skills but poor fluency and comprehension. So targeting each student's specific needs is critical to responding effectively. And finally, these students must receive this intensive support in addition to Tier 1 and Tier 2, not in place of it. Asking individual teachers to diagnose, target, prioritize, and monitor this level of help is unreasonable and unrealistic. The site intervention team, collectively experienced in all the foundational skills that must be retaught at Tier 3, is a school's best hope to achieve these outcomes.

These students must improve multiple grade levels in a single school year. If a fifth grader is reading at a third-grade level and improves one year's growth in reading at the end of the year, then this student is now a sixth grader reading at a fourth-grade level—still two years below grade level. So Tier 3 interventions must be highly effective for these students to have any realistic chance of reaching high levels of learning.

Here's Why

In almost every case, students in need of Tier 3 interventions have been attending school for years. Dedicated, professional educators have provided core instruction and most likely additional help, when possible; yet, these students are still *years* below grade level. A school must assume that finding solutions for these students is going to be very difficult. If simple interventions would work for them, prior years' teachers would have used them.

Faced with this challenge, the best way to brainstorm and identify potential solutions is through a team approach. However, unlike Tier 2 where we advocate that teacher teams lead the intervention process, we recommend that an intervention team with diverse expertise lead Tier 3. When students struggle to master specific essential academic standards, teachers who teach the same grade or course can brainstorm together to identify better ways to teach the standard. For example, if a student is struggling in a specific essential academic skill—such as the ability to solve a linear equation in mathematics—then algebra teachers with similar training would be perfectly qualified to identify effective interventions for this singular need. However, if a student has significant gaps in foundational reading, number sense, and behavior, the algebra team is not the most effective for this student. A team composed of expertise in all the student's areas of need is best. Because the site intervention team is purposefully designed to include educators highly trained in the universal skills focused in Tier 3, it has the best chance to diagnose, target, prioritize, and monitor the intervention needs of students who face daunting problems.

Here's How

The first step is for the school leadership team to create a site intervention team comprising experts in the universal skills of reading, writing, number sense, native language, and social and academic behaviors. Also, the leadership team must dedicate time during the workday for this team to meet frequently. When the site intervention team is only called together as needed, it is not frequent enough to effectively monitor and revise student intervention plans.

Like any other team on campus, the site intervention team should develop norms. Our experience is that this team will discuss very sensitive information regarding both students and staff. Team members must be honest, which requires an environment of trust and confidentiality. Also, meeting time for this team will likely be limited, so protocols to keep the conversations focused and on task are critical.

> Team members must be honest, which requires an environment of trust and confidentiality.

In regard to protocols, we introduced our RTI at Work pro-solve process in chapter 5—a series of questions designed to diagnose and target interventions (see page 169). We apply these five questions to the universal skills taught at Tier 3, creating a "RTI at Work Pro-Solve Intervention Targeting Process: Tier 3" (see page 244) and "RTI at Work Pro-Solve Intervention Monitoring Plan: Tier 3" (see page 248).

The RTI at Work Pro-Solve Intervention Targeting Process helps the team focus on a particular student's areas of need. These six areas include:

1. Reading (decoding, fluency, or comprehension)

2. Writing

3. Number sense

4. English language (primary language spoken in the school)

5. Academic and social behaviors

6. Health and home

It is likely that the school's most at-risk students need intensive interventions in most of these areas. Providing intensive interventions in them all at once—and still guaranteeing the student access to Tier 1 and Tier 2—might not be possible. When this is the case, the site intervention team must also prioritize the student's needs, determining the best sequence of supports.

While the school leadership team and site intervention team focus on different essential actions at Tier 3, coordination between both teams is critical. As the site intervention team determines a specific student's needs, it might realize that his or her current schedule prohibits the recommended interventions. At this point, the leadership team would consider if it can adjust the school's scheduling and resources to meet the student's needs. Likewise, it is difficult for the leadership team to allocate resources unless it knows each student's specific needs for Tier 3 support.

We recommend the principal serve on both the school leadership team and the site intervention team to help with coordinating. While additional people might serve on both teams, the principal has more direct control over schoolwide resources. When the principal defers site intervention team responsibilities to another site administrator, the site intervention team likely finds it difficult to make immediate decisions because it could require the principal's approval. This just adds an extra, unnecessary step. In the end, we cannot think of a more important use of the principal's time than to help the school's most at-risk students succeed.

There are two last critical points. First, the site intervention team should assume that its initial plan will *not* work perfectly. The identified students have been failing for years and their problems are complex, so the team should not expect easy solutions. This is why the site intervention team meets frequently. These students are moving targets, and so are their interventions.

Second, and most important, the site intervention team must commit to the mindset that not every at-risk student needs special education. Later in this chapter, we detail how this team makes the final recommendation if a student should receive special education identification and services. But here is what we know—if the site intervention team begins a student's Tier 3 intervention process assuming that the student probably has a disability, the odds are good that the RTI process will lead to that outcome for the student. The site intervention team must assume that the student is capable of learning at high levels if he or she receives targeted, effective instruction at Tier 1, Tier 2, and Tier 3.

Helpful Tools

The following tools will help you accomplish the work for this essential action.

▶ **"RTI at Work Pro-Solve Intervention Targeting Process: Tier 3" (see chapter 7, page 244):** This activity is designed to help the site intervention team identify, diagnose, target, and monitor Tier 3 academic and behavior interventions.

▶ **"RTI at Work Pro-Solve Intervention Monitoring Plan: Tier 3" (see chapter 7, page 248):** Teams should use this activity in coordination with the "RTI at Work Pro-Solve Intervention Targeting Process: Tier 3" reproducible. Members can record a student's progress in meeting his or her academic and behavior goals at Tier 3.

Coaching Tips

The site intervention team must create a team culture built on trust, honesty, and respect. When working with teams who are struggling to achieve this culture, the mistaken beliefs we most often hear are, "We don't need team norms, because we get along just fine," and "We don't have time for protocols; we can get this done by talking to each other."

> The site intervention team must create a team culture built on trust, honesty, and respect.

Becoming a highly productive, true site intervention team requires much more than getting along. It requires a shared understanding of the goals the team is seeking to achieve and the tasks required to reach those goals. Norms define the playing field for accomplishing that work. Not only is it essential for site intervention team members to agree on the ground rules for their dialogue, but members must also agree on how to monitor themselves and respond when a team member does not adhere to the team's agreed-on norms.

Using protocols is equally important. As Joseph McDonald, Nancy Mohr, Alan Dichter, and Elizabeth McDonald (2003) state in *The Power of Protocols: An Educator's Guide to Better Practice*, "The kind of talking needed to educate ourselves cannot rise spontaneously and unaided from just talking. It needs to be carefully planned and scaffolded" (p. 4). Site intervention team discussions require careful planning and scaffolding so team members can learn from each other as well as improve learning for the school's students most in need. Protocols do just that. They are tools and strategies that create conversations in which:

▶ All members get time to speak and time to listen, thus ensuring all voices are heard

▶ Dialogue proves to be optimally honest and respectful

▶ Members are open to others' perspectives

> ▸ Members maintain balance among presenting information, examining data, questioning the current reality, and responding to the information and data

> ▸ Members achieve positive outcomes

The tools in this section include two critical protocols to assist the site intervention team's work. We included additional resources in the References and Resources (page 283), and you can find more protocols available online at National School Reform Faculty (www.nsrfharmony.org), the School Reform Initiative (www .schoolreforminitiative.org), and Teachers College Press's (n.d.) "Protocols" (http:// bit.ly/2vFMR46). (Visit **go.SolutionTree.com/RTIatWork** to access live links to the websites mentioned in this book.) You can adjust these protocols to meet your needs or make up some of your own—but be sure to use them!

Action 2

Ensure Proper Intervention Intensity

Intensity clarifies. It creates not only momentum, but also the pressure you need to feel either friction, or fulfillment.

—Marcus Buckingham

In chapter 5, we use the analogy of a sick child to discuss the concept of progress monitoring. Here we will use a similar analogy to discuss intervention intensity. Imagine that you discover your child has a temperature of 103.5 degrees. You rush your child to the pediatrician who discovers that he or she is suffering from streptococcal pharyngitis (strep throat). Your doctor prescribes four hundred milligrams of amoxicillin, which you have to give your child four times per day. As a conscientious parent, you dutifully carry out these instructions with fidelity, but your child's condition does not improve. Unbeknownst to you, the pharmacist misread the doctor's prescription and only filled each capsule with forty milligrams of amoxicillin rather than four hundred. Right medicine, wrong intensity.

Similarly, students requiring Tier 3 interventions are failing academically or behaviorally and need our strongest possible "medicine" or interventions. They are often years behind in terms of academic skills and frequently experience social behaviors and academic behaviors that make it impossible for them to improve. Students requiring intensive support often have more than one area of concern, and their struggles often impact multiple subjects as well as their motivation, attendance, and behavior.

We should not provide Tier 3 interventions solely to students in special education with an IEP. Many students who do not have a specific learning disability are nonetheless drowning academically and should receive these intensive interventions. Tier 3, as defined by the National Association of State Directors of Special Education and many other professionals who advocate for intensive instruction, may or may not include special education services (Daly, Glover, & McCurdy, 2006).

Here's Why

Some students advance from grade to grade yet have not mastered the fundamental skills necessary for success in school and in life. These universal skills are reading, writing, number sense, English language, social and academic behaviors, and health and home. It is clear that students who do not read fluently and who struggle with reading comprehension will be unable to experience success across the curriculum, throughout the various grade levels, despite the fact that they are capable of high levels of learning. Similarly, students may understand instruction for a science unit perfectly well but are unable to organize and express their understanding in writing. Other students may not have developed fluency with numbers that allows them to understand and solve more complex equations.

Many students who are highly capable of learning suffer because they do not yet possess the academic vocabulary needed to understand classroom instruction. Other students are at risk in school due to their lack of motivation, self-monitoring and control, and infrequent attendance. Finally, many students requiring intensive Tier 3 interventions lack several of these universal learning skills.

Because the mission PLC at Work expresses is "to ensure high levels of learning for all students," schools must attend to students most in need of Tier 3 help because they will continue to fail until we address and close their gaps in universal skills. Students who are not successful in school are highly correlated with a shortened life span, poor health, poverty, and incarceration (Buffum et al., 2012; Buffum et al., 2015; Burrus & Roberts, 2012). It is a moral imperative that we do not allow these students to drop out of school or simply drift through school without obtaining the skills and dispositions necessary for success in the 21st century. While the goal of RTI at Work is early prevention, we must do everything possible to help those students who are drowning inside our schools.

Here's How

Tier 3 interventions must be directive, not invitational. Many students who are far behind in school may have become so disengaged with learning that they decline invitations for help. For this reason, Tier 3 interventions should be part of the regular school day, and we must carve out time for these students to receive help without missing Tier 1 instruction in essential grade-level standards. See Buffum and Mattos (2015) and Mattos and Buffum (2015) for multiple examples of how real elementary and middle schools have modified their timetables to do this.

It is also important to consider how to make Tier 3 interventions so intensive and effective that both students and teachers can see the achievement gap closing. Sharon Vaughn and Greg Roberts (2007), of the University of Texas at Austin's Meadows Center for Preventing Educational Risk, note that Tier 3 interventions should:

> Be intensive enough to provide students with a reasonable opportunity to 'catch up' to grade-level expectations. Students should not be 'locked into' the intervention for long periods of time without ongoing progress monitoring and consideration of their trajectory for meeting grade-level expectations. (p. 44)

Tier 3 interventions must be directive, not invitational.

So, how do we make these interventions of sufficient intensity? First, we consider the frequency with which they are delivered. Based on our experience as practitioners in schools, Tier 3 interventions are best delivered daily. Psychologists Rachel Brown-Chidsey, Louise Bronaugh, and Kelly McGraw (2009) also support this viewpoint.

Next, we consider the intervention's duration. While schools might successfully deliver Tier 2 interventions (a little more help with essential grade-level standards) twice per week for approximately thirty minutes, we have found that schools must deliver Tier 3 interventions five days per week for approximately fifty minutes.

For secondary schools, this works out nicely because most class periods for schools not utilizing a block schedule fall in the range of fifty to sixty minutes. Struggling students can then receive daily Tier 3 intensive interventions during one of their five to seven regularly scheduled periods without being removed from their grade-level instruction in language arts or mathematics. Students in kindergarten and grade 1 should not receive fifty straight minutes of intervention but instead, have these minutes dispersed throughout the day. The combination of daily interventions, each totaling around fifty minutes, gives students the support necessary to make overwhelming progress. But duration and frequency alone are not enough.

Group size is another consideration in regard to Tier 3 interventions. In fact, many studies recommend group sizes as small as three to one or even one to one (Haager, Klingner, & Vaughn, 2007; Simmons et al., 2007; Vaughn, Linan-Thompson, & Hickman, 2003). As practitioners, we recognize this ratio is extremely daunting for many schools today. For that reason, the following two factors make more of a difference than group size alone: (1) targeting Tier 3 interventions and (2) training staff for delivering Tier 3 interventions.

Targeting Tier 3 Interventions

We must target
Tier 3 interventions
like a laser beam
on the cause of the
student's struggles.

While focusing Tier 2 interventions on causes rather than symptoms is important, it is absolutely critical at Tier 3. It is not enough to know that students are low readers or far below basic or "red," the color teachers often use to represent students who are struggling. We must target Tier 3 interventions like a laser beam on the cause of the student's struggles. Is the student struggling with phonological awareness, phonemic awareness, decoding, fluency, comprehension, or some combination thereof? Accurate targeting can actually overcome the fact that staff may deliver some Tier 3 interventions to groups as large as six or eight.

Think about it this way: as a teacher, would you prefer to have a Tier 3 intervention group consisting of three students from the same grade level—one struggling with phonemic awareness, one struggling with fluency, and the third struggling with comprehension (all far below basic or red), or would you prefer a group as large as eight with every student needing exactly the same help?

Training Staff for Delivering Tier 3 Interventions

The final consideration in organizing Tier 3 interventions is the level of training of those delivering the intervention. Many secondary schools assign new teachers the lowest-achieving students with the greatest needs. While some new teachers might indeed be the most highly trained people in the school to help students struggling in English language arts or mathematics, it is clear that schools often assign new teachers merely because they won't complain. In many secondary schools, a pecking order has evolved in which the most highly trained teachers work only with the highest-achieving students. While we wouldn't suggest these highly trained teachers never be able to work with high-achieving students, could they—for perhaps one class period a day—accept collective responsibility for the welfare of the students who need the most help? These are not someone else's students; they are all *our* students.

In elementary schools, we often see one caring teacher who loves children so much he or she always takes the lowest-achieving group without considering if he or she is actually the most highly trained person to help. We also see rotations that involve conversations such as, "You had them the last six weeks, so I guess it's my turn," without considering who might be the most highly trained person to deliver these intensive interventions.

With regard to assigning the most highly trained teachers to the students most in need of Tier 3 intervention, let's not forget the wonderful special education teachers, speech and language pathologists, occupational therapists, and other itinerant teachers who come to a school, service their caseload, but are too seldom involved with helping prevent our students with Tier 3 needs from falling even further behind. Increasingly, we see schools using these kinds of specialists to inform their Tier 3 interventions if not actually deliver them.

How do we make certain that the intensity of our Tier 3 interventions is sufficient— that they do indeed represent four hundred milligrams of amoxicillin and not forty milligrams? We increase the frequency to five days per week, increase the duration to a total of fifty minutes daily, and decrease the group size as much as possible and feasible to do this. However, even more important are the concepts of highly targeted interventions—targeted on causes and not symptoms, and assigning the most highly trained educators to work with our students most in need of interventions.

Helpful Tool

The following tool will help you accomplish the work for this essential action.

▸ **"Ensuring Proper Intensity for Tier 3 Interventions" (page 269):** Teams can use this form to determine if their Tier 3 interventions have the proper intensity for struggling students by assessing their current reality, obstacles, and next steps.

Coaching Tips

Because establishing Tier 3 interventions is primarily the site intervention team's responsibility, the most important tip to keep in mind, once again, is to communicate! Teachers and staff members who are not directly involved in Tier 3 still must be fully informed and share a deep understanding of the rationale and process for providing Tier 3 support. In other words, even if a teacher does not have a student in need of

> These are not someone else's students; they are all *our* students.

Tier 3 intervention, that teacher still shares responsibility for ensuring high levels of learning for *all* students and must be informed, committed, and able to articulate the process. Why? Because that same teacher may be called on to deliver an intervention or receive a new student who needs Tier 3 support.

Equally importantly, parents also must understand the RTI at Work process's rationale and structure. Proactive, consistent communication is often the most valuable strategy the site intervention team has to build understanding and minimize resistance. It is only when all stakeholders understand the system as a whole that teachers, support staff, and parents alike can advocate for every student.

Former classroom teacher James A. Beane (1995) says it this way, "None of the pieces means anything taken alone, only when the pieces are put together do they mean something" (p. 1). These "pieces" are essential in making sure all students achieve success.

Ensuring Proper Intensity for Tier 3 Interventions

To assess the current reality, use a 3-point scale:
1 point = not in place   2 points = partially in place   3 points = 100 percent in place

Critical Criteria to Consider	Current Reality	Challenges or Obstacles	What are our next steps to effectively meet these criteria?
Frequency ☐ Daily: Five times per week			
Duration ☐ Fifty minutes per day			
Group Size ☐ As small as possible ☐ All students require the same intervention for the same cause.			
Targeting ☐ Focused on cause, not symptoms			
Training ☐ The staff member with the best training provides the intervention matched to his or her training.			

Action 3

Determine if Special Education Is Needed and Justifiable

> Our duty is to believe that for which we have sufficient evidence, and to suspend our judgment when we have not.
>
> **—John Lubbock**

The premise of RTI is that schools should not delay providing help for struggling students until they fall far enough behind to qualify for special education. Instead, we should provide timely, targeted, systematic interventions to all students in need. Because RTI is a multitiered system of supports, students who are years behind in foundational skills can receive intensive remediation while still learning essential grade-level curriculum. Regardless if a student qualifies for special education, the RTI process should collaboratively build on the collective training and skills of all site educators to meet that student's unique needs.

> We should provide timely, targeted, systematic interventions to all students in need.

RTI does have a secondary benefit—schools can use it as a process to identify students with learning disabilities and potentially qualify them for special education services. But a school must be sure the student's lack of response to previous interventions is due to a potential learning disability and not because the school failed to provide highly effective core instruction and interventions that meet the student's individual needs. It would be both unprofessional and unethical to convince a parent that his or her child has a learning disability, when in fact the child's problem is that the school has not done its due diligence to help the child.

Here's Why

Prior to the reauthorization of IDEIA (2004), the only legally required systematic intervention process to provide students additional time and support was special education. In order to qualify students for special education services prior to 2004, schools traditionally used the discrepancy model—also known as the wait to fail model. Utilizing a combination of IQ and achievement testing, this model required students to demonstrate a discrepancy of at least two standard deviations between their perceived ability and their current level of achievement to qualify for special education. Standard deviations are used to determine if scores are significantly above or below average—or in this case, significantly below what might be expected of students of similar IQ. Two standard deviations would indicate a very significant difference.

Unfortunately, research confirms that once a student falls this far behind (two or more standard deviations), it is nearly impossible for him or her to catch up (Fuchs & Young, 2006; Vellutino, Scanlon, Zhang, & Schatschneider, 2008). In many cases, a student's struggles are not due to a disability. However, the school waits so long to systematically respond that the student drops significantly behind and this achievement gap becomes his or her qualifying disability. In other words, the student is not born with a disability—the school's neglect creates it.

This is why the RTI process is a superior way to identify students with true disabilities. Because the process is timely and proactive, students do not have to fall too far behind to receive the help. And because the site intervention team is the most diverse team—expertise-wise—on campus, and has coordinated the most intensive interventions for students it considers for special education, it is in the best position to determine if a student's continued struggles are evidence of a learning disability. This decision has profound implications for students, so the site intervention team must have clearly defined criteria and processes for making these decisions.

Here's How

As previously discussed, when RTI focuses on identifying students for special education, the process often becomes overly driven by rigid time lines, a predetermined sequence of interventions, and laborious documentation. We acknowledge that schools must consider laws and regulations, especially when special education is a possibility. A school must be confident, beyond a reasonable doubt, that the student truly has special learning needs. The site intervention team should answer the following questions at each tier when considering identifying a student for special education to achieve this goal. (See "Critical Questions for Special Education Identification" on page 274 or **go.SolutionTree.com/RTIatWork** to access a free reproducible version of these questions.)

> A school must be confident, beyond a reasonable doubt, that the student truly has special learning needs.

Tier 1

▶ Did the student have ready access to essential grade-level curriculum as part of his or her core instruction?

▶ Did the student receive effective supports, accommodations, or differentiation to support his or her success in learning essential grade-level standards? What were these supports?

▶ Is there evidence that the school's core instructional practices are working for a large majority of students, including similar students?

Tier 2

▶ Did the school identify the student for supplemental support in a timely manner?

▶ What were the student's specific learning needs at Tier 2? (The team should be able to list exact standards, learning targets, and behaviors.)

▶ What caused the student to not learn these essential learning outcomes?

▶ What research- or evidence-based interventions did teachers use to address the student's specific learning needs?

▶ Did the school provide these interventions in addition to Tier 1?

▶ Is there evidence that these interventions were effective for similar students?

Tier 3

▶ Did the school identify the student for Tier 3 interventions in a timely, proactive manner?

▶ What quality problem-solving process did the school use to better identify the student's specific learning needs and the cause of the student's struggles?

▶ What were the student's specific learning needs at Tier 3? (The team should be able to list exact standards, learning targets, and behaviors.)

▶ What research and evidence-based interventions did the school use to address the student's specific learning needs?

▶ Did highly trained professionals in the student's areas of need provide these interventions?

▶ Did the school provide these interventions in addition to Tier 1 and Tier 2?

▶ How often did the school monitor the student's progress for each intervention? What revisions or modifications did the school make based on this information?

▶ Is there evidence that these interventions were effective for similar students?

▶ Are there any other interventions or supports the school should try before considering special education placement?

▶ Does the site intervention team unanimously feel that special education identification is necessary and appropriate for this student? What benefits will the student receive due to this recommendation that could not be provided without it?

▶ Would team members make the same recommendation if the student in question were their child?

If the site intervention team can't successfully and affirmatively answer each question, then it should not be recommending the student for special education. Student-assessment data undoubtedly play a critical role in answering these questions. The decision should not rest on whether a school satisfactorily completes all the necessary paperwork and protocols. Instead, special education eligibility should measure the school's confidence that it has served the student well and that he or she truly has unique learning needs that the school's general education and RTI resources cannot meet or maintain (Buffum et al., 2012). Qualifying a student for special education is not in itself the solution to the student's learning needs, but it creates opportunities to provide the student with even more highly specialized, targeted, and personalized support.

Helpful Tool

The following tool will help you accomplish the work for this essential action.

▶ **"Critical Questions for Special Education Identification" (page 274):** This form offers questions for the site intervention team when considering identifying a student for special education.

Coaching Tips

The most important tip the site intervention team should consider as it determines if special education is needed and justifiable is to keep an open mind. That may sound simple, but it is, in reality, very difficult. Given the fact that special education has historically been the only intervention available to struggling students, many educators still approach support for their students with a singular focus—get them into special education! Shifting that mindset is what this entire book is all about, from working to establish a culture of collective responsibility to implementing a multitiered system of supports.

With that in mind, the leadership team and the site intervention team must be prepared and proactive about countering the rush to identify students for special education. Talking about the history, pros, and cons of special education needs to be a part of conversations on a consistent basis. The challenge is never to diminish the special educators' work, while simultaneously highlighting the reasons why special education has not been the best solution for many students.

There are no magic bullets for keeping minds open or for shifting people's mindsets. Rather, it is part of a school's never-ending mission to ensure high levels of learning for all students. Reeves (2009b) reminds us, "Failure in change strategies need not be inevitable. In fact, it is avoidable if change leaders will balance their sense of urgency with a more thoughtful approach to implementing change" (p. 7). That said, never is it more important for members of the leadership and intervention teams to walk the talk.

It is part of a school's never-ending mission to ensure high levels of learning for all students.

Critical Questions for Special Education Identification

The site intervention team must ask the following questions when considering a student for special education placement.

Tier 1

- Did the student have ready access to essential grade-level curriculum as part of his or her core instruction?

- Did the student receive effective supports, accommodations, or differentiation to support his or her success in learning essential grade-level standards? What were these supports?

- Is there evidence that the school's core instructional practices are working for a large majority of students, including similar students?

Tier 2

- Did the school identify the student for supplemental support in a timely manner?

- What were the student's specific learning needs at Tier 2? (The team should be able to list exact standards, learning targets, and behaviors.)

- What caused the student to not learn these essential learning outcomes?

- What research or evidence-based interventions did teachers use to address the student's specific learning needs?

- Did the school provide these interventions in addition to Tier 1?

- Is there evidence that these interventions were effective for similar students?

Tier 3

- Did the school identify the student for Tier 3 interventions in a timely, proactive manner?

- What quality problem-solving process did the school use to better identify the student's specific learning needs and the cause of the student's struggles?

- What were the student's specific learning needs at Tier 3? (The team should be able to list exact standards, learning targets, and behaviors.)

- What research- and evidence-based interventions did the school use to address the student's specific learning needs?

- Did highly trained professionals in the student's areas of need provide these interventions?

- Did the school provide these interventions in addition to Tier 1 and Tier 2?

- How often did the school monitor the student's progress for each intervention? What revisions or modifications did the school make based on this information?

- Is there evidence that these interventions were effective for similar students?

- Are there any other interventions or supports the school should try before considering special education placement?

- Does the site intervention team unanimously feel that special education identification is necessary and appropriate for this student? What benefits will the student receive due to this recommendation that could not be provided without it?

- Would team members make the same recommendation if the student in question were their child?

Conclusion

The most at-risk students in a school face complex problems. They are like a knot—a bundle of needs that intertwine into a ball of frustration. A student might be below grade level in reading, *and* have weak number-sense skills, *and* be an English learner, *and* consistently demonstrate impulsive behaviors in class. Schools often ask us what intervention program to provide for a student like this. Our initial answer is, "We don't know what the right intervention is—there is no effective reading, mathematics, English language program that you can buy."

What we can offer, instead of a program recommendation, is the right problem-solving *process*. The solution to a knot like this is to carefully unravel and untangle each thread that makes up the knot, and address each with the dedication, focus, and perseverance that you would want for your own child. We can't promise that the recommendations and processes this chapter described guarantee that a site intervention team always finds the right solution for each student in need of intensive support—we never achieved perfection at our schools. What we know is that these ongoing processes give your school the best chance to successfully help your most at-risk students.

> The solution to a knot like this is to carefully unravel and untangle each thread that makes up the knot, and address each with the dedication, focus, and perseverance that you would want for your own child.

Eating the Elephant

Not I, nor anyone else can travel that road for you. You must travel it by yourself. It is not far. It is within reach.

—Walt Whitman

Within the eight chapters of this book, we outlined the essential actions a school must take to create a highly effective, multitiered system of supports to ensure every student learns at high levels—we provided a cumulative list of these actions at the end of this epilogue (see page 281). For each action, we provided specific steps and proven tools to help achieve each outcome. Our goal in writing an RTI at Work handbook was to make the work understandable, logical, and achievable. Nevertheless, as you reflect back on what you read, the totality of the PLC and RTI processes might seem daunting. You *should* feel that way. It would be naïve to think that guaranteeing every student's success in school is a trivial, easy-to-achieve endeavor. Radically rethinking and restructuring an education system that successfully served the United States for more than two hundred years is monumental work. We don't acknowledge this point to dissuade you from the journey but to honestly confirm that the challenges in your path are formidable. This is not a sprint, but a marathon.

> This is not a sprint, but a marathon.

Facing this reality, educators often ask us, "Our school has none of these practices in place. It all seems so overwhelming—where do we start?" As we noted in the book: *How do you eat an elephant? One bite at a time.* The same approach is true here; you create a system of interventions one "bite" at a time.

We know that successful PLC at Work implementation does not happen accidently, serendipitously, or through random individual efforts. This is why the first essential action in this book is to build a guiding coalition—the right team of people to lead the process. After establishing this leadership team, this team's first job is to build consensus on the school's fundamental purpose—to ensure high levels of learning for *all* students. Achieving this mission takes a collaborative effort, so forming teams and scheduling time for frequent collaboration is the logical next step. *Learning by Doing* (2016) and *Taking Action* were written to provide that step-by-step pathway—one bite at a time.

Another question educators ask us is how long it should take to build an effective system of interventions within a PLC school. To this, we offer three answers: one year, three years, and forever. With effective leadership, the essential foundational elements can be in place in one year. These steps would include:

1. Create a guiding coalition.

2. Build consensus on the school's mission.

3. Create teacher teams and a site intervention team.

4. Schedule weekly collaboration time.

5. Identify a limited number of essential standards (academic and behavior).

6. Ensure all students have access to this essential curriculum.

7. Create and use common assessments on essential standards.

8. Create a schoolwide teacher-recommendation process for Tier 2 interventions.

9. Schedule time for Tier 2 interventions on a limited number of essential standards (will and skill).

10. Identify students who need intensive interventions.

11. Have the leadership team begin to diagnose, target, and monitor the most at-risk students.

12. Begin Tier 3 interventions in one subject area.

13. Evaluate current site interventions.

Notice that the preceding list has some critical qualifiers, such as focus on a *limited number* of essential standards, and begin Tier 3 interventions in *one* subject area. When Mike served as principal of Marjorie Veeh Elementary School, which served predominately at-risk youth, the staff focused on one subject—reading—to begin its PLC journey. Each grade-level team selected a limited number of essential reading standards for its collaborative focus. The school modified its schedule to ensure students were not pulled from class while these essential standards were being taught at Tier 1 or retaught during each team's daily supplemental intervention time. Tier 3 resources focused on students that needed intensive reading support. While students had needs in other subjects, the school was not ready to address them all.

For the first year, it made more sense to do a few things well rather than many things poorly. As one might suspect, the school saw increases on its end-of-year reading assessments. But to the staff's surprise, the school also saw growth in its end-of-year assessments in mathematics, science, and social studies. The staff concluded that because more students could read and comprehend grade-level texts, this universal skill helped students across the curriculum. The second year, the staff continued their focus on reading, but because they had some parts in place in that subject, they began to identify essential standards in writing. They included mathematics the third year—one bite at a time.

While it is possible to get the foundational pieces in place for at least one subject per year, a school will probably not be overly efficient or effective at these new processes. A school should expect it to take closer to three years of focused efforts to get good at the work. The first year, many of the initial steps create the conditions to begin to do the work. Because the second year begins with those structures already in place, the staff can hit the ground running, identify what isn't working, and make refinements. By the third year, the school can begin to reap the benefits of its efforts, confirming that the processes work. This reinforces the staff's commitment to the process. As time progresses, the faculty will stop talking about implementing PLCs and RTI, and instead, see the PLC at Work process as the new school norm.

And because the school's reason for implementing the PLC process is to achieve its mission of ensuring high levels of learning for all students, the work does not stop until it achieves this mission. As long as there is at least one student who is not succeeding, the staff must commit to continuously seeking better ways to serve their students, making the implementation time line forever.

When we suggest that schools implement RTI one bite at a time, we would *not* suggest the following approach: let's just focus on Tier 1 this year. We will form teams and begin to identify essential standards. In the second year, we will have teams start to create and administer common assessments while exploring ways to create intervention time during the school day. In the third year, we will begin providing systematic interventions.

There are two significant drawbacks to this approach. First, at-risk students can't wait two years to start getting extra time and support. There is urgency to this work. Every day in which a student is not succeeding means he or she is probably falling further behind. Second, the key to creating staff commitment to the RTI process is when teachers see it work—and the staff achieve this when students who are failing start to succeed. If it takes two years to begin systematic interventions, then it is unlikely that teachers will start to see more of their struggling students succeed until then. Momentum is often lost in drawn-out implementation. It is better to start with a fewer number of essential standards but then begin to assess and intervene on these during the first year. This provides opportunities for short-term wins. For teachers, the most rewarding part of their job is when they see their students succeed.

Finally, as you begin your journey we offer a few cautionary suggestions.

> ▸ **There are no shortcuts:** It is tempting to have a district committee identify essential standards, removing most teachers from the process. Yet, when teacher teams roll up their sleeves and dig deeply into the curriculum, they become students of the standards. They gain a deeper understanding of the essential curriculum and an ownership of the process that creates deep levels of commitment.

A school should expect it to take closer to three years of focused efforts to get good at the work.

For teachers, the most rewarding part of their job is when they see their students succeed.

It can also be tempting to simply buy packaged assessment systems and intervention programs instead of committing to the processes necessary to target interventions to the unique needs of each student. These shortcuts are seductive. But in the end, the educators in the building are the school's greatest resource. The foundational assumption of the PLC process is that the best way to improve student learning is through the job-embedded, collaborative learning of the adults. The people doing the work are doing the learning (DuFour et al., 2016). Avoid the work, and the learning stops.

- ▸ **There is never going to be a perfect time to begin:** All the stars in the education universe—district, state or province, and federal leadership—are unlikely to align. Regardless, we are doubtful any existing laws or regulations would prohibit a school from working in teams, identifying essential curriculum, giving common assessments, and providing targeted students with extra help. The key is to get started, then get better. Mistakes are inevitable. The only mistake you cannot tolerate is not getting started in the first place.

- ▸ **There are sufficient resources to get started:** Having worked with schools around the world, we can say with confidence that no school *ever* has enough resources. For every school that claims a lack of resources for its inability to start, we can provide model schools that have done it with less. We are not suggesting it is easy, but schools are doing it.

- ▸ **There is a difference between uncomfortable and unreasonable:** Unreasonable demands are unjust, but change sometimes requires discomfort.

Undoubtedly, the work will be hard. That is the nature of our work as educators. If there is one thing for certain at the start of every school year, it is this: educators are going to work hard. The question is not whether we will work hard, but will we work hard and succeed or work hard and fail?

We deal in futures— the futures of our students.

Our profession does not build widgets, nor do we measure our success in profit margins. We deal in futures—the futures of our students. Every day that we get collectively better at doing the right work right, it is measured in the life of a child. One more student gains an essential academic skill or behavior that can open doors of opportunity for a lifetime. Achieving this outcome for every child takes more than proven research and good intentions . . . it requires *taking action*. So let's get at it!

RTI at Work Essential Actions for Tiers 1, 2, and 3

A Culture of Collective Responsibility

ACTION 1: Establish a Guiding Coalition

ACTION 2: Build a Culture of Collective Responsibility

ACTION 3: Form Collaborative Teacher Teams

ACTION 4: Create Time for Collaboration

ACTION 5: Commit to Team Norms

Tier 1

Teacher Team Essential Actions	Schoolwide Essential Actions
ACTION 1: Identify Essential Standards for Each Grade Level or Course	ACTION 1: Ensure Access to Essential Grade-Level Curriculum
ACTION 2: Create an Essential Standards Unit Plan	ACTION 2: Identify and Teach Essential Academic and Social Behaviors
ACTION 3: Implement the Team Teaching-Assessing Cycle	ACTION 3: Provide Preventions to Proactively Support Student Success
ACTION 4: Give Common End-of-Unit Assessment for Essential Standards	
ACTION 5: Identify Students for Tier 2 Support by Student, Standard, and Learning Target	

Tier 2

Teacher Team Essential Actions	Schoolwide Essential Actions
ACTION 1: Design and Lead Supplemental Interventions for Academic Essential Standards	ACTION 1: Schedule Time for Supplemental Interventions
ACTION 2: Consider Screening in Immediate Prerequisite Skills	ACTION 2: Establish a Process for School-wide Student Intervention Identification
ACTION 3: Monitor the Progress of Students Receiving Supplemental Supports	ACTION 3: Plan and Implement Supplemental Interventions for Essential Social and Academic Behaviors
ACTION 4: Extend Student Learning	ACTION 4: Coordinate Interventions for Students Needing Skill *and* Will Supports

Tier 3

Schoolwide Essential Actions	Intervention Team Essential Actions
ACTION 1: Identify Students Needing Intensive Support	**ACTION 1:** Diagnose, Treat, Prioritize, and Monitor Tier 3 Interventions
ACTION 2: Create a Dynamic, Problem-Solving Site Intervention Team	**ACTION 2:** Ensure Proper Intervention Intensity
ACTION 3: Prioritize Resources Based on Greatest Student Needs	**ACTION 3:** Determine if Special Education Is Needed and Justifiable
ACTION 4: Create a Systematic and Timely Process to Refer Students to the Site Intervention Team	
ACTION 5: Assess Intervention Effectiveness	

REFERENCES AND RESOURCES

American Diploma Project. (2004). *Ready or not: Creating a high school diploma that counts*. Washington, DC: Achieve. Accessed at www.achieve.org/les/ReadyorNot.pdf on March 5, 2014.

AZQuotes. (n.d.). *Margot Fonteyn quotes*. Accessed at www.azquotes.com/author/4969-Margot_Fonteyn on February 20, 2017.

Bailey, M. J., & Dynarski, S. M. (2011). *Gains and gaps: Changing inequality in U.S. college entry and completion* (NBER Working Paper No. 17633). Cambridge, MA: National Bureau of Economic Research.

Balu, R., Zhu, P., Doolittle, F., Schiller, E., Jenkins, J., & Gersten, R. (2015). *Evaluation of response to intervention practices for elementary school reading*. Washington, DC: National Center for Education Evaluation and Regional Assistance. Accessed at https://ies.ed.gov/ncee/pubs/20164000/pdf/20164000.pdf on February 24, 2017.

Barber, M., Chijioke, C., & Mourshed, M. (2010). *How the world's most improved school systems keep getting better*. Accessed at www.mckinsey.com/industries/social-sector/our-insights/how-the-worlds-most-improved-school-systems-keep-getting-better on February 24, 2017.

Barber, M., & Mourshed, M. (2007). *How the world's best-performing school systems come out on top*. Accessed at http://mckinseyonsociety.com/how-the-worlds-best-performing-schools-come-out-on-top on February 24, 2017.

Beane, J. (1995). *Toward a coherent curriculum*. Alexandria, VA: Association for Supervision and Curriculum Development.

Bloom, B. S. (1968). Learning for mastery. *Evaluation Comment, 1*(2), 1–12.

Bloom, B. S. (1971). Mastery learning. In J. H. Block (Ed.), *Mastery learning: Theory and practice* (pp. 47–63). New York: Holt, Rinehart & Winston.

Brantlinger, E. A. (Ed.). (2006). *Who benefits from special education? Remediating (fixing) other people's children*. Mahwah, NJ: Erlbaum Associates.

Breslow, J. M. (2012, September 21). *By the numbers: Dropping out of high school*. Accessed at www.pbs.org/wgbh/frontline/article/by-the-numbers-dropping-out-of-high-school on February 24, 2017.

Brooks-Gunn, J., & Duncan, G. J. (1997). The effects of poverty on children. *Future of Children, 7*(2), 55–71.

Brown-Chidsey, R., Bronaugh, L., & McGraw, K. (2009). *RTI in the classroom: Guidelines and recipes for success.* New York: Guilford Press.

Brown-Chidsey, R., & Steege, M. W. (2005). *Response to intervention: Principles and strategies for effective practice.* New York: Guilford Press.

Buffum, A., & Mattos, M. (2014, May). *Criteria for selecting essential standards.* Presented at the Simplifying Response to Intervention Workshop, Prince George, British Columbia.

Buffum, A., & Mattos, M. (2015). *It's about time: Planning interventions and extensions in elementary school.* Bloomington, IN: Solution Tree Press.

Buffum, A., Mattos, M., & Weber, C. (2009). *Pyramid response to intervention: RTI, professional learning communities, and how to respond when kids don't learn.* Bloomington, IN: Solution Tree Press.

Buffum, A., Mattos, M., & Weber, C. (2012). *Simplifying response to intervention: Four essential guiding principles.* Bloomington, IN: Solution Tree Press.

Buffum, A., Mattos, M., Weber, C., & Hierck, T. (2015). *Uniting academic and behavior interventions: Solving the skill or will dilemma.* Bloomington, IN: Solution Tree Press.

Burrus, J., & Roberts, R. D. (2012). Dropping out of high school: Prevalence, risk factors, and remediation strategies. *R and D Connections, 18*, 1–9. Accessed at http://bit.ly/1a3S213 on May 9, 2017.

Center for Health and Justice. (2009). *Incarceration and jobless rates among young male drop-outs highest for African Americans.* Accessed at www .centerforhealthandjustice.org/FOY%2010-09.pdf on March 1, 2017.

Chappuis, J., Stiggins, R., Chappuis, S., & Arter, J. (2012). *Classroom assessment for student learning: Doing it right—using it well* (2nd ed.). Boston: Pearson.

Cleveland Clinic. (n.d.). *The very best way to lose weight and keep it off.* Accessed at http://my.clevelandclinic.org/health/healthy_living/getting_fit/hic _Maintaining_a_Healthy_Weight/hic_The_Very_Best_Way_To_Lose_Weight _and_Keep_It_Off on February 24, 2017.

Collins, J. (2001). *Good to great: Why some companies make the leap . . . and others don't.* New York: HarperBusiness.

Conley, D. T. (2007). *Redefining college readiness.* Eugene, OR: Educational Policy Improvement Center.

Conzemius, A. E., & O'Neill, J. (2014). *The handbook for SMART school teams: Revitalizing best practices for collaboration* (2nd ed.). Bloomington, IN: Solution Tree Press.

Cooper, H., Charlton, K., Valentine, J. C., Muhlenbruck, L., & Borman, G. D. (2000). Making the most of summer school: A meta-analytic and narrative review. *Monographs of the Society for Research in Child Development, 65*(1), i–v, 1–127.

Covey, S. R. (1989). *The 7 habits of highly effective people: Powerful lessons in personal change.* New York: Fireside.

Daly, E., Glover, T., & McCurdy, M. (2006). *Response to intervention: Technical assistance document.* Lincoln: Nebraska Department of Education.

Deal, T. E., & Peterson, K. D. (1999). *Shaping school culture: The heart of leadership.* San Francisco: Jossey-Bass.

Deno, E. (1970). Special education as developmental capital. *Exceptional Children, 37,* 229–237.

Dexter, D. D., & Hughes, C. (n.d.). *Progress monitoring within a response-to-intervention model.* Accessed at http://rtinetwork.org/component/content /article/10/22-progress-monitoring-within-a-response on April 18, 2017.

Diament, M. (2014, April 29). Graduation rates fall short for students with disabilities. *Disability Scoop.* Accessed at www.disabilityscoop.com/2014/04/29 /graduation-rates-disabilities/19317 on December 17, 2015.

Donovan, M. S., & Cross, C. T. (Eds.). (2002). *Minority students in special and gifted education.* Washington, DC: National Academies Press.

Dorn, S. (1996). *Creating the dropout: An institutional and social history of school failure.* Westport, CT: Praeger.

DuFour, R. (2015). *In praise of American educators: And how they can become even better.* Bloomington, IN: Solution Tree Press.

DuFour, R. (2016). *Advocates for professional learning communities: Finding common ground in education reform.* Accessed at www.allthingsplc.info/files/uploads /AdvocatesforPLCs-Updated11-9-15.pdf on February 27, 2017.

DuFour, R., DuFour, R., Eaker, R., & Many, T. W. (2006). *Learning by doing: A handbook for Professional Learning Communities at Work.* Bloomington, IN: Solution Tree Press.

DuFour, R., DuFour, R., Eaker, R., & Many, T. W. (2010). *Learning by doing: A handbook for Professional Learning Communities at Work* (2nd ed.). Bloomington, IN: Solution Tree Press.

DuFour, R., DuFour, R., Eaker, R., Many, T. W., & Mattos, M. (2016). *Learning by doing: A handbook for Professional Learning Communities at Work* (3rd ed.). Bloomington, IN: Solution Tree Press.

DuFour, R., Eaker, R., & DuFour, R. (2007). *The power of Professional Learning Communities at Work: Bringing the big ideas to life* [DVD]. Bloomington, IN: Solution Tree Press.

Education for All Handicapped Children Act of 1975, Pub. L. No. 94–142, 20 U.S.C. § 1401 (1975).

Effective Schools. (n.d.). In *Wikipedia*. Accessed at https://en.wikipedia.org/wiki /Effective_schools on March 1, 2017.

Eller, J. (2004). *Effective group facilitation in education: How to energize meetings and manage difficult groups*. Thousand Oaks, CA: Corwin Press.

Erkens, C., Jakicic, C., Jessie, L. G., King, D., Kramer, S. V., Many T. W., et al. (2008). *The collaborative teacher: Working together as a professional learning community*. Bloomington, IN: Solution Tree Press.

Fendler, L., & Muzaffar, I. (2008). The history of the bell curve: Sorting and the idea of normal. *Educational Theory, 58*(1), 63–82.

Ferri, B. A., & Connor, D. J. (2006). *Reading resistance: Discourses of exclusion in desegregation and inclusion debates*. New York: Peter Lang.

Fischhoff, B. (1992). Risk taking: A developmental perspective. In J. F. Yates (Ed.), *Risk-taking behavior* (pp. 133–162). Chichester, England: Wiley.

Fischhoff, B., Crowell, N. A., & Kipke, M. (Eds.). (1999). *Adolescent decision making: Implications for prevention programs—Summary of a workshop*. Washington, DC: National Academies Press.

Fleming, C. B., Harachi, T. W., Cortes, R. C., Abbott, R. D., & Catalano, R. F. (2004). Level and change in reading scores and attention problems during elementary school as predictors of problem behavior in middle school. *Journal of Emotional and Behavioral Disorders, 12*(3), 130–144.

Fuchs, D., Compton, D. L., Fuchs, L. S., Bryant, J., & Davis, G. N. (2008). Making "secondary intervention" work in a three-tier responsiveness-to-intervention model: Findings from the first-grade longitudinal reading study at the National Research Center on Learning Disabilities. *Reading and Writing, 21*(4), 413–436.

Fuchs, D., & Young, C. L. (2006). On their relevance of intelligence in predicting responsiveness to reading instruction. *Exceptional Children, 73*(1), 8–30.

Fuchs, L. S., & Fuchs, D. (2007). A model for implementing responsiveness to intervention. *Teaching Exceptional Children, 39*(5), 14–20.

Fullan, M. (1994, May 5–7). *Keynote address*. Presented at the symposium sponsored by the California Center for Restructuring Schools, Anaheim.

Gallimore, R., Ermeling, B. A., Saunders, W. M., & Goldenberg, C. (2009). Moving the learning of teaching closer to practice: Teacher education implications of school-based inquiry teams. *Elementary School Journal, 109*(5), 537–553.

Gandhi, M. (n.d.). You must be the change you wish to see in the world. In *BrainyQuote.com*. Accessed at https://brainyquote.com/quotes/quotes/m /mahatmagan109075.html on May 27, 2017.

Garmston, R. J., & Wellman, B. M. (2009). *The adaptive school: A sourcebook for developing collaborative groups* (2nd ed.). Norwood, MA: Christopher-Gordon.

Gerstner, L. V., Jr. (1995). *Reinventing education: Entrepreneurship in America's public schools.* New York: Penguin.

Goodreads.com. (n.d.). *Abraham H. Maslow.* Accessed at www.goodreads.com /author/show/4570807.Abraham_H_Maslow on February 24, 2017.

Graham, P., & Ferriter, W. M. (2010). *Building a Professional Learning Community at Work: A guide to the first year.* Bloomington, IN: Solution Tree Press.

Guskey, T. R. (2010). Lessons of mastery learning. *Educational Leadership, 68*(2), 52–57.

Guskey, T. R., & Pigott, T. D. (1988). Research on group-based mastery learning programs: A meta-analysis. *Journal of Educational Research, 81*(4), 197–216.

Haager, D., Klingner, J., & Vaughn, S. (Eds.). (2007). *Evidence-based reading practices for response to intervention.* Baltimore, MD: Brookes.

Hallowell, T. (Executive Producer), & Howard, R. (Director). (1995). *Apollo 13* [Motion picture]. United States: Universal Pictures.

Harris, J. (n.d.). *Facilitative leadership: Balancing the dimensions of success.* Accessed at http://interactionassociates.com/insights/blog/facilitative-leadership-balancing -dimensions-success#.WVFGhjOZPUo on June 25, 2017.

Hattie, J. (2009). *Visible learning: A synthesis of over 800 meta-analyses relating to achievement.* New York: Routledge.

Hattie, J. (2012). *Visible learning for teachers: Maximizing impact on learning.* New York: Routledge.

Hattie, J., & Yates, G. (2014). *Visible learning and the science of how we learn.* New York: Routledge.

Hierck, T., Coleman, C., & Weber, C. (2011). *Pyramid of behavior interventions: Seven keys to a positive learning environment.* Bloomington, IN: Solution Tree Press.

Horner, R. H., Sugai, G., & Lewis, T. (2015, April). *Is school-wide positive behavior support an evidence-based practice?* Accessed at www.pbis.org/research on June 13, 2017.

Individuals With Disabilities Education Improvement Act of 2004, 20 U.S.C. §§ 1400 *et. seq.* (2004).

Interaction Associates. (1997). *Facilitative leadership: Tapping the power of participation.* San Francisco: Author.

Jacobs, H. H. (2001). New trends in curriculum: An interview with Heidi Hayes Jacobs. *Independent School, 61*(1), 18–24.

Jefferson, T. (n.d.). There is nothing more unequal than the equal treatment of unequal people. In *Goodreads.com*. Accessed at www.goodreads.com/quotes/178043-there -is-nothing-more-unequal-treatment-of on August 8, 2017.

Jerald, C. D. (2009). *Defining a 21st century education*. Alexandria, VA: Center for Public Education.

Kallick, B., & Colosimo, J. (2009). *Using curriculum mapping and assessment data to improve learning*. Thousand Oaks, CA: Corwin Press.

Killion, J. (2008). *Assessing impact: Evaluating staff development* (2nd ed.). Thousand Oaks, CA: Corwin Press.

Killion, J., & Roy, P. (2009). *Becoming a learning school*. Oxford, OH: Learning Forward.

Kotter, J. P. (1996). *Leading change*. Boston: Harvard Business School Press.

Kotter, J. P. (2007, January). Leading change: Why transformation efforts fail. *Harvard Business Review*. Accessed at https://hbr.org/2007/01/leading-change -why-transformation-efforts-fail on March 1, 2017.

Landry, T. (n.d.). A coach is someone who tells you what you don't want to hear, who has you see what you don't want to see, so you can be who you have always known you could be. In *Goodreads.com*. Accessed at www.goodreads.com/quotes/58284-a -coach-is-someone-who-tells-you-what-you-don-t on June 20, 2017.

Lencioni, P. (2002). *The five dysfunctions of a team: A leadership fable*. San Francisco: Jossey-Bass.

Lencioni, P. (2005). *Overcoming the five dysfunctions of a team: A field guide for leaders, managers, and facilitators*. San Francisco: Jossey-Bass.

Lezotte, L. W. (2005). More effective schools: Professional learning communities in action. In R. DuFour, R. Eaker, & R. DuFour (Eds.), *On common ground: The power of professional learning communities* (pp. 177–192). Bloomington, IN: Solution Tree Press.

Mader, J., & Butrymowicz, S. (2014, October 29). The Hechinger Report: For many with disabilities, special education leads to jail. *Disability Scoop*. Accessed at www .disabilityscoop.com/2014/10/29/for-sped-leads-jail/19800 on January 26, 2016.

Malone, J. (2006, August 17). *Are we a group or a team? 2006 Getting Results Conference— The impact of one, the power of many* [Handout]. Accessed at http://results.ocde.us /downloads/JMalone-Group_Team_Handout.pdf on April 17, 2017.

Marzano, R. J. (2003). *What works in schools: Translating research into action*. Alexandria, VA: Association for Supervision and Curriculum Development.

Marzano, R. J., Heflebower, T., Hoegh, J. K., Warrick, P., & Grift, G. (2016). *Collaborative teams that transform schools: The next step in PLCs*. Bloomington, IN: Marzano Research.

Marzano, R. J., Warrick, P., & Simms, J. A. (2014). *A handbook for high reliability schools: The next step in school reform.* Bloomington, IN: Marzano Research.

Mattos, M. (2015). *Making time at Tier 2: Creating a supplemental intervention period in secondary schools* [DVD]. Bloomington, IN: Solution Tree Press.

Mattos, M. (2017). *Timebomb: The cost of dropping out* [DVD]. Bloomington, IN: Solution Tree Press.

Mattos, M., & Buffum, A. (2015). *It's about time: Planning interventions and extensions in secondary school.* Bloomington, IN: Solution Tree Press.

Mattos, M., DuFour, R., DuFour, R., Eaker, R., & Many, T. W. (2016). *Concise answers to frequently asked questions about Professional Learning Communities at Work.* Bloomington, IN: Solution Tree Press.

Mayer, D. P., Mullens, J. E., & Moore, M. T. (2000). *Monitoring school quality: An indicators report* (NCES 2001–030). Washington, DC: National Center for Education Statistics. Accessed at https://nces.ed.gov/pubs2001/2001030.pdf on March 1, 2017.

McDonald, J. P., Mohr, N., Dichter, A., & McDonald, E. C. (2003). *The power of protocols: An educator's guide to better practice.* New York: Teachers College Press.

Mehta, J. (2013). Why American education fails: And how lessons from abroad could improve it. *Foreign Affairs, 92*(3). Accessed at www.foreignaffairs.com /articles/united-states/2013-04-03/why-american-education-fails on December 30, 2015.

Morrison, G. M., Anthony, S., Storino, M., & Dillon, C. (2001). An examination of the disciplinary histories and the individual and educational characteristics of students who participate in an in-school suspension program. *Education and Treatment of Children, 24*(3), 276–293.

Muhammad, A. (2018). *Transforming school culture: How to overcome staff division* (2nd ed.). Bloomington, IN: Solution Tree Press.

Musgrove, M. (2013, March 7). *Response to Troy Couillard* [Memorandum]. Accessed at www2.ed.gov/policy/speced/guid/idea/memosdcltrs/12-011637r-wi-couillard -rti3-8-13.doc on August 16, 2017.

National Governors Association Center for Best Practices & Council of Chief State School Officers. (2010). *Common Core State Standards for English language arts and literacy in history/social studies, science, and technical subjects.* Washington, DC: Authors. Accessed at www.corestandards.org/assets/CCSSI_ELA%20 Standards.pdf on February 24, 2017.

Nelson, J. R., Benner, G. J., Lane, K., & Smith, B. W. (2004). Academic achievement of K–12 students with emotional and behavioral disorders. *Exceptional Children, 71*(1), 59–73.

No Child Left Behind Act of 2001, Pub. L. No. 107–110, 20 U.S.C. § 6319 (2002).

Oakes, J. (2005). *Keeping track: How schools structure inequality* (2nd ed.). New Haven, CT: Yale University Press.

O'Connor, C., & Fernandez, S. D. (2006). Race, class, and disproportionality: Reevaluating the relationship between poverty and special education placement. *Educational Researcher, 35*(6), 6–11.

Peterson, D. B., & Hicks, M. D. (1996). *Leader as coach: Strategies for coaching and developing others.* Minneapolis, MN: Personnel Decisions International.

Pierce, C. (2015). *Revised—RTI2 implementation guide July 2014—State of Tennessee.* Accessed at www.noexperiencenecessarybook.com/W85Wa/revised-rti2 -implementation-guide-july-2014-state-of-tennessee.html on May 8, 2017.

Powers, K. M., Hagans-Murillo, K. S., & Restori, A. F. (2004). Twenty-five years after Larry P.: The California response to overrepresentation of African Americans in special education. *California School Psychologist, 9*(1). Accessed at www.researchgate.net /publication/271405207_Twenty-five_Years_after_Larry_P_The_California _Response_to_Overrepresentation_of_African_Americans_in_Special_Education on June 14, 2017.

Prasse, D. P. (n.d.). *Why adopt an RTI model?* Accessed at www.rtinetwork.org/learn /what/whyrti on February 24, 2017.

Profession. (n.d.). In *Merriam-Webster.com.* Accessed at www.merriam-webster.com /dictionary/profession on February 24, 2017.

Proust, M. (1923). The prisoner (5th of 7 volumes) in *Remembrance of things past.* Paris, France: Grasset and Gallimard.

Reardon, S. F. (2011). The widening academic achievement gap between the rich and the poor: New evidence and possible explanations. In G. J. Duncan & R. J. Murnane (Eds.), *Whither opportunity? Rising inequality, schools, and children's life chances* (pp. 91–116). New York: Russell Sage Foundation.

Reeves, D. B. (2002). *The leader's guide to standards: A blueprint for educational equity and excellence.* San Francisco: Jossey-Bass.

Reeves, D. B. (2009a, July 13). In education, standards aren't enough. *The Hill, 16*(82). Accessed at https://thehill.com/opinion/op-ed/50089-in-education -standards-arent-enough on June 3, 2017.

Reeves, D. B. (2009b). *Leading change in your school: How to conquer myths, build commitment, and get results.* Alexandria, VA: Association for Supervision and Curriculum Development.

Reis, S. M., & Fogarty, E. A. (2006). Savoring reading, schoolwide. *Educational Leadership, 64*(2), 32–36.

Rodriguez, L. (2010, March 12). Why diets fail, and how weight control works. *Tampa Bay Times.* Accessed at www.tampabay.com/features/fitness/why-diets -fail-and-how-weight-control-works/1079221 on March 1, 2017.

Rouse, C. E. (2005, October 24–26). *The labor market consequences of an inadequate education.* Paper presented at the Teachers College Symposium on Educational Equity, Columbia University, New York.

Samuels, C. A. (2010). Learning-disabled enrollment dips after long climb. *Education Week, 30*(3), 1, 14–15.

Santos, J. L., & Haycock, K. (2016). Higher education's critical role in increasing opportunity in America: What boards should know and 10 questions they should ask. *Trusteeship Magazine, 24,* 14–20.

Saphier, J. (2005). *John Adams' promise: How to have good schools for all our children, not just for some.* Acton, MA: Research for Better Teaching.

Schmoker, M. (2011). *Focus: Elevating the essentials to radically improve student learning.* Alexandria, VA: Association for Supervision and Curriculum Development.

Sergiovanni, T. J. (1996). *Leadership for the schoolhouse: How is it different? Why is it important?* San Francisco: Jossey-Bass.

Sickbert-Bennett, E. E., DiBiase, L. M., Willis, T. M. S., Wolak, E. S., Weber, D. J., & Rutala, W. A. (2016). Reduction of healthcare-associated infections by exceeding high compliance with hand hygiene practices. *Emerging Infectious Diseases, 22*(9), 1628–1630.

Siegle, D., & McCoach, D. B. (2005). Making a difference: Motivating gifted students who are not achieving. *Teaching Exceptional Children, 38*(1), 22–27.

Simmons, D. C., Kame'enui, E. J., Harn, B., Coyne, M. D., Stoolmiller, M., Santoro, L. E., et al. (2007). Attributes of effective and efficient kindergarten reading intervention: An examination of instructional time and design specificity. *Journal of Learning Disabilities, 40*(4), 331–347.

Simonsen, B., Sugai, G., & Negron, M. (2008). Schoolwide positive behavior supports: Primary systems and practices. *Teaching Exceptional Children, 40*(6), 32–40.

Skiba, R. J., Poloni-Staudinger, L., Gallini, S., Simmons, A. B., & Feggins-Azziz, R. (2006). Disparate access: The disproportionality of African American students with disabilities across educational environments. *Exceptional Children, 72*(4), 411–424.

Skiba, R. J., Simmons, A. B., Ritter, S., Gibb, A. C., Rausch, M. K., Cuadrado, J., et al. (2008). Achieving equity in special education: History, status, and current challenges. *Exceptional Children, 74*(3), 264–288.

Sparks, D. (2005a). *Leading for results: Transforming teaching, learning, and relationships in schools.* Thousand Oaks, CA: Corwin Press.

Sparks, D. (2005b). Leading for transformation in teaching, learning, and relationships. In R. DuFour, R. Eaker, & R. DuFour (Eds.), *On common ground: The power of professional learning communities* (pp. 155–176). Bloomington, IN: Solution Tree Press.

Sparks, S. D. (2015). Study: RTI practice falls short of promise. *Education Week, 35*(12), 1, 12.

Sparks, S. K. (2008). Creating intentional collaboration. In C. Erkens, C. Jakicic, L. G. Jessie, D. King, S. V. Kramer, T. W. Many et al. *The collaborative teacher: Working together as a professional learning community* (pp. 31–55). Bloomington, IN: Solution Tree Press.

Tavernise, S. (2012, February 9). Education gap grows between rich and poor, studies say. *The New York Times.* Accessed at www.nytimes.com/2012/02/10 /education/education-gap-grows-between-rich-and-poor-studies-show.html on February 10, 2012.

Teachers College Press. (n.d.). *Protocols.* Accessed at www.tcpress.com/filebin/PDFs /mcdonaldprot.pdf on July 25, 2017.

Tomlinson, C. A. (2000). Differentiation of instruction in the elementary grades. *ERIC Digest.* Accessed at http://education.ky.gov/educational/diff/Documents /tomlin00.pdf on February 24, 2017.

Tomlinson, C. A., & McTighe, J. (2006). *Integrating differentiated instruction and understanding by design: Connecting content and kids.* Alexandria, VA: Association for Supervision and Curriculum Development.

Vaughn, S., Linan-Thompson, S., & Hickman, P. (2003). Response to intervention as a means of identifying students with reading/learning disabilities. *Exceptional Children, 69*(4), 391–409.

Vaughn, S., & Roberts, G. (2007). Secondary interventions in reading: Providing additional instruction for students at risk. *Teaching Exceptional Children, 39*(5), 40–46.

Vellutino, F. R., Scanlon, D. M., Zhang, H., & Schatschneider, C. (2008). Using response to kindergarten and first grade intervention to identify children at-risk for long-term reading difficulties. *Reading and Writing, 21*(4), 437–480.

Wiliam, D. (2011). *Embedded formative assessment.* Bloomington, IN: Solution Tree Press.

Wyner, J. S., Bridgeland, J. M., & Diiulio, J. J., Jr. (2007). *Achievement trap: How America is failing millions of high-achieving students from lower-income families—A report by the Jack Kent Cooke Foundation and Civic Enterprises with original research by Westat.* Accessed at www.jkcf.org/assets/1/7/Achievement _Trap.pdf on February 24, 2017.

Zimmerman, B. J., & Schunk, D. H. (Eds.). (2003). *Educational psychology: A century of contributions.* New York: Routledge.

INDEX

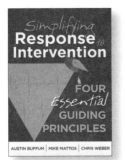

Simplifying Response to Intervention
Austin Buffum, Mike Mattos, and Chris Weber

The follow-up to *Pyramid Response to Intervention* advocates that a successful RTI model begins by asking the right questions to create a fundamentally effective learning environment for every student. RTI is not a series of implementation steps, but rather a way of thinking. Understand why bureaucratic, paperwork-heavy, compliance-oriented, test-score-driven approaches fail. Then, learn how to create a focused RTI model that works.
BKF506

Uniting Academic and Behavior Interventions
Austin Buffum, Mike Mattos, Chris Weber, and Tom Hierck

Ensure students acquire the academic skills, dispositions, and knowledge necessary for long-term success. The authors examine effective academic and behavior supports and offer a step-by-step process for determining, targeting, and observing academic and behavior interventions. You'll discover how to work in collaborative teams using a research-based framework to provide united and simultaneous interventions to students at risk.
BKF595

RTI at Work™: Grades K–12
Mike Mattos, Austin Buffum, and Chris Weber

Learn how to develop timely, targeted interventions at all three tiers of the RTI pyramid for grades K–12. Explore the rationale and strategic steps needed to design a successful plan, and discover a user-friendly framework for overcoming implementation challenges. Includes assigned reading from *Simplifying Response to Intervention* (PDF).
OTK022

Timebomb
Mike Mattos

Timebomb addresses the urgency of reducing dropout rates and preparing students for a better future. Ideal for team meetings and whole-school professional development, the video's bold message will inspire and energize you and your team to provide the best education possible by collaborating at high levels and establishing quality systems of support.
DVF074

Learning by Doing
Richard DuFour, Rebecca DuFour, Robert Eaker, Thomas W. Many, and Mike Mattos

Discover how to close the knowing-doing gap and transform your school or district into a high-performing professional learning community. The powerful third edition of this comprehensive action guide updates and expands on new and significant PLC topics. Explore fresh strategies, tools, and tips for hiring and retaining new staff, creating team-developed common formative assessments, implementing systematic interventions, and more.
BKF746

Solution Tree | Press

a division of

Solution Tree

Visit SolutionTree.com or call 800.733.6786 to order.

" WOW!

I liked how I was given
an effective, organized plan
to help EVERY child."

 PD Services

Our experts draw from decades of research and their own experiences to bring you practical strategies for providing timely, targeted interventions. You can choose from a range of customizable services, from a one-day overview to a multiyear process.

Book your RTI PD today!
888.763.9045

Solution Tree